Defending Women's Rights in Europe

Defending Women's Rights in Europe

Gender Equality and EU Enlargement

Olga A. Avdeyeva

Published by State University of New York Press, Albany

For information, contact State University of New York Press, Albany, NY
www.sunypress.edu

Production, Jenn Bennett
Marketing, Michael Campochiaro

Library of Congress Cataloging-in-Publication Data

Avdeyeva, Olga A., 1976–
    Defending women's rights in Europe : gender equality and EU enlargement /
Olga A. Avdeyeva.
        pages cm
    Includes bibliographical references and index.
    ISBN 978-1-4384-5591-4 (hardcover : alk. paper)
    ISBN 978-1-4384-8 (ebook)
    1. Women's rights—European Union countries.   2. Sex discrimination against
women—European Union countries.   I. Title.

    HQ1236.5.E85A93 2014
    305.42094—dc23   2014020292

10 9 8 7 6 5 4 3 2 1

For my parents

Contents

Contents

Illustrations

Figures

Tables

Acknowledgments

I am grateful to so many people who helped me and encouraged me at different stages of this project. I have had many mentors. In graduate school, seminars with Laurel Weldon and Patricia Boling encouraged my interest in women's rights and made me aware of multiple barriers to achieving gender parity. They taught me to think critically about the impact of public policies on the opportunities of people, men and women, to advance in education, careers, and politics. I learned that the life chances of people are not random; they are structured by a deep gender divide which greatly impacts our life opportunities. Interactions with such scholars as Aaron Hofmann and Ann Clark led me to ask questions about the role of external actors in shaping states' behavior. This book developed from my initial interest in how international norms on women's rights encourage states to change domestic policies in support of working women. With time, this project grew into a larger inquiry about the mechanisms that international actors use to influence domestic politics.

I was fortunate to have encouraging and enthusiastic scholars on my dissertation committee. Perhaps they did not realize it, but my advisors encouraged me to elaborate this project in opposite directions: while Laurel Weldon and Rosalee Clawson recommended exploring a broader range of cases, Oxana Shevel and Robert Bartlett advocated a more nuanced and fine-grained analysis of a limited set of states. I have always kept this advice in my mind. In my dissertation and in this book, I try to strike a balance between these two goals by grounding my large n-statistical comparative analysis in detailed and nuanced case studies. My gratitude goes to my advisors. Most of all, Laurel Weldon has been a steadfast, forthright, and caring advisor. Always offering solid constructive advice, she has been an intellectual role model whose contribution went far beyond the obligations of a dissertation advisor. She introduced me to a field of gender and politics and to a world of the best feminist scholars. I also owe a special thanks to Amy Mazur for her confidence in me, her support and encouragement of young scholars and graduate students, and her willingness to read through some of the earlier drafts of this project. Amy is integrity defined.

Many of the ideas that appear in this book developed during the course of conversations at various conferences and workshops. I am tremendously grateful to many people who shared their ideas with me: Liza Baldez, Lee Ann Banaszak, Karen Beckwith, Christina Chiva, Katalin Fabian, Emilie Hafner-Burton, Mala Htun, Janet Johnson, Dorothy McBride, Celeste Montoya, Mark Pollack, Leigh Raymond, Meg Rincker, Aili Marie Tripp, Georgina Waylen, Christina Wolbrecht, and Kathrin Zippel. I received invaluable comments on early drafts of this work from the discussants at the American Political Science Association in August 2011, Midwest Political Science Association in April 2012, and the European Conference on Politics and Gender in March 2013. I am also indebted for comments and suggestions from the participants of Purdue Workshop on Informal Institutions and Intractable Global Problems held in West Lafayette in April, 2013. I was very fortunate to be part of the workshop, and my book benefited tremendously from the advice, questions, and encouragement I received. My special thanks go to my editor, Michael Rinella, and two anonymous reviewers who saw the value in this manuscript and helped me make this book a reality.

I would like to thank my colleagues at Loyola University Chicago for their interest, questions, and support of this endeavor. My special thanks go to Richard Matland, a good friend and colleague, with whom we spent long evenings talking about politics and Japanese cinematography in Siberia, Russia. Thank you for encouraging this project and always reminding me that smart women should be confident in what they do. David Doherty walked me through the mazes of statistical analysis and helped me to develop a model for this research, while correcting multiple mathematical errors I made; thank you for your patience and advice! My conversations and friendship with Molly Melin and Alex Grigorescu have inspired my work and helped me cope with the multiple competing tasks a young professor faces: doing research, writing, teaching, and raising children. Your friendship is very important to me and I greatly value our conversations. Vince Mahler read first drafts of this book and Raymond Tatalovich read the final version of the manuscript. I deeply appreciate your comments and suggestions!

This project would not be possible without support of my dearest friends, Sangmin Bae, Martyn De Bryn, Germano Franzoni, Inna Hannan, Evie Malaia, Mariya Omelicheva, Anna Pak Burdin, Kate Ralston,

Sarah Robinson, and Anna Sokolovska. My husband, Keith Gordon, has been an incredible partner throughout the process of writing and revising the manuscript for publication, taking up the household duties and spending time with our two little children, Gabe and Natasha. This book, though, is dedicated to my parents, Galina and Alexander Avdeev, two surgeons from Siberia, whose sole goal was to give the best to their children and support us in all our endeavors and undertakings. It is to them I am indebted for everything.

I

EU Enlargement, Accession Conditionality, and Gender Equality

Theoretical Departures and Research Design

1

Introduction

On May 1, 2004, eight countries of the former communist bloc entered the European Union (EU) after almost a decade of accession negotiations and considerable reforms to their domestic institutions and legal codes.[1] Two and a half years later on January 1, 2007, two other post-communist countries, Romania and Bulgaria, joined the European Union. These long-awaited events marked a historic moment and "a decisive phase" in eliminating "divisive structures in Europe" (Polish Government Delegation 1998).[2] They also demonstrated a remarkable commitment by candidate states to transform their domestic policies, institutions, and practices, in order to fulfill accession requirements imposed by the European Commission (EC). In total, candidate states had to comply with thirty-five chapters of the European Community Law, also known as *Aquis Communautaire*. These documents comprise the primary and secondary legislation, objectives, substantive rules, policies, and case law which form the legal order of the European Union in social, political, economic, and legal affairs.

After the collapse of communism across Central and Eastern Europe (CEE) in 1989, the prospect of EU membership became a strong incentive for newly independent states to comply with EU accession requirements. They fervently sought membership in the European Union despite the potential high costs of domestic reforms and legal transformation. EU membership implied unprecedented support in the development of a market economy and the strengthening of democratic political institutions from Brussels, full integration with the EU economic and financial institutions, free movement of labor and goods, substantial investment in states' infrastructures, and finally, but very importantly, acceptance and recognition of these states as members of the European community.

Each accession agreement, overseen by the European Commission, included a Social Chapter which encompassed ten directives on gender equality in the workplace and in social security calculation. Candidate states were required both to transpose these legal prescriptions into national law as well as to establish government institutions capable of enforcing these new codes at the national and local levels. While gender equality laws were not of prime importance to most of the governments in the post-communist Enlargement states, the European Commission emphasized the significance of gender equality directives by making them an indispensable part of membership conditionality.[3] Regardless of the strong incentives to comply, the commentators of EU accession noted substantial variation in states' commitment to transposing and enforcing gender equality directives (Avdeyeva 2009, 2010; Sedelmeyer 2009, 2012; Sloat 2004b; Watson and Lindenberg 2002). Lithuania and Slovenia were the frontrunners of state compliance with EU requirements on gender equality. Bulgaria, Estonia, Latvia, and Romania were reform laggards, only meeting the accession requirements shortly before the accession deadline. Poland, Hungary, and Slovakia saw periods of progressive reforms and dramatic reversals on gender equality while the neighboring Czech Republic made very modest steps in complying with minimum requirements. Until today, Latvia continues to lag behind in policy and institutional adjustment. What explains these puzzling variations in levels of state compliance with EU accession requirements on gender equality? To answer this question, I examine how domestic state and non-state political actors—women's groups, political parties, opposition groups, and women politicians—influence national policy and policy enforcement.

The domestic dimension of compliance, however, is refracted by the international dimension, or the status of EU Enlargement states as regards to the European Union. The status of these states changed from aspirants seeking EU candidacy to EU candidate states, and finally, to EU member states. Each of these periods was characterized by a particular set of instruments used by the European Union to influence the behavior of Enlargement states. I identify three distinct mechanisms of EU influence, which I collectively call international pressures: conditionality, normative pressures, and social pressures. I explore the role of these mechanisms in the process of EU accession and their ability to produce a sustained change in state behavior. By normative pressures, or socialization, I mean EU strategies to influence normative positions of elites and public in EU Enlargement states. Such strategies are based on persuasion and include the following: recommendations for government policy, policy advice, and "policy teaching," including soft law, training, conferences, and dissemination of educational policy materials. Importantly, these measures offer no reward or punishment for compliant or non-compliant behavior.

The goal of these strategies is to produce congruence in values, beliefs, and policy positions on gender equality amongst the elites and public in EU Enlargement states, which I refer to as "normative congruence" throughout this book.

By social pressures or social influence, I mean a self-imposed and/or a group-imposed pressure to conform to practices and behaviors shared by other group members. The main assumptions for describing this mechanism of social influence are derived from social psychology and are based on the argument that actors' environment influences their behavior (Aronson, Wilson, and Akert 2002). Social environment and actors that constitute it can alter the behavior of group members by emphasizing the role of social and cognitive costs (such as shaming, exclusion, and shunning) and social benefits (including praise, prestige, reputation, and recognition by others). Political scientists investigated the role of social pressures for explaining state behavior and found empirical support for the theory of social influence as applied to states (Johnston 2001, 2005; Kelley and Simmons 2012; Hafner-Burton and Tsutsui 2005). This mechanism of influence is distinctively different from normative pressures, where behavior of actors is explained by the degree of their normative fit or congruence (the more similar beliefs they hold, the more likely they are to act similarly). It is also very different from rationalist-, interest-, and preference-based explanations of behavior: actors are driven by social and cognitive benefits, such as group recognition and prestige, rather than by purely material interests. Another distinctive feature of social influence is in the degree of compliance with group expectations. In response to social pressures, actors demonstrate to other group members their respect and recognition of group practices and values even if they do not wholeheartedly embrace these values. Their goal is to assimilate others in the group and signal conformity with group values. The conformal behavior, however, does not necessarily produce changes in actors' normative positions (change in deep-seated beliefs and values) and often result in formal superficial compliance with group norms. The conformal behavior, therefore, produces poor compliance with international requirements.

Finally, by conditional pressures, or conditionality, I mean the explicit connection between material incentives and compliant behavior. The extension of EU membership to candidate states is conditioned on their compliance with EU accession requirements. The transfer of conditional laws and institutions is often described as a coercive imposition of EU policy and institutional models on candidate states. During the accession process, the European Commission (EC) received unprecedented powers

to review and evaluate the degree of state compliance with EU requirements and had powers to put accession negotiations at a halt in case of
candidate state noncompliance. It is widely acknowledged that EU conditionality significantly altered the incentive structure for candidate states
and enabled the EU to impose laws and institutions which these states
would not have adopted otherwise (Grabbe 2006; Schimmelfennig and
Sedelmeier 2005a,b; Vachudova 2005). The EC powers to punish states
decreased significantly after states gained membership in the European
Union, because it becomes costly and procedurally difficult to expel states
from EU for noncompliance. This fact changes government calculation
about the costs and benefits of compliance with EU requirements, especially if policy changes are costly and unpopular at home. While in some
policy areas the European Commission continues to maintain similar
conditional powers toward the member states (such as agricultural and
competition policy areas), for most other policy areas the European Union
relies on state voluntary observance of EU Directives. The European
Commission does not have the same monitoring and enforcement capacity in member and candidate states. The monitoring process in a member
state is not so rigorous and often relies on the third-party monitoring
(such as interest groups and the public). The European Commission can
initiate the infringement procedures against noncomplying states, but in
the area of social policy in general, and gender equality in particular, the
cases of infringement procedures are limited to legal violations of EU
Directives (e.g., policy incongruence in member states with EU Directives). The powers of the Commission to monitor the enforcement of new
policies are very limited. For instance, there are no cases of infringement
procedures initiated against new member states which do not enforce
adopted gender equality laws. For this reason, some commentators feared
that conditional imposition of EU laws could regress upon states' accession to the European Union; that is, once conditional requirements were
removed, the states would no longer have any incentive to comply with
Commission-imposed requirements, leading to institutional and policy
reversals (Epstein and Sedelmeier 2008). But findings from various policy
areas, including gender equality in the workplace, demonstrate the opposite: the EU Enlargement states strengthened their compliance with EU
laws upon the accession and in a number of cases outperformed EU-15
states in levels of compliance with EU regulations (Blauberger 2009;
Faulkner, Treib and Holzleithner 2008a,b; Grabbe 2005; Sedelmeier
2008; Toshkov 2008). What explains the stability of these reforms following accession? I offer several theoretical explanations to the question

of compliance in the pre- and post-accession periods and explore the mechanisms of conditionality, normative congruence, and social pressures in shaping states' compliance with international laws.

Argument

In my evaluation of international influences on state compliance, I find that EU conditionality based on the credible promise of membership had a large effect on (a) the adoption of policies and (b) the enforcement capacities of institutions regarding gender equality in the EU accession states. A detailed analysis reveals that candidate states significantly changed their domestic policies and established government institutions on gender equality to comply with EU accession requirements. Upon accession, new member states generally maintained those same high levels of reform and showed no signs of dramatically dismantling the policies or the institutions meant to support gender equality. This study speaks to the debate about the respective role of norms, social pressures, and incentives in explaining state compliance with international requirements. I emphasize the importance of membership conditionality, perceived and real incentives or benefits derived from compliance, and considerations of costs at the initial stages of inducing state compliance with EU accession requirements. Once granted membership, however, states become responsive to social pressures generated by the expectations of the European Commission and self-imposed by new member states of the Union. Such social pressures include the states' desire to act in congruence with their formal commitments to the Union, thus signaling to all other parties that they are not deviant actors and that they can keep their promise to fulfill the obligations associated with membership. We observe that social pressures prevent the reversal of reforms upon state accession to European Union; however, they do not guarantee that compliance will continue to strengthen rapidly following their membership. Instead, we observe state conformity with EU requirements on gender equality that prevents dramatic reversals of policies or discontinuation of institutions, on the one hand, but which does not result in a strong state commitment to reforms, on the other hand. Rapid reforms during the accession period, therefore, lead to conformity with EU requirements after accession and result in superficial formalistic enforcement of new laws.

To explore the variations in state compliance with EU gender equality requirements, I test several hypotheses about the importance of domestic political actors and the levels of their mobilization in support of, or in opposition to, gender equality requirements. Specifically, I demonstrate that certain configurations of domestic political actors who support policies and institutions on gender equality significantly strengthened state compliance with EU requirements before and after accession to the European Union. In particular, I find that state compliance with gender equality directives was highest in times when a left-wing majority in national parliaments coincided with active advocacy from non-governmental organizations (NGOs) specializing in gender equality. These two actors produce a joint effect that is important for explaining the difference in state commitment to gender equality policies. I observe that left-wing governments, while on average more responsive to gender equality demands than right-wing governments, did not reach the highest levels of compliance without pressure from women's NGOs. Active advocacy women's NGOs often could not overcome the resistance of right-wing parties to gender equality requirements. Thus, a combination of these two factors, left-wing majority in parliaments and active NGOs on gender equality, were important for the success of policy change and enforcement. Among other political actors, female cabinet members are found to support the creation of stronger institutions on gender equality, but they do not have any impact on the process of policy adoption. In addition, while individual feminist advocates of gender equality reforms in parliaments can significantly strengthen the reforms, the number of female parliamentarians cannot directly explain state compliance with gender equality requirements. Party affiliation of female deputies, however, will often determine their position on reforms and can explain why some women in parliaments oppose these laws.

Why Study Gender Equality and EU Enlargement?

There are several reasons to examine the enforcement of gender equality policies in EU Enlargement countries. First, a large literature on gender and transition notes that the principle of gender equality has a unique history in the post-communist countries of Central and Eastern Europe.[4] The communist states introduced this principle during industrialization, creating a greater labor supply by pushing women into the labor market. As a result, the rates of female labor participation expanded across the communist states. Because of the introduction of a quota system, women also received representation in political offices and in many communist parliaments. The communist states achieved high visibility of women in economy and politics which created the illusion of equal treatment between men and women in the labor market; consequently, marked resistance to the recognition of EU equality requirements by the post-communist accession states followed (Einhorn 2006). Both the public and the government widely believed that women were already on an equal footing with men and that no additional provisions were required for improving their status. Moreover, post-transition sentiments against communist legacies and norms revived conservative norms which reestablished the traditional roles of "male breadwinners" and a "female caretakers" (Einhorn and Sever 2003). The rising nationalist sentiments, as well, embraced the idea of a traditional family unit by linking it to patriotism and nation-building. The EU regulations on gender equality were confronted by domestic opposition and low public awareness, but in the end, the membership conditionality changed elite rhetoric and turned the course of government policies toward compliance.[5] The examination of the EU accession process demonstrates the power of international conditionality to reverse the course of discriminatory national policies in societies with low public awareness and insufficient support for gender equality norms. Thus, the investigation of methods and degrees of international involvement provides excellent material for studying the role of international institutions as domestic policy actors and for examining the compelling questions about institutional intervention in support of gender justice.

Second, international organizations emphasize the importance of gender equality principles for their member states. Along with the European Union, such organizations as the Council of Europe, the United Nations, and the International Labor Organization explicitly recognize the importance of gender equality principles in the labor market and provide recommendations for policy reform to their member states. The case of the European Union, though, is unique among these international organizations. It is the only one that establishes a range of stringent gender equality directives in numerous areas of labor relations and links them to a conditional reward, for example, membership for candidate states, or punishment, such as warnings and fines for existing members. The process of EU enlargement is especially distinct and exceptional in the history of international organizations because it grants discretionary powers to the European Commission. The span of this study from the pre- to post-accession periods allows for investigating the role of conditional pressures and other mechanisms of institutional influence on the policy and its outcomes.

Third, gender equality in the labor market is a normative principle, not an economic treaty that implies material incentives for compliance and cooperation. In this sense, gender equality policy provides some parallels and insights into other human rights issues and the role of international intervention in their advancement and enforcement worldwide. Finally, it is a gendered policy issue which suggests that countries with a strong patriarchal tradition will show poor compliance with international requirements on gender equality in the labor market, while also assuming that more progressive and liberal countries will score higher on this measure. The data, however, reveal puzzling results: patriarchal societies with Catholic values ingrained in social policies, such as Poland, demonstrate higher levels of compliance with EU gender equality requirements. Conversely, a secular nation like the Czech Republic scores poorly when judged on its adoption of required policies and the establishment of strong institutions for enforcing gender equality. A comparative examination of domestic political actors and their mobilization in support of gender equality norms provides an invaluable explanation to this puzzle, and can potentially provide worthwhile insights to those studying the many other gender policy issues in world politics.

The rest of this chapter will provide contextual introduction for the book. First, it will introduce the main principles of EU Directives on gender equality and will briefly review the history of Community legislation on equal treatment for women and men. Second, it will review the EU enforcement tools and describe the types of EU institutional influence. Third, it will describe the context of gender equality policies, institutions, and practices in EU Enlargement states. Finally, it will introduce the methods and research design of this study and set the stage for the following chapters.

EU Engagement and Gender Equality in the Labor Market

Overview of Community Legislation on Equal Treatment for Men and Women

Since the mid-1950s, the European Union has developed a major body of legislation in the field of gender equality. The principle of equal pay was introduced in the Treaty of Rome in 1957.[6] Forty years later, the 1997 Amsterdam Treaty significantly enhanced that law by giving the European Commission a specific legal basis to take action in the area of establishing equal opportunities and equal treatment for women and men (Articles 13, 137, and 141 of the Amsterdam Treaty). In particular, Article 141 is a critical legal provision which establishes the principle of "equal pay for equal work." Because it represents the Community not only as an economic union, but also as a community concerned with social progress and improvements in living and working conditions, the European Court of Justice recognized this article as one of the most important Community objectives.[7]

The Lisbon Treaty adopted in 2009 largely reaffirmed these principles. The wording of Article 19 (formerly Article 13) and Article 157 (formerly Article 141) did not change, except for new specification of some procedural aspects. The scope of EU law on the protection of women's rights expanded once again with the adoption of the Charter of Fundamental Rights of the EU in 2010. Article 21 of the Charter prohibited discrimination on the grounds of sex and sexual orientation. Article 23 called for positive action in promotion of gender equality. Article 33 created legal rights for work and family reconciliation by establishing rights for paid maternity and parental leave.

Over the years, there has been a proliferation of normative instruments designed to ensure equal rights and opportunities for women and men in the fields of employment, vocational training, and social protection.[8] Until recently, eleven European directives constituted the entire legal corpus governing gender equality: ten in the field of employment and one focused on the equal treatment of women and men to access goods and services).[9] This diversity of protective sources, as well as the ever-expanding body of case law at the European Court of Justice, eventually prompted the European Commission to consider recasting these directives as a single text. The purpose of drawing up an integrated "equality directive" was to "simplify, modernize and improve the Community law in the area of equal treatment between men and women" in employment and occupation.[10] The aim was to make available a single document that would be clearer and more practical for all citizens and to enhance the *acquis communautaire* by incorporating case law from the Court of Justice. In response to this call, the Recast Directive 2006/54/EC was promulgated on 5 July 2006. It was designed to coordinate six directives relating to equal pay, equal treatment for men and women in employment, training, promotion, working conditions, social security schemes and the burden of proof—all within a single text.[11]

All members and candidate states are required to transpose legal provisions from these directives in appropriate national laws and ensure their enforcement. The European Community language on enforcement is clear and direct. It applies to all existing member and candidate states, and provides a detailed timetable of action to ensure compliance. For instance, in regards to the implementation of the new Recast Directive, Article 33 of the directive states the following:[12]

> Member States shall bring into force the laws, regulations and administrative provisions necessary to comply with this Directive by 15 August 2008 at the latest or shall ensure, by that date, that management and labor introduce the requisite provisions by way of agreement. Member States may, if necessary to take account of particular difficulties, have up to one additional year to comply with this Directive. Member States shall take all necessary steps to be able to guarantee the results imposed by this Directive. They shall forthwith communicate to the Commission the texts of those measures.

To ensure state compliance with EU directives, the European Commission requires member states to establish and maintain specific offices on gender equality, to promote the principle of equal treatment for men and women, to monitor the enforcement of these policies, and to help the victims of discrimination. Furthermore, it encourages the engagement of social partners and NGOs in the promotion of the principal of equal treatment and the establishing of cooperative links with governmental equality bodies.

In general, the EU gender equality directives establish the principles of equal treatment for men and women in the labor market and in social security and benefit calculations, provide definitions of direct and indirect discrimination against workers on the bases of sex, and outline provisions for combating it. They oblige member and candidate states to consider the objective of equality between men and women when formulating and implementing laws, regulations, administrative provisions, policies and other activities mentioned in the text of the directives. Ten directives on gender equality were part of the EU accession requirements. Together they comprise a comprehensive set of policies that could be organized in five subcategories: (1) parental and maternity leave; (2) care and informal work; (3) equal pay and gender pay gap; (4) tax and benefit policies; and finally (5) nondiscrimination and equal access to labor market.[13] Candidate states had to transpose legal provisions of these directives in major domestic laws regulating labor relations, including Labor Codes,

Pay Acts, Administrative Codes, Social Security and Pension laws, and adopt an all-encompassing Act on Equal Treatment of Men and Women or Gender Equality Law. In addition, candidate states were required to ensure the enforcement of these new laws by establishing government institutions on gender equality whose responsibility it would be to coordinate, monitor, and enforce new policies, as well as to investigate cases of discrimination on the basis of sex and assist victims of discrimination in courts and settlement agreements with employers.

EU Enforcement Tools: Types of Institutional Influence

The European Union employs an extensive arsenal of tools, mechanisms, and strategies to influence the behavior of its member and candidate states. The EU Enlargement made extensive use of *membership conditionality* in shaping the political environment, policies, and economic development of EU candidate states. In international relations and comparative politics literature, political and economic conditionality refers to coercive pressures to change state behavior by altering their cost-benefit calculations (Downs, Rocke, and Barsoom 1996; Keohane 1984). In particular, EU membership conditionality relied on the use of material rewards to encourage state compliance, and used threats of either delaying or withdrawing membership in cases of noncompliant behavior. The European Union did not use material punishments against candidate states; during the accession period, the most serious punishment entailed the withholding of material benefits and the termination of accession negotiations (Schimmelfennig 2007; Schimmelfennig and Sedelmeier 2004). This mechanism implies a direct link between state behavior and admission to the European Union, which is viewed as an incentive for state behavior. Membership conditionality fits rationalist theories and assumptions that define states as cost-benefit calculating and utility-maximizing actors. Under this mechanism, states positively respond to an international institution's incentive and sanction structure when they believe that compliance will maximize their interests and preferences.

Assessing the effectiveness of conditionality produces different opinions among scholars and commentators. Many scholars and politicians recognize the importance of conditionality and credit it with the successful achievement of accession goals by Enlargement states. Other scholars believe that the coercive imposition of rules and laws could lead to reversal of those reforms in the future (Bird 2001*a,b*; Vermeersch 2002); moral hazard, destruction of traditional practices, and general ineffectiveness (Bird 2001*a,b*; Collier, Guillaumont, Guillaumont, and Gunning 1997; Drezner 2000; Martinez-Vasquez, Rioja, Skogstad, and Valev 2001). Similarly, EU conditionality was criticized for coercive imposition of rules on candidate states which lead to anger and public disapproval of EU policies (Grabbe 2001; Fierke and Wiener 1999). On several occasions, government officials in candidate states severely criticized the EU conditional requirements for lacking an understanding of the region and potentially destabilizing regional economies. For instance, the Bulgarian Prime Minister Ivan Kostov said in an interview with Reuters that the European Union was exerting "meaningless diktat" by demanding Bulgaria shut down parts of its Kozlodoui nuclear power plant. He reiterated, "The aggressive demand to close the nuclear power plant will destroy even what little competitiveness the country now has. What will remain of the Bulgarian economy?"[14] In the same interview, the Bulgarian Prime Minister showed a high degree of dissatisfaction with the allocation of EU funds. By dividing the candidate countries into outcasts, of which Bulgaria was one, and favorites, Sophia's advancement towards its accession goals were seriously impeded.

In the area of gender equality, we observe a similar variation in the assessment of EU conditionality. There is general recognition that the EU impacted states' agendas on gender equality, often regardless of states' preference (Ellina 2003; Sedelmeier 2009; Wahl 2008). Some commentators note negative effects from the top-down reform on gender equality, which created tensions between the international policy agenda and the goals of grassroots women's movements in EU candidate and member states (Roth 2007, 2008*a,b*). Some commentators, on the other hand, criticized underdeveloped EU conditionality in the area of gender equality and gender mainstreaming, noting a lack of commitment on the part of the European Commission and the member states to fully embracing the principles of gender equality, thus resulting in poor outcomes in these policy areas (Bretherton 2001; Hafner-Burton and Pollack 2009; Hoskyns 1996; Pascall and Lewis 2004; Walby 2004). Such a diversity of opinions and reactions calls for further research into the question of EU conditionality and its effects on policy and policy outcomes in new member states of the European Union.

Conditionality was not the only strategy used by the European Union to stimulate compliance with EU accession requirements in the field of gender equality. Extensive socialization, referred to in this book as normative pressure or strategic efforts to change the normative positions of state elites and the public about the issues in question, accompanied membership conditionality. The EU developed a broad range of soft law, or policy recommendations and programs, on gender equality and recommended that candidate states take part in these programs while also incorporating these new rules into their domestic practices. Gender equality became an integral part of the European Employment Strategy and later the Lisbon Strategy, which together generated recommendations for changing employment practices in member and candidate states by reforming wages, providing child care, establishing flexible work hours and part-time work, ensuring equal treatment of men and women, and closing the gender pay gap. To accommodate these new policies, states were asked to develop and adopt National Strategies and Action Plans on gender equality and gender mainstreaming as domestic policy instruments for achieving the goals prescribed by the directives.

To assist in developing and initiating these programs, the European Union channeled financial resources to state governments and social partners. The Structural Funds represent the EU's financial commitment of the organization to helping states meet their accession goals. In the area of employment, state and non-state organizations could apply for EU financial grants provided by the European Social Fund to sponsor programs and campaigns on gender equality. Many EU programs required national co-funding, which stimulated cooperation between governmental and non-governmental sectors of society. Additional funding was also available for NGOs and state institutions through programs such as PHARE, SOCRATES, and INTERREG.[15]

The European Union encouraged multilevel cooperation between national, regional, and international state and non-state actors in the area of gender equality by supporting twinning programs between the governments of Western democracies (EU-15) and candidate states. These programs included the training of civil servants, government officials, social workers, judges, and NGO representatives in various aspects of gender equality, including representing victims of discrimination in courts and running national offices on gender equality. Some experts refer to such practices or strategies of socialization not only as a way to pass on the knowledge of gender equality institutionalization, or to change the normative positions of people, but also as the capacity-building of actors in support of these policies on the national and local levels (Montoya 2009).

How effective is normative pressure in changing state behavior? The literature offers an abundance of contradictory and inconsistent responses to this question. Some skeptics claim that "talk is cheap" and that governmental rhetoric in support of a norm is merely window dressing if material incentives and coercive mechanisms are not used (Shannon 2000). Others believe that initial strategic rhetorical recognition of international human rights norms can lead to deeper normative changes in the future (Keck and Sikkink 1998). These debates reflect much broader questions about how states behave and under which conditions their behavior changes. The dominant scholarship in international relations identifies two main mechanisms whereby states and international organizations can influence the behavior of other states: coercion (realist and rationalist approach) and persuasion (constructivist approach). In this book, I argue that while two of the dominant theoretical approaches, rationalism and constructivism, provide an indispensable framework of analysis for state behavior, their approach to international influence is underspecified and incomplete because such analyses do not take into consideration the intricate system of social environment and state social commitments and pressures that often drive state behavior in the absence of coercive pressures and normative congruence.

In this book, I draw scholars' attention to a more complete conceptual framework by identifying and testing a third mechanism by which international organizations and groups of states affect the behavior of states: social pressures. In response to perceived or real pressures to assimilate or conform to other states in a group, social pressure is a mechanism which induces changes in state behavior (Avdeyeva 2007; Goodman and Jinks 2004; Johnston 2001; Kelley and Simmons 2013). The main theoretical assumptions of this approach for explaining state behavior are imported from social psychology and are based on a premise that actors' environment will influence behavior (Aronson, Wilson, and Akert 2002). Social pressures entail a number of processes by which the social environment (and actors that constitute this social environment) impacts state behavior, including mimicry; social approval, such as praise, inclusion in group activities and decision making; elevation of state prestige and reputation in a group; and social punishment, such as shaming, exclusion from group activities and decision making, and marginalization in a group. This mechanism describes and analyzes the role of social and cognitive costs and benefits for state behavior, as opposed to material costs and benefits analyzed in the realist and rationalist paradigms, and normative congruence and noncongruence of constructivism (Avdeyeva 2007). To account for the influence of international social pressures on state behavior, I introduce the notion of international social environment to my analysis of the outcomes of state compliance with EU requirements on gender equality in the work place. I recognize the complexity of state responses to EU conditionality and socialization efforts by disentangling these processes and placing them in the multifaceted social environment in which states operate and interact. In addition, I test the effect of international pressures against domestic political environments: the analysis will investigate the positions of various political domestic actors in support of or in opposition to gender equality norms and their effect on the levels of state compliance with international pressures.

The Context of EU Enlargement States

Policies and Institutions on Gender Equality

The principles of gender equality in the CEE states' labor markets were introduced by the Marxist-Leninist economic doctrine of state-planned socialist economies, which instantiated full employment as a primary right and primary obligation for every capable citizen. In communist ideology, the principle of full employment was viewed as a major precondition for ensuring the equal rights of citizens, including women. In all ten countries examined in this book, the key provisions declaring gender equality were contained in national labor codes and constitutions which replicated Stalin's 1936 constitution. These regulations asserted the equal rights of women and men in all areas of state, political, economic, cultural, and social life. Constitutional provisions prohibited any form of discrimination, gave citizens the right to work and choose their occupation, required equal remuneration for an equal job, ensured the rights of workers to vacation and time off, and guaranteed state social security support during sickness and after retirement. Constitutions provided financial and legal support to mothers and children, including protection for pregnant women, paid leave of absence prior to and after giving birth, guaranteed medical and obstetric care to expecting mothers and children, and a network of nurseries and kindergartens. Overall, entitlements such as free education, free childcare, maternity and parental leave, health care, paid sick leave and pensions were broader and more generous than in many Western democracies at that time. While these provisions resulted in greater participation of women in the paid workforce and greater visibility of women in political and social arenas, they failed to fully eliminate discriminatory practices against women workers during the socialist period (Daskalova 2007; Deacon 2000; Einhorn 1993; Nechemias 2006). Moreover, these provisions failed to protect women workers at the time of transition which resulted in marginalizing women in the labor market, raising social inequality, increasing unemployment, and growing the poverty gap between women and men.

The remainder of this chapter will briefly review socialist provisions concerning gender equality to provide an idea of how closely they fit (or do not fit) the EU requirements outlined in the equality directives. The provisions concerning *equal pay* were stipulated both in national constitutions and labor codes of post-communist countries. However, the commentators noted a lack of equal pay stipulations in the administrative orders and wage tariff calculations (Sloat 2004*b*). Typically wage tariffs, evaluation and classification of work, were established by the central ministries of labor and social affairs in cooperation with trade unions. While they formally observed the principle of remuneration for work according to its amount, quality, and societal value, the documents did not define the concept of remuneration itself and did not determine how the principle of "equal pay for equal work" should be established. Thus, we detect formal recognition of the principle, but no administrative stipulation or guidelines for how to enforce this principle.

Similarly, *equal treatment* provisions were formally recognized in socialist labor codes and constitutions, but there were no definitions of these principles and no clear administrative orders for enforcing them. Equal treatment was narrowly understood as equal access to employment and the free pursuit of education. Women's equal participation in the public sphere was assured through the specialized regulations of work conditions, special care during pregnancy and maternity, and extensive provisions of social services, such as childcare. Protective legislation also included a range of limitations and bans on many jobs that were viewed to be inappropriate for women, especially pregnant women and working mothers. For instance, in Poland women could not be drivers of public buses and trams (Fuszara 2005*b*). In Romania, women with children younger than six years old could not work night shifts (Ghebrea, Tataram, and Cretoiu 2005). Numerous jobs in industrial, construction, and transportation sectors were prohibited for women. Legal access to shift work was highly regulated as well. These protective measures, considered "women's privilege" during socialist times, backfired against female workers during the time of transition (Zielinski 1995).

None of the countries had extensive provisions to ensure the *equal treatment of self-employed* workers. The phenomenon of self-employment was extremely rare in socialist countries. With gradual economic liberalization in the 1980s, Slovenia and Hungary established minimum provisions for ensuring the rights of self-employed individuals in areas of social security and maternity and health benefits; however, these cases were rare. Other states did not have such legislation before the 1990s.

The *equal treatment in the calculation of social security* is a problematic area of gender equality legislation for all post-communist countries. None of the countries had occupational social security; all states managed statutory social security insurance funds requiring all working individuals and employers to pay a certain percentage of their income to the fund. In addition, state governments transferred some portion of the GDP to the national social security fund to pay social security benefits to retired individuals. The calculation of retirement benefits under the state-planned economy violated the principal assumptions of gender justice. First, it reflected a gender pay gap embedded in wages, which resulted in a conspicuously gendered benefit gap. Second, the gender gap in social security benefits was exacerbated by the different retirement ages for men and women workers: on average, female workers retired five years earlier than male workers. All socialist states considered the early retirement age of women to be a special privilege. It was viewed as the state's recognition of women's hard work and a special way to reward this work. This principle, however, disguised indirect discrimination against women, whose wages and social security contributions and, therefore, benefit entitlements, were much lower than those of working men. In addition, social security benefits reflected the life expectancy of the recipients, decreasing women's benefits even more, because on average, female life expectancy is longer than that of males. Meager pensions resulted in greater rates of impoverished, retired women across these socialist states.

CEE states had minimum provisions to ensure the rights of *part-time workers*. In general, part-time work was a rare practice in socialist states because insufficient wages earned from those jobs could not cover basic survival needs (Sloat 2004*b*). Hungary was the only state where similar social security calculation and eligibility for full-time and part-time workers were established. In other states, these provisions were not explicit or nonexistent. Often socialist labor codes guaranteed part-time and reduced-hour work upon request by the employee in cases of special needs, such as sickness or childbirth.

No countries included in this study had provisions, or a defined concept, for the reversal of the *burden of proof* in cases of discrimination. Discrimination on the basis of sex was prohibited in state constitutions and in national labor codes. Some countries, Czechoslovakia and Hungary for example, stipulated minimal provisions of how to seek redress in cases of discrimination against workers. Nevertheless, socialist states did not have a tradition of litigation and case law. Overall, it was difficult and not advisable to seek remedy in cases of discrimination through legal means. There were very limited administrative avenues for seeking redress through negotiations and disputes with the help of trade unions and women's organizations (Fuszara 2004). At any rate, organizations, which represented the interests of individuals and criticized discriminatory practices, should have taken the lead in cases of discrimination instead of leaving individuals to seek redress personally.

Social policies in socialist states had an explicit pro-natalist focus. *Maternity and parental leave* provisions were intended to help women combine care giving responsibilities with work. All socialist states had an extensive list of leaves available to working mothers and pregnant women. In fact, state socialist provisions in the area of paid leaves in all examined states exceeded EU provisions. At the same time, there was no *paternity leave* for caring fathers. In some states, fathers could enjoy the same leave and benefit provisions only if they could prove that they were the primary caretaker of a child (divorced, single, widowed, or unmarried fathers).[16]

Institutional oversight and regulation of issues related to work and family were divided between several ministries, which typically included the Ministries of Labor and Social Affairs, the Ministries of Youth and Families, and the Ministries of Health. Such ministries had departments that dealt with issues of women and families, family and child benefits, and welfare services. The Ministries of Health were involved in the enforcement and monitoring of pro-natalist policies and policies protecting the health of working, pregnant women and mothers of young children. Poland was the only socialist state that had a specific government office that dealt with women's issues, the Government Plenipotentiary on Women. This office was established in 1986 in the aftermath of the World Women's Conference in Nairobi (Nowakowska 2000). Poland was also the first country to establish the office of the Ombudsperson for Civil Rights in 1987, which opened legal opportunities for seeking redress in cases of discrimination, including discrimination on the grounds of sex.

In addition to ministry-level institutions, several socialist countries established administrative inspectorates to monitor and enforce labor code provisions and detect violations. For instance, by mid-1980s Poland, Hungary, and Czechoslovakia had centralized Labor Inspection Offices with regional branches. In other states, like the three Baltic states, the functions of monitoring labor code violations were performed by trade unions. Trade unions were often involved in the elaboration and enforcement of regulations concerning worker's rights and obligations, including worker protection, leave, bonuses, and family vacation and recreational activities. In addition, they were involved in the distribution of social benefits (including housing, food stamps, vacation and recreation, and scarce resources, such as clothing, home appliances, cars, etc.). Labor offices and trade unions did not have a direct mandate to promote and monitor the enforcement of gender equality provisions outlined in national labor codes, however. These offices represented the rights of all workers and often supported the segregation of occupations by gender because they viewed women's income and work as secondary to that of men. Some women's issues were handled by women's organizations. But the primary function of these organizations during the socialist time was ensuring political support and satisfaction with communist party politics among working women.

Policy Outcomes in the 1990s

Socialist provisions for gender equality did not withstand the trying times of transition: state guarantees of full employment and access to benefits collapsed alongside the planned socialist economies which supported them. A dramatic neoliberal turn and austerity measures adopted by many post-communist, transition states in the early 1990s exacerbated the effects of economic transformation on social outcomes: social benefits and welfare provisions disappeared, unemployment skyrocketed, and hyperinflation dramatically reduced the value of wages (Cook, Orenstein, and Rueschemeyer 1999). Nationalist sentiments came to dominate public agendas reinstating traditional family values with gendered divisions of labor between a male breadwinner and a female caretaker (Nowakowska 1997; Pollert 2003; Renne 1997).

Women, who experienced a significant decline in levels of employment, living standards, political participation, and cutbacks on reproduction rights, are often characterized as the "losers" during this time of economic transition (Einhorn 1993; Gal and Kligman 2000; Ghodsee 2004). While no one debated that reproductive freedoms and levels of political participation declined dramatically, the data for women's participation in the labor market is suggestive of a different interpretation (Van der Lippe and Fodor 1998; Wahl 2008). Van der Lippe and Fodor argue that economic liberalization allowed for greater competition in the service sector, traditionally dominated by women (1998). This had a positive effect on women's employment and wages. Pascall and Manning note that although female labor participation rates declined after the collapse of socialist economies, their employment rates are still high in comparison to Western European countries (2000). Table 1.1 displays the rates of women's employment in a comparative perspective: all states experienced significant decline in female employment rates, but they remained quite high in comparison to the EU-15 average (Pascall and Manning 2000). Overall, employment rates of women in Eastern European countries resemble female employment rates in Scandinavian countries rather than the lower totals and particularly the full-time employment rates in other Western European countries (Fagan, Grimshaw, Smith, Hebson and Figueiredo 2005).

According to Table 1.1, levels of unemployment varied across states: some countries demonstrated high unemployment levels (Poland, Bulgaria, Latvia, and Slovakia), whereas others illustrate that levels of unemployment remained quite low taking into consideration the degree of economic transformation the countries were experiencing. Table 1.2 displays levels of female unemployment across post-communist states over time. Female unemployment rates are not significantly different from male unemployment rates in transition states. Some experts argue that relatively low unemployment was sustained mainly because of an afford-

Table 1.1. Total Female Labor Force Participation, Age 15–65, Central and Eastern European Countries, 1985–2005

Year / Lithuania	Bulgaria / Poland	Czech Republic / Romania	Estonia / Slovakia	Hungary / Slovenia		Latvia
1985	70.8	73.9	77.4	58.1	76.4	72.3
66.4	62.1	69.7	64.6			
1990	72.2	74	76	57.3	75	70.3
65	61.1	70.7	63.2			
1995	64.3	64.5	66.4	50.5	66.1	67.5
60	66.2	61.6	63.1			
2000	54.5	63.7	65.2	52.6	62.8	67.1
59	62	63.2	63.5			
2005	52.3	64	64.3	53.5	63	65.9
57.6	55.3	62.4	65.6			

Source: *Eurostat and European Commission database on Women and Men in Decision-Making,* different years.

Table 1.2. Total Female Unemployment Rate, Central and Eastern European Countries, 1990–2004

Year Lithuania	Bulgaria Poland	Czech Republic Romania	Estonia Slovakia	Hungary Slovenia	Latvia	
1990	22 (1993)	5.4 (1993)	0.7	8.7 (1992)	n/a	n/a
n/a	n/a	n/a	9.1 (1993)			
1995	15.8	4.8	8.6	8.7	20.7	13.9
14.7	8.6	13.8	7			
2000	15.9	10.6	12	5.6	13.1	13
18.1	6.4	18.6	7.4			
2004	11.5	9.9	8.9	6.1	8.4	11.8
19.1	6.9	19.1	6.5			

Source: *Eurostat and European Commission database on Women and Men in Decision-Making, different years.*

able and highly flexible labor market. For this reason, enterprises had little reason to fire staff (Clarke 1998). Ashwin and Yakubovich explain why in some countries rates of female unemployment were lower than those of men: women were more likely to take the first offered, poorly paid job, while men remained on the job market longer while trying to find a more lucrative initial job (2005). Heinen and Portet reported high levels of discrimination of women in hiring and promotion regardless of their education and training in transition states (2002).

Data on the post-communist gender gap suggests that there is a steady trend in closing the wage gap during the post-transition period (see Table 1.3). Another positive remark is that the overall wage gap in post-transition states is not as high as in EU-15 states (Wahl 2008). While these findings are quite encouraging, it is difficult to explain the decline in the wage gap in EU Enlargement states. One explanation suggests a positive effect of EU directives on combating gendered pay difference. Another explanation concerns male job loss and male pay cuts experienced in post-transition economies (Pollert 2005). A conclusive analysis to investigate the causality of declining wage gap, however, has yet to be explored.

Public perception of gender equality in CEE countries remains heavily influenced by the legacy of state-sponsored inclusion. As Nagy succinctly put it: "after forty years of socialism people are not enthusiastic

Table 1.3. Gender Pay Gap, Central and Eastern European Countries, 1995–2010

Year	Bulgaria	Czech Republic	Estonia	Hungary	Latvia	Lithuania	Poland	Romania	Slovakia	Slovenia
1995	17	30	35	25	20	30	16	17	30	15
2000	15	27	35	21	15	26	14	15	27	13
2005	13	25	33	19	13	21	13	12	25	10
2010	13	26	30	17	13	21	10	9	20	8

Sources: *Eurostat and European Commission database on Women and Men in Decision-Making, different years.*

about emancipation or even about positive discrimination" (2003, 164). Post-communist transitions, with their search for new identities and painstaking economic transformations, became a fertile ground for the revival of traditional stereotypes surrounding the role of women. Pushing women into the private sphere was also convenient and justifiable when the state could no longer perform its welfare functions anymore and had to close down nurseries and kindergartens while also abolishing other welfare responsibilities. Furthermore, in times of high economic uncertainty many people began to value job security as one of the key aspects of employment, regardless of pay and discriminatory practices. A 2001 public opinion poll in Lithuania showed that respondents consistently supported the statement, "A better paid job is more important for men than for women (Sloat 2004*b*, 78)." Similarly, describing public attitudes towards gender equality in CEE states, Pollert notes that neither men nor women seem to be concerned with gender inequality in society (2005, 228). Galligan, Clavero, and Calloni note that there is a great variation in public attitudes on gender equality in ten Eastern European countries they have studied, but these attitudes are much more conservative than the average of citizens in Western Europe (2007). These observations are consistent with the World Values Survey (WVS) and the European Values Survey (EVS) data. In the distribution of sixty-one nations on the gender equality scale for 1995–2001, the CEE countries sprawl from the high-middle to low-middle ranges, revealing strong conservative sentiments (see Table 1.4).[17] Bulgaria and the Czech Republic demonstrate the most progressive attitudes in the group; Lithuania, Hungary, Latvia, Poland, and Estonia cluster in the middle; and Romania, Slovakia, and Slovenia held the least progressive public attitudes toward gender equality. It is clear that gender equality norms propagated by the European Union do not resonate with public norms and public agenda, which helps to explain weak feminist mobilization in the region, on the one hand, and reveals the top-down direction of state compliance with EU requirements on gender equality, on the other hand.

Methods and Data

This analysis focuses on ten post-communist countries of Central and Eastern Europe, newly accepted members of the European Union. The study uses both quantitative and qualitative methods. I use panel data analysis to investigate institutional and policy change over fifteen years.

Table 1.4. Gender Equality Score (Adopted from Gender Equality Scale), Pooled 1995–2001

Year	Bulgaria	Czech Republic	Estonia	Hungary	Latvia	Lithuania	Poland	Romania	Slovakia	Slovenia
Score*	74	70	68.5	68	67	66.5	66	64	63.5	63
Position**	16	24	27	28	29	31	32	37	41	43

Source: Author's calculations from Gender Equality Scale, Inglehart and Norris 2003, 33.

*Score out of 100-point scale of the 5 items of the survey (see Notes for more details on the GES).

**Position refers to nation's rank among sixty one nations included in analysis; 1 being the most progressive state (Finland) and 61 being least progressive state (Jordan).

The analysis begins in 1995 and ends in 2010, which allows this study to look at the state of gender equality policies and institutions before conditionality was applied (until 1998 for some and 2000 for other states), during accession conditionality (1998/2000 to 2004/2007 depending on the year of accession negotiations and year of accession), and beyond conditionality (2004/2007 to 2010). State compliance with EU gender equality requirements is conceptualized as a twofold process: legislative adjustment and institutional reform, which measures institutional capacity to enforce gender equality policies. Thus, I present two scores for state compliance: legislative and institutional compliance. Such a division exposes the variation in state compliance across and within the separate countries in order to make the analysis more efficient and systematic; furthermore, it allows the study to explore the differences in state *formal compliance* (legislative change) and *enforcement compliance* (institutional capacity to enforce new policies). Many commentators recognize legislative change as a formal statement of government commitment to international requirements, which may remain unenforced (Hafner-Burton and Tsutsui 2005; Simmons 2000). The focus on institutional capacity to enforce new policies allows this analysis to investigate government activity beyond legislative commitments, on the one hand, and to capture the gap between formal commitment and enforcement, on the other hand. Chapter 3 will address issues of nominal and operational conceptualization of the study variables in greater detail and will also present the distribution of compliance scores among accession countries.

Qualitative analysis of this study complements, explores, and illustrates the results of the statistical analysis. In chapter 4, I evaluate the role of international factors, namely conditionality, normative pressures, and social pressures, in a substantive qualitative discussion of theoretical premises and empirical findings. To overcome the problem of design and to disentangle the responses to conditional, normative, and social pressures, I employ an analysis of counterfactuals by examining the case of violence against women, a policy area regulated only by soft measures. Based on the findings from this policy area, I discuss the role of conditionality in state adjustments to EU accession pressures and offer an inclusive framework for the analysis of international factors on state compliance.

Country case studies presented in chapters 5 to 7 allow for disentangling the effects of international factors in detail. In these chapters, I evaluate the impact of conditionality, normative pressures, and social pressures against the domestic political environment in three accession states. I employ process tracing techniques to analyze how individual government decisions to adjust policies and to establish institutions on gender equality changed with a change of international incentive structure. The goal of the case studies is to identify political and civic actors critical for the development of gender equality policy and institutions, to analyze their incentives and debates, to reveal their motives, attitudes, and actions, to reflect any changes in their positions when the state status *vis a vis* EU changed, and to evaluate their effect on government policy. The focus of the case studies is on political actors and the degree of their mobilization and activity in three accession states: the Czech Republic, Lithuania, and Poland. The analysis is centered on critical policy issues and relies on systematic evaluation of statements, actions, levels of mobilization in support or in opposition to gender equality regulations of major political actors: social actors, most notably women's groups and NGOs; political parties and their positions on gender equality; women parliamentarians and women members of cabinets. The detailed case studies reveal the timing of events and actions, the motives and attitudes of actors, and the interaction between international and domestic players.

Sources of Data

This study relies on a careful analysis of legislative activity and government actions to establish, promote, and revoke powers of state institutions related to gender equality in ten post-communist states, new members of the European Union, from 1995 to 2010. I followed each of these legislative and institutional changes over time, observing how various political actors were involved, or not involved, in these decisions and how various forms of engagement with the European Union in domestic politics affected government decisions and compliance with EU directives on gender equality in the labor market. To explore levels of compliance I examined primary sources, such as existing laws, amended laws, administrative orders, official documents, special resolutions and declarations by relevant institutions on the issue, and formal communications from the government to relevant institutional bodies when available. I also examined government reports to the European Union on compliance, press releases, parliamentary debate records, and official opinions of the government officials and members of parliaments concerning new legislation and institutions. In addition, I used secondary data as a check for my evaluation of compliance. This data included the European Commission Opinions on compliance in the area of gender equality as well as reports from independent experts and agencies, such as the Open Society Institute, Network Women's Project, Karat Coalition, Enlargement, Gender and Government dataset (EGG), and the QUING Project (Quality in Gender + Equality Policies).

Original data was collected during my field research in Poland and the Czech Republic. This data includes interviews with governmental officials and officers in labor inspection institutions and trade unions; interviews with activists from non-governmental organizations; and interviews with scholars and experts on gender and social policy. This field research helped identify key actors and events in the policy process and refine the research strategies for studying policy development in the eight other countries. A broad array of documents surveyed in this study include transcripts of parliamentary debates pertaining to gender equality issues and EU directives in this area; governmental programs, electoral platforms of governmental officials, and winning parties and party coalitions in regards to the social policies in question was analyzed in all ten countries. In addition, statistical information on socioeconomic development in the ten countries of analysis is obtained from the International Labor Organization, the European Commission, and the World Bank.

Data is rarely perfect and this study is no exception. My major concern relates to the evaluation of institutional mechanisms and institutional engagement on state compliance. I had the opportunity to study a quasi-natural experiment and evaluate the effect of institutional engagement on levels of state compliance: no conditional requirement, conditional requirement, and post-conditional requirement. Since it is not a perfect experiment, it is difficult to separate the effect of conditional treatment from the normative and social treatments because normative engagement and social pressures were present in all three stages mentioned above. Detailed case studies, however, allow investigating how the incentive structure of domestic actors changed when the structure of international relations changed. Thus, I do not aim to test the causal pathway of the different mechanisms, but I do discuss the theoretical underpinnings of each, and from there I derive a set of consistent, theoretically rooted propositions. These limitations prompt some caution; the findings about the role of institutional influence should be taken as suggestive rather than conclusive.

Plan of the Book

Chapter 2 discusses the theoretical framework of the study in greater depth. The study taps into two research questions relating first, to variations in state compliance, and second, to the effect of international institutional engagement on state compliance. A theoretical discussion situates the study in the current literature on these questions and sets the stage for theoretical propositions which will drive the empirical analysis in the following chapters. Chapter 3 accomplishes two goals. First, it presents the research design of the study. It clarifies conceptual definitions of study variables and presents the framework for their operationalization of the quantitative and qualitative analyses. It discusses the data and its limitations, presents coding rules, and provides a simple tabular overview of the data on government compliance. Second, it presents findings from the quantitative analysis and discusses them. It sets the stage for the qualitative discussion of the case studies that follow.

Chapter 4 analyzes the impact of international factors focusing on specific periods in EU-applicant state negotiations: pre-accession negotiations, accession conditionality, and the post-accession period. It revisits the theoretical premises of three accounts by considering policy and institutional changes in ten Enlargement countries in an alternative case of violence against women. Chapters 5 through 7 present the case study evidence from Poland, the Czech Republic, and Lithuania with the goal of examining the findings derived from the statistical analysis in greater depth. Each of these chapters begins by introducing the current state of gender equality policies in the country and then briefly summarizes the domestic politics since the mid-1990s. It then discusses the level of compliance with EU requirements on gender equality over time, focusing on major debates on critical issues and the configuration of domestic political actors as well as their influence on policy decisions. The chapters conclude with a brief analytical summary of reform milestones.

Chapter 8 concludes the book with a summative overview of major findings and a brief review of a theoretical model of state compliance. It then draws some policy lessons and recommendations and discusses some questions raised by the findings, including the durability of compliance, the relationship between conditional, normative, and social pressures, and issues of policy implementation. I conclude by suggesting routes for future research.

2

Theoretical Framework

What Explains State Compliance with International Requirements?

While international actors, using various treaties and agreements, have promoted the protection of women's rights and advocated for the equal treatment of men and women in the labor market since the late 1950s, the case of EU Enlargement is quite distinct from other cases where international organizations have been involved. In this chapter, I examine theoretical discussions on institutional efforts to influence legislation on gender equality in states and domestic factors known to inhibit or facilitate international efforts and influence the outcome of gender equality policies. In the first part of this chapter, I will consider international factors of influence and propose testable hypothesis for examining their effectiveness. In the second part of this chapter, I will discuss the effect of domestic state and non-state actors, as well as other domestic factors, including economic development and the costs of reforms, on state compliance with gender equality requirements.

International Influences

The question of state compliance with international requirements has been at the center of recent research both in international relations and comparative politics scholarship. Recent research has generated several compelling explanations for state compliance and noncompliance. These explanations reflect much broader theoretical debates about how states behave and under which conditions their behavior changes. In general, scholars identify three dominant mechanisms for explaining how international institutions can influence the behavior of states: material incentives and coercion, persuasion and normative change, and social pressures such as shaming and praising, inclusion and exclusion (Checkel 1998; Downs, Rocke, and Barsoom 1996; Finnemore and Sikkink 1998; Keck and Sikkink 1998; Keohane 1984; Meyer, Boli, Thomas, and Ramirez 1997; Risse 2000). Respectively, these mechanisms represent rationalist, constructivist, and sociological institutionalism theories. The study of Europeanization benefitted from all theoretical perspectives and developed a significant body of scholarship.[1] The study of EU Enlargement, however, was dominated by rationalist explanations that linked candidate state compliance with EU accession requirements to EU conditionality, or a strategy of "reinforcement by reward" (Schimmelfennig 2007; Schimmelfennig and Sedelmeier 2004). Rationalist accounts were well-suited for examining the EU Enlargement because EU conditionality governed the pre-accession stage. This theoretical starting point limited our understanding about the influence of other institutional mechanisms on state compliance and left questions about the effects of EU normative and international social pressures unanswered. This study will address this limitation by demonstrating the importance of other, non-conditionality based, mechanisms of international influence in EU Enlargement states. In doing so, I recognize the difficulty in the task of differentiating the effects of three simultaneous processes—conditionality, normative and social pressures—and suggest ways for working around these circumstances, while understanding the limits of plausible conclusions.

The Role of Conditionality

State compliance with EU rules, including EU gender equality policies, was set as a condition for extending membership to candidate states and reflects the coercive incentive structure of the EU Enlargement. EU incentives for candidate states require change in policies, institutions, and practices in accordance with EU law in exchange for financial, institutional, and technical support, as well as inclusion in the European Single Market. Some commentators on Enlargement consider EU conditionality "a positive incentive structure" (Schimmelfennig, Engert, and Knobel 2003). The European Union rewards compliant states by extending assistance and the promise of membership, and it withholds such assistance if the target government fails to comply with EU accession rules. The positive direction of the incentives here means that the European Union did not punish noncomplying states with fines or other coercive measures; the EU relied solely on the extension or denial of rewards, the main incentive being membership in the European Union.

The conditionality explanation of compliance uses the rationalist bargaining model in which actors, the governments of candidate states, are strategic utility-maximizers interested in achieving EU membership (Schimmelfennig 2007). Actor calculations about the feasibility of achieving rewards and the costs of compliance influence their propensity to comply with conditional requirements. The rationalist bargaining literature identifies several factors that influence state transfer and institutionalization of EU rules. First, it is the *credibility* of EU promise to grant the reward (Grabbe 2005; Kelley 2004; Schimmelfennig 2007; Schimmelfennig and Sedelmeier 2004*a,b*, 2005; Vachudova 2005). In the case of membership conditionality, measures targeted at increasing the credibility of Brussels' commitment to EU Enlargement greatly improved state compliance with EU accession requirements, such as associational agreements, rhetorical recognition, and commitment to Enlargement, and thereby hastened the accession of other candidate states. Secondly, the *size and speed of rewards* tend to improve state compliance. Commentators on EU Enlargement observe that as the day of accession approaches, states speed up their harmonization reforms, which demonstrates that states postpone policy harmonization until the last moment (Schimmelfennig and Sedelmeier 2004). The third factor is the cost of compliance: the smaller the costs of compliance, the easier it is for the candidate states to change and enforce new rules (Dimitrova 2002; Jacoby 2001; Kelley 2004; Schimmelfennig et al. 2003). Some other scholars refer to the cost of compliance as the fit between existing domestic legislation and the norms prescribed by the European Union—states with the highest fit between domestic policies and EU regulations are expected to comply at a higher rate than states with a larger gap (Cowles, Caporaso, and Risse 2001).

The rationalist explanations provide a solid understanding of why candidate states succeeded in meeting the EU accession requirements. In general, most commentators credit the EU membership conditionality employed in the 2004 and 2007 Enlargements with the successful alignment of political institutions, also the legal and economic structures in candidate states, with the *acquis communautaire*. In the area of gender equality policies, we observe similar rapid and satisfactory reform, especially in the legislative part of compliance. While all countries created offices to oversee the enforcement of gender equality policies, the status and functions of these offices varied greatly. Thus, conditionality improved formal compliance with EU requirements. The conditionality effects on levels of compliance are debated and will be addressed later in this book.

From this theoretical discussion on conditionality, I posit the following proposition about the effects of conditionality on state behavior:

Hypothesis 1: *Conditionality greatly improved states compliance with gender equality requirements.* Overall, I expect to see satisfactory state compliance by the time of accession. In addition, I expect to find that candidate states harmonized their laws and established government offices on gender equality during their candidacy status, not before or after it. If compliance with conditional requirements implies rational behavior under coercive pressures with little domestic interest or resonance with international norms and with compliance positing certain costs to state governments, I expect that states will postpone compliance with gender equality reforms until the last possible moment in their negotiations with the European Union. We can expect rapid legislative and institutional reforms right before the accession in most candidate states.

Hypothesis 2: *State compliance with gender equality requirements will deteriorate once states receive the membership status and conditional requirements are lifted.* Indeed, if conditional compliance implies only a minimal level of state compliance under coercive external incentives, then once the structure of conditional incentives is dismantled, compliance with gender equality requirements might not be among the immediate interests of state governments. The removal of conditionality, therefore, can change the cost-benefit structure of states, which can negatively impact their levels of compliance upon the accession.

Thus, the removal of conditionality in the post-accession period poses several questions about the consistency of the rationalist incentive-based model. If state behavior were driven by the promise of rewards, then once the reward is achieved, we should expect to see the deterioration of compliance (Epstein and Sedelmeier 2008). Commentators on Enlargement identified several factors that could negatively influence state compliance with international requirements in the post-accession period. First, the mere elimination of a membership incentive could change cost-benefit calculations for new member states and consequently diminish their levels of compliance with EU rules. Second, the coercive imposition of EU rules on candidate states could pose a question of legitimacy in the Enlargement countries. New legislation was not subject to democratic parliamentary scrutiny; the states had to follow the orders of the EU in order to achieve their membership reward. This legislative process could delegitimize the new laws and suppress their enforcement. Third, the lack of broad public support could also prevent the enforcement and stall state compliance (Epstein and Sedelmeier 2008). Despite these skeptical expectations, empirical evidence demonstrates that while the EU's enforcement capacities decreased substantially, the degree of compliance in different areas of policy did not deteriorate upon accession (Epstein and Sedelmeier 2008; Gray 2009; Hollyer 2010; Johnson 2008; Levitz and Pop 2009; Pridham 2008; Sasse 2008; Sedelmeier 2008, 2009). These findings suggest that other mechanisms of influence on state behavior were at play during the pre-accession period and became dominant in the post-accession stage.

The Role of Normative and Social Pressures

While the pre-accession period was best suited for testing the rationalist bargaining model because of attached conditionality, the post-accession period demonstrates the theoretical utility of other causal mechanisms for explaining state behavior. Constructivists and scholars of the sociological tradition posit several convincing explanations for evaluating the behavior of post-Enlargement member states. Constructivist accounts credit socialization, or the process of regular and sustained interaction by which actors obtain new knowledge and values which reshape their identity and form their new interests, generating lasting changes in states' behavior (Checkel 1999, 548). International governmental and non-governmental organizations are viewed as "sites of socialization" and as "promoters of socialization" (Johnston 2001, 508–509). EU socialization accompanied accession conditionality. The EU used soft law and recommendations for state policy, relying heavily on the exchange of expertise between governmental officials and non-governmental actors and encouraging the development of accountability of governmental offices to a specific public—NGOs.

Socialization is a strenuous process; it relies on sustained interaction between norm promoters and norm learners. Constructivists distinguish the depth of change in an actor's behavior by defining Type I and Type II socialization (Checkel 2005, 804). Type I socialization describes a strategic situation in which actors rhetorically recognize the importance of new norms and change their behavior accordingly to these norms, but do not incorporate this norm in their identity. In other words, we observe a shallow acceptance of a new norm. Type II socialization describes the situation of a profound normative change, in which actors internalize a new norm that becomes part of their identity and produces a long-lasting effect on their behavior.

A large body of international relations (IR) literature has examined the effect of international socialization on state behavior, including the behavior of EU Enlargement states (Bearce and Bondanella 2007; Check-el 1999, 2001, 2005; Epstein 2008a,b; Finnemore and Sikkink 1998; Keck and Sikkink 1998; Hollyer 2010; Gheciu 2005; Kelley 2004; Risse 2001). While the findings regarding socialization effects are mixed,[2] scholars agree that in situations where high normative incongruence between the state's observable behavior and international norms exist, it is improbable to see the effects of international socialization immediately, because they would require dramatic changes in the actors' normative positions. This assertion has important implications for this study because it suggests that the effects of EU socialization in Enlargement countries had a positive cumulative impact on state actors and therefore prevented compliance deterioration in the post accession period. In other words, because EU socialization accompanied accession conditionality, its effects strengthened the impact of conditionality by changing prospective member states' normative positions which sustained behavioral change.

Sociological accounts of compliance offer another important explanation for why the commitments of Enlargement states to EU policies endure. Building on theories of social psychology, sociologists view relations between actors as shaped by social pressures and driven by the logic of appropriateness, as opposed to the rationalist logic of consequences or the constructivist logic of normative congruence (March and Olsen 1989). In social relations, the behavior of actors is driven by their assessment of how they may satisfy the expectations of the other members within the group; to avoid disappointing the group, they conform to expectations, and therefore become recognized as a legitimate peer. Operating in a social environment, actors are responsive to social pressures (such as social rewards and punishments), as opposed to normative charges or material incentives. Social rewards include praise, social inclusiveness, and recognition by other members of the group; social punishments include shaming, exclusion, marginalization, and the general labeling of the divergent actor as a deviant group member (Goodman and Jinks 2004; Hafner-Burton and Tsutsui 2005; Meyer and Rowan 1977; Meyer, Boli, Thomas, and Ramirez 1997). The sociological accounts of compliance offer two useful explanations of state behavior. First, from a socio-psychological perspective, the conditional agreement between the European Union and Enlargement established a social contract in which both parties had a number of agreed-upon mutual responsibilities: the candidate states agreed to comply with EU requirements, the European Union agreed to grant membership. Once the European Union admitted candidate states into the community, it fulfilled its obligation toward accession states and created a "social trap" for accession states, who now had to act according to their promises. The term "social trap" was coined by psychologist John Platt in his 1973 article to describe a strategic situation in which the behavior of social actors is determined by their assessment of the future actions of other actors. The social trap situation is studied extensively in research on cooperation and non-cooperation, dilemmas of collective action, and the provision of public goods (Ostrom 1990, 1998, 1999; Putnam 1995, 2002; Rothstein 2005). At the heart of the social trap dilemma are the principles of trust, reciprocity, and social exchange that can explain cooperative or non-cooperative behaviors among actors (Fukuyama 1995; Heinrich, Boyd, Bowles, Camerer, Fehr and Gintis 2004). By granting membership to accession states, the European Union confirmed the legitimacy of their social contract, signaled respect and trust toward the new member states and their future behavior, and suggested a path for positive reciprocity in the social transaction between the actors. In response, governments of new member states felt bound by self-imposed pressures to fulfill their part of the contract in order to maintain their reputation among other group members.[3]

The second explanation refers to direct social pressures—shaming for deviant behavior and praising for compliant behavior. While employing soft strategies of influence, social pressures engage reputational concerns of states about their position in a group of other states (Avdeyeva 2012). No state wants to be known and treated by others as a "deviant actor" (Hafner-Burton and Tsutsui 2005). Thus, states will continue their compliance with EU requirements upon the accession to avoid an undesirable reputation. Research in social psychology shows that new group members are more likely to respond to social pressures and comply with group rules even when these actors normatively disagree with those rules. Social pressures, however, cannot force states into compliance; in order to satisfy group expectations states can formally embrace group rules, signaling to others that they are in compliance, but then do not enforce new behaviors (Meyer et al. 1997). Social pressures, therefore, generate conformity, rather than compliance with group rules, and result in low or partial enforcement of group norms.[4]

Theoretical discussion of normative pressures (socialization) and social pressures (acculturation) generates several expectations about state behavior in response to these mechanisms of international influence that could be tested on EU Enlargement states. The differentiation of these mechanisms for inducing compliance is profoundly important for predicting state behavior upon accession. Each mechanism, I argue, has distinct implications for the degree of compliance, durability of compliance, and the possibility of compliance reversal when the conditional pressures are lifted. Below, I review these expectations and generate testable hypotheses.

The literature on normative pressures and socialization postulates that states comply when they accept the promoted norms and change their behavior according to these new beliefs. If normative pressures are successful, and actors (in this case political elites) actively accept new norms about gender equality in the work place, we expect to see lasting changes in state behavior. We can expect comprehensive compliance in the post-accession period, such as further alignment of policies on gender equality with EU requirements, and the strengthening of state institutions on gender equality in the absence of conditional pressures. In this case, the chances of reform reversals are very low. Moreover, we can expect that the speed and scope of reforms (the slope of compliance) will be similar to that of the conditionality period. Norm acceptance, indeed, ensures durable and comprehensive compliance with international requirements.

Hypothesis 3: *Successful socialization (normative congruence) ensures comprehensive compliance with EU requirements on gender equality and prevents states from compliance deterioration upon their accession to the European Union.* Comprehensive compliance means that the speed and scope of reforms in accession and post-accession periods will be similar. New member states will achieve full compliance with EU equality *acquis* upon accession. If normative change among the elites does not occur, then we can expect the dismantling of policies and institutions; if state elites do not normatively embrace the EU norms, why would they choose to maintain them? Lack of normative support among the elites, therefore, would not prevent policy and institutional dismantling.

The sociological accounts of compliance generate different expectations of compliance when states are driven by social pressures to comply with group requirements. Social pressures do not generate compliance; they lead to conformal behavior, which can result in partial enforcement of new policies, stagnation of policy and institutional development, and their marginalization; but social pressures would prevent dramatic reversal of new policies and institutions as long as these requirements remain on the group's agenda. Social pressures do not lead to normative acceptance of promoted rules and laws; therefore, state actors are not going to be compelled by internal need to enforce these laws. But they will respond to the need to signal to other states that they are in compliance with group requirements and maintain policies and institutions on gender equality as expected of them.

Hypothesis 4: *Self-imposed or group-imposed social pressures ensure state conformity with EU formal requirements on gender equality and prevent states from dramatic compliance deterioration upon their accession to the European Union.* Often social pressures generate formalistic response to international pressures, such as rhetorical recognition of a norm, creation of weak institutions for norm enforcement and monitoring, and the adoption of legislation "on the books." Since policies and institutions in EU Enlargement states were adopted during the conditionality period, in the post-conditionality period, conformity may mean stagnation in this policy area with no radical changes to their structures in either a positive or negative direction. However, we can expect to see slight changes in either direction.

In the summary of this section, I recognize the methodological limitations of this research design and the difficulty in separating the effects of conditionality, social pressures, and normative pressures from one another, since each occurred simultaneously during the pre-accession stage. I address the issues of the compounding effects of international influences on states' compliance in two different ways: first, I look at three periods of compliance, pre-negotiation period, accession conditionality and post-accession; and second, I test the effects of social and normative pressures on the example of another gendered policy area which was not part of the accession conditionality—violence against women. The case of violence against women policies will be presented in chapter 4 to assess the influence of international socialization (normative pressure) and social pressures in the absence of international conditionality.

Domestic Factors of States' Compliance

Much of the research on conditionality and compliance tends to neglect the domestic political environment and institutional characteristics of states which inhibit the capacity of international conditionality to streamline domestic reforms and achieve desired policy outcomes (Collier, Guillaumont, Guillaumont, and Gunning 1997). Research on conditionality has also been criticized for disregarding historical continuities that resulted in disastrous outcomes for some international conditional aid (Killick 1998, 156). Increasingly, scholars begin to pay attention to domestic, political, and economic structures and recognize that the impact of conditionality depended on opportunities presented by the domestic developments and relations of the recipient state with the wider international system (Collier 1997; Cowles, Caporaso, and Risse 1999; Risse Kappen 1995; Kelley 2004; Pridham 1997). Scholars of ideational accounts note the importance of domestic resonance of international norms and argue that the normative environment of nation-states accounts for the variation in the impact of international norms embedded in conditional treaties (Checkel 2001; Johnston 2001, 2005; Risse-Kappen 1995; Risse 2000; Schwellnus 2005).

Numerous studies note that domestic politics can hinder international influences. Kelley reveals that authoritarian governments resisted pressures from the European Union to change discriminatory minority policy accordingly, even when the compliance was linked to membership conditionality (2004). For instance, in Slovakia, it was only after the authoritarian government of Vladimir Mečiar was voted out of power that the adoption of new minority policies occurred. Ross posits that the impact of conditionality in contested areas of policy is unclear, especially "when powerful domestic interests oppose the reform" (1996, 1223). In the context of Europeanization, scholars recognize the difficulty of reform in the face of a strong nationalist opposition (Kelley 2004; Pridham 1999). Pridham notes that the presence of strong nationalist opposition in a country can limit the predisposition of the domestic political elite to engage in international dialogue (1999). Other scholars argue that the existence of multiple veto points in a given policymaking structure can become a significant impeding factor in policy adoption and enforcement (Tsebelis 1995; Cowles, Caporaso, and Risse 2001). The more power is dispersed across a political system and the more actors that have a say in political decision making, the harder it becomes to arrive at an agreement that could satisfy all players.

Other institutional structures, however, can facilitate the adaptation of policies. For instance, such institutions can provide political actors with policy expertise and support and can induce more rapid policy change. Women's policy machineries are widely considered to facilitate state institutions in advancing gender equality policies in many Western European states (Caporaso and Jupille 2001; Stetson and Mazur 2011). Other studies have found that external attempts to push reforms depend, to a large degree, on whether the relevant interest groups are part of the government coalition (Berkovitch 1999; Risse-Kappen 1995). Risse-Kappen argues that transnational actors are able to translate international norms into domestic policies if they can find domestic partners able to establish a strong coalition with the government (1995). When examining domestic politics as an independent variable, the challenge clearly is to identify whose opposition matters, how much it matters, and under which conditions the effect of resistance cease to exert pressure/influence. To answer these questions, I refer to a large comparative literature on gender and the state. This literature informs my analysis of domestic political actors and structures relevant for facilitating state compliance with EU requirements on gender equality in the labor market.

Gender and the State

Comparative research on gender and the state has investigated international and domestic conditions favorable for the advancement of feminist policies at the national, regional, and local levels. While recognizing the crucial importance of international influences for domestic policy change in a number of gendered policy areas (Berkovitch 1999; Boyle and Preves 2000; Htun and Weldon 2012; Johnson 2007; Katzenstein and Mueller 1987; Krook 2009; Krook and O'Brien 2010; True and Mintrom 2001; Zippel 2006),[5] this scholarship generated testable hypotheses supported by rich comparative data about the importance of the state, its institutional structures and domestic political environment, for the articulation, adoption, and enforcement of feminist policies by national and local governments. Mounting comparative research demonstrates the role of political actors in supporting the feminist cause. It shows that particular characteristics of state and non-state political actors, their level of mobilization and activist strategies, their connections to each other, and the political environment in which they operate are crucial for explaining the existence of feminist policies and their outcomes (Banaszak 1996; Htun 2003; Stetson and Mazur 1995; McBride and Mazur 2010; Morgan and Zippel 2003; Soule and King 2006; Weldon 2002, 2011).

In addition, scholars note the importance of historical and cultural contexts for creating similar policy patterns in some countries, thus allowing for typological categorization of states into "families of nations" (Castles 1993; Esping-Andersen 1993; 1999; Korpi and Palme 2003; Orloff 2002; O'Connor, Orloff and Shaver 1999). Other research has demonstrated that various "policy styles" have an influence on policy outcomes and can explain differences in the development of gendered policies within specific subsectors, such as employment, professional training, or violence against women (Mazur 2002; Htun and Weldon 2012). Drawing on this broad body of research, I identify several important predictors of reforms on gender equality in the labor market in ten EU Enlargement states: female mobilization in support of gender equality legislation, the inclination of political elites to cooperate with women's NGOs on the issue of equality (most commonly predicted by party politics), and the role of female political actors, specifically female members of national parliaments and women holding positions in the government cabinet. The rest of the chapter will discuss theoretical premises and major research findings from each individual account and generate hypotheses for the study's analysis.

Women's Movements

Research on public policy has long recognized social mobilization as an important predictor of change in the political environment and the addition of new issues to the government agenda (Kingdon 1984; Baumgartner and Mahoney 2005; Rochon and Mazmanian 1993).[6] Democratic theorists convincingly demonstrated that social mobilization is critical for advancing inclusion and democracy (Costain 2005; Dryzek 1990; McBride and Mazur 2010; Tarrow 1998; Waylen 2007; Weldon 2011). Research on women's movements reflects the broader social movement literature and uses its major analytical components, such as political opportunity structure, resource mobilization, and cultural framing of feminist ideas. Not all women's movements are feminist movements. Women, organizing as women and aiming to advance the status of women, raise awareness about the critical issues of gender discrimination and gender injustices, while also placing feminist policies on the national and global agendas. Women organizing for other causes, social or political, are widely recognized as women's movements, but are not considered feminist movements (Beckwith 2000).

Using the models developed by social movement theories in sociology, women's movement scholarship has generated data on specific campaigns and movements, studying the sequence of events and explicating conditions for a movement's success or failure (Banaszak, Beckwith, and Rucht 2003; Beckwith 2000, 2005; Mazur 2002; Weldon 2011). Research consistently demonstrates that certain characteristics of women's movements account for their success in producing an enduring policy change. The strength of its mobilization and its autonomy relative to other pressure groups are listed among the most important conditions for a movement's success (Amenta, Caren, Chiarello and Su 2010; Beckwith 2007*b*, Mazur 2002; Weldon 2002; 2011). Several explanations are helpful in understanding how these characteristics of women's organizations are important for the advancement of feminist policies across the globe. First, women have a social knowledge of their position in society, which helps them to articulate critical issues cast aside by mainstream politics (Mansbridge 1995, 2001; Young 2000). Second, issues of gender injustice, including inequality in the labor market, challenge established gender roles and male privileges in economic matters. Mainstreaming such policies in state institutions can lead to state cooptation of the feminist agenda and result in half-hearted outcomes of government measures meant only to appease international authorities and demands from women's groups (Avdeyeva 2009; Geller Schwartz 1995; Mazur 2002; Stetson and Mazur 1995). Nevertheless, the ability of women's groups to hold the government accountable to its policies is important. Finally, women organized within the mainstream political institutions, such as parties and trade unions, often do not give feminist issues the highest priority in the organization. This is because such issues are often perceived as being solely the concern of women and, therefore, are pushed to the margins of the organizational agenda, giving way to more "inclusive" issues such as increasing wages and benefits for all workers, combating poverty and unemployment, and other social priorities (Caiazza 2007; Leira 2002; Sainsbury 2001; Weldon 2011). Current research also demonstrates that a high level of mobilization is required for a movement to be influential (Amenta et al. 2010).

Very few studies investigate the impact of women's movements on social policy in large-scale cross-national studies (Htun and Weldon 2012; McBride and Mazur 2010; Montoya 2012; Weldon 2002). This shortcoming is due to a lack of adequate comparable data.[7] Some studies focus on movements across several countries, but they usually employ historical and descriptive methods and have relaxed criteria for comparison (e.g., Bull, Diamond and Marsh 2000; Bystydzienski 1992; Dahlerup 1986; Ferree and Martin 1995; Katzenstein and Mueller 1987). Most commonly, the studies on women's movements investigate their impact on the advancement of feminist policies in individual countries or a small number case studies (e.g., Banaszak 2006; Banaszak et al. 2003; Gelb 2003; Kaplan 1992; Lewis 1997; Meehan and Sevenhuisjen 1991; Singh 1998; Hantrais 2000). The growing body of research on women's NGOs and their role in shaping government social policy in CEE countries bears similar limitations: it is widely centered on one or two movements and does not engage the issue in a systematic, comparative cross-regional analysis. This book seeks to fill this gap and to examine the impact of women's movement actors on levels of government compliance with EU Enlargement requirements in a systematic, comparative analysis of ten states over fifteen years.

I posit the following hypotheses from the above discussion on the impact of women's movement on public policy:

Hypothesis 5: *Women's non-state mobilization and organization in support of EU regulations on gender equality policies increases the likelihood that the state will comply with accession gender equality requirements.* In testing this proposition, I outline the importance of non-governmental feminist organizations operating at the national and local levels in candidate states which explicitly articulate the issue of gender inequality and gender discrimination occurring in the labor market in their public statements and interactions with the government. I control for their strength and activist strategies.

Not all women's groups are advocating feminist causes. Conservative women's organizations promote the revival of traditional family values and "maternal" policies, such as long parental leaves for working women. Social groups, other than women's organizations, influence government decisions as well, and their sentiments toward gender equality can range from neutral to disapproving. Conservative social activism can divert government attention from gender equality policies to traditional family values policies, impeding the course of reforms (Watson 2000). These activists include religious organizations, nationalist movements, labor organizations threatened by the expansion of women's rights on the labor market, and the conservative public (Fuszara 2001, 2003, 2005*a*,*b*; Lohmann and Seibert 2003; Matynia 2003; Nowakowska 1997). I posit the following proposition:

Hypothesis 6: *Conservative social organizing decreases the likelihood of state compliance with EU gender equality regulations.*

Party Politics and Gender Equality

Scholars of gender politics generated comparative propositions about how political parties affect the outcomes of women's policies (Kittelson 2011; Sanbonmatsu 2002; Swers 2002; Wolbrecht 2000; Wolbrecht and Hero 2005). In general, political parties have established agendas on issues related to women's interests, and in some countries left-wing parties have become aligned with women's movements by incorporating their demands into policy platforms, establishing women's organizations, and instituting quotas for women in leadership positions. When women's movement actors become close political allies with left-wing parties and the left-wing parties dominate national parliaments, this combination produces a political environment favorable for gaining access to the policy agenda. Thus, governments formed by left-wing political parties with close ties to women's movements are more likely than any other governments to respond favorably to women's movement demands (McBride and Mazur 2010).

Political parties provide or deny political access to various interest groups and trigger realignments within the political system. Extensive research on women's movements has considered political parties as explaining the successes or failures of the movement (Banaszak 1996; Bashevkin 1998; Costain 1992, 1998, 2005; Gelb 1989, 2003; Hellman 1987; Katzenstein 1987; Katzenstein and Mueller 1987; Mueller 1988; Ray 1999). Several studies analyzed the interactions between women's movements and parties in power and examined how changes in democratic states impacted movement strategies (Banaszak et al. 2003). Scholars are increasingly emphasizing that the party positions on women's rights vary by issue (Htun 2003; Sanbonmatsu 2002; Weldon 2011; Wolbrecht 2001; Wobrecht and Hero 2005). Comparative research demonstrates that the left-wing parties are found to be supportive of gender equality in the labor market whereas right-wing parties often view provisions for working women as a special accommodation which interferes with open competition in a free-market economy, so they consistently deny the expansion of gender equality provisions (Esping-Andersen 1993; Mazur 2002). In post-communist states, it is possible to find communist legacies instilled in the party platforms of socialist and social-democratic parties, in addition to their continuous alliances with women's organizations, which can suggest that left-wing parties will be inclined to support women's movement demands. In contrast, I expect to find that right-wing nationalist parties and Christian democratic parties can be a serious impediment to feminist group access to agenda setting and, as a result, we can expect to observe low compliance with EU gender equality requirements under right-wing parties.

Hypothesis 7: *Left-wing parties in power are more likely to promote legislative and institutional compliance with EU requirements on gender equality.*

Hypothesis 8: *Left-wing parties in power are more likely to collaborate with women's NGOs on issues of gender equality and promote compliance with EU requirements on this issue.* In this proposition, I aim to test the interaction between women's NGOs and the parties in power and to assess how the effect of women's movements on state compliance is mediated by political parties.

Women in Positions of Political Power and Gender Equality

Feminist research has criticized contemporary free-market democracies for the systematic exclusion of women from political representation (Pateman 1988; Phillips 1991, 1995; Pitkin 1967). The lack of women in political decision making not only violates the principles of the "politics of presence," but it most importantly fails to represent women's interests and needs, either through direct placement of women in positions of power or indirectly through the incorporation of gender perspectives in the policy process (Phillips 1995). Empirical studies convincingly demonstrate that the absence of women in positions of power is central for explaining why public policies in many postindustrial societies are gender biased and often discriminate against women (Bratton and Ray 2002; Kittilson 2008; Lovenduski and Norris 1993; Mainsbridge 2005; Norris, Vallance, and Lovenduski 1992; Schwindt-Bayer and Mishler 2005). Some researchers credit gender as having a considerable effect on policy preferences. In their study of the British parliament, Lovenduski and Norris find that women have more feminist and leftist values than men (Norris and Lovenduski 1993, 224). Similarly, in her analysis of parliamentary surveys in the Swedish Rikstag, Wängnerud finds that female politicians advance policies on social welfare and gender equality to a greater extent than male politicians (2000). Gender equality policies are almost exclusively pursued by the female members of parliament (MPs). Bochel and Briggs find that female MPs bring women's concerns to parliament. While exploring examples of an act against female circumcision and an attempt to abolish a tax on sanitary products, the authors emphasize that both concerns were undertaken by female MPs in Westminster (2000). Numerous female-directed policies and programs have been adopted by the Scottish parliament, in large part due to the 37 percent female representation within the chamber (Ross 2002). Substantial research demonstrates that the adoption of family leave policies is strongly associated with a greater number of women in national parliaments (Kittelson 2008; Schwindt-Bayer and Mishler 2005). Similarly, Swers demonstrates that even though representatives often vote according to party line, their gender is politically significant and does indeed influence policymaking. Swers argues that the gender of members of Congress moderates their party identification (2002).

Other researchers are more skeptical about the effect of gender on MPs' policy preferences (Reingold 1996). Esaiasson and Holmberg reviewed policy attitudes of female and male members of the Swedish

Rikstag and concluded that overall the difference between men's and women's attitudes on most of the investigated issues was insignificant (Esaiasson and Holmberg 1996). Weldon finds that the percentage of women in legislature is a weak predictor of policy outcomes on violence against women (2002). McAlister and Studlar find very limited differences between female and male parliamentarians in one party in Australia (1992). Celis finds that increasing the number of women in Belgian parliament did not result in greater substantive representation of women (2008). These inconclusive findings on the effect of female parliamentarians on the promotion of women's policies call for further research on the subject and justify careful analysis of individual policy cases. Previous research on female members of parliament in Central and Eastern Europe and their effects on influencing policy production or enforcement is virtually absent. So far, studies have only addressed the issue of institutional barriers to women's advancements (electoral rules, party strategies, and women's organizations), party ideology, and cultural norms (Matland 2004; Matland and Montgomery 2003; Renc-Roe 2003; Petö 1997; Saxonberg 2000; Siemenska 2004; Ðilović 2004; Sloat 2004b). While it is established and widely recognized that there are institutional barriers to women's participation in politics (Matland 1993; Matland and Studlar 1996), there is no scholarly consensus about whether female politicians make dramatically different decisions than male politicians in various policy areas. This study adds to the scholarship on the role of female MPs in promoting women's policies by introducing new cases dealing with the EU Enlargement states and by also testing the effect of female MPs on the level of state compliance with EU requirements on gender equality:

Hypothesis 9: *A greater proportion of female deputies in national parliaments is likely to increase the degree of state compliance with legislative and institutional requirements of the European Union on gender equality in the labor market.*

In recent years, gender disparity in cabinet appointments has gained significant scholarly attention (Atchison and Down 2009; Escobar-Lemmon and Taylor Robinson 2009; Krook and O'Brien 2012). The pattern of gender disparity in cabinet appointments is similar to gender imbalance in other political positions: women hold fewer cabinet positions than men, and where they have received an appointment, they often are marginalized to "feminine," low-prestige, policy areas. While cabinet members are among the most powerful positions in state hierarchies, little is known about the status of women as cabinet ministers and their effect on public policy. Several studies have addressed the issue of relative status of female members of cabinets to reveal the pattern of power distribution in port-folio assignments (Davis 1997; Escobar-Lemmon and Taylor Robinson 2009; Krook and O'Brien 2012; Studlar and Moncrief 1999). In their recent study Krook and O'Brien develop a new measure, the Gender Power Score, to measure the status of women in cabinets across nations (2012). This measure takes into consideration the prestige of assigned appointments and the number of assigned appointments held by women.

Executive dominance in policymaking is evident and well-docu-mented (James 1999; Laver and Shepsle 1994). In parliamentary democ-racies, cabinets set the main policy agenda and generate the largest number of policy initiatives. Cabinets can also exert significant control over the legislative agenda by deciding which proposals incur legisla-tive scrutiny and which proposals remain in control of the executive branch. In addition, individual ministers have a tremendous influence on the substantive content of policies (Atchison and Down 2009). With so much policymaking power, cabinet ministers can either facilitate or impede the adoption and implementation of contested policies. The pres-ence of women among cabinet ministers can have a significant impact on the state propensity to adopt and enforce gender equality policies. I will test the effect of female cabinet members on state compliance with EU requirements on gender equality. The underlying assumption of the following proposition is grounded on the notion of a common interest shared by women and advanced by female political leaders.

Hypothesis 10: *A greater proportion of female cabinet members is likely to increase the degree of state compliance with legislative and institutional requirements of the European Union on gender equality in the labor market.*

Conclusion

In this chapter, I reviewed an extensive theoretical literature on interna-tional institutional mechanisms of influence on state policies and insti-tutions on gender equality. I argued that the case of EU Enlargement presented the opportunity to identify and analyze three distinct mecha-nisms of international involvement: conditionality (conditional pressures), which used coercive strategies to change the behavior states; normative pressures (socialization), which used persuasion to change normative posi-tions of elites and the public on gender equality; and social pressures generated by group expectations about the appropriate behavior among group members. I argue that each of these mechanisms has distinct implications for compliance. Conditional pressures are expected to generate high compliance; however, chances of reform reversal are high once the conditional requirements are lifted. Normative pressures are able to generate high compliance only if elites in accession states embrace the norms of gender equality. Social pressures are expected to generate formalistic conformity with group norms, which may never lead to high levels of compliance, on the one hand; and may prevent the dramatic reform reversal, on the other hand.

Various domestic actors have an impact on reform stability and comprehensiveness. I reviewed substantial literature on gender and the state to identify several important factors that could explain variation in state compliance with international gender equality requirements, including women's movements and social opposition, women as political actors, and parties in power. In the following chapter, I introduce the research design of the study, discuss the operationalization of study variables, and present the findings of the statistical analysis which evaluates the explanatory power of these factors in the context of EU Enlargement states.

3

Exploring the Data

To analyze government compliance with EU accession requirements on gender equality from 1995 to 2010, I traced state actions on policy harmonization and the creation of institutions on gender equality over this time period. I observed the involvement of the European Union in the issue, the way it was received by national legislatures, how the legislatures addressed the issue, and how the issue fit into such domestic events as parliamentary changes, social mobilization, parliamentary and governmental debates.[1] The first step in this analysis was to create systematic timelines by placing all domestic and European events into a larger context. From these I was able to develop the dimension for international pressures: a timetable of accession talks between the European Union and accession states,[2] the beginning of EU monitoring of state compliance, and the timelines of accession.

My analysis of international pressures begins prior to the accession talks, covers the period of EU accession conditionality, and then culminates in the post-conditionality stage. To understand state actions in response to EU conditionality, I outline all parliamentary and government activity in relation to gender equality in the market from 1995 to 2010, beginning with existing policies on gender equality and their compatibility, or fit, with EU requirements. The ten directives on gender equality in the labor market were divided into five policy areas of analysis: parental and maternity leave, care and informal work, equal pay and gender pay gap, tax and benefit policies, and nondiscrimination and equal access to work. This division was suggested by the analysis of policy changes in EU Enlargement countries conducted by scholars of the QUING Project. I note that all accession states already had some of the policy provisions in these areas before their accession negotiation began; moreover, in some areas of policy, such as parental and maternity leave, the existing provisions at that time were more generous than the European Union required.[3] Thus, my analytical task in assessing state compliance is to evaluate the compatibility of existing pre-negotiation laws on gender equality with EU requirements, assess policy, and institutional reform in closing the gap between the EU requirements and state laws in the pre-accession period, and assess the maintenance of these standards in the post-accession period. I then evaluate institutional compatibility with EU requirements by tracing the creation of state institutions on gender equality, their status, their mandate, and their functions. Some countries like Poland have had an institution on women's affairs since 1986; other countries like Latvia, Estonia, and Bulgaria created their institutions on gender equality right before the accession. My task is to document these institutional reforms and to assess the powers of existing or newly created offices for each given year, capturing changes over time. In the quantitative analysis, my observations reflect yearly changes in policy and institutional adjustment. In the following section on data coding, I provide a detailed overview of how measuring policy and institutional compatibility with EU requirements proceeded. First, this chapter will introduce the study variables and coding rules. Second, it will present the findings from the statistical analysis. Finally, it will introduce the qualitative case studies.

Coding the Variables

The Outcome Variable: State Compliance with EU Requirements on Gender Equality

For the quantitative analysis, the study evaluates if the outcomes of policy and institutional reform "were not compatible with EU requirements on gender equality requirements and standards," "were minimally compatible with EU requirements on gender equality requirements and standards," "were partly compatible with EU requirements on gender equality requirements and standards," or "were compatible with EU requirements on gender equality requirements and standards." The measurement of government compliance explores government input in policy and institutional reform rather than the outcomes of these policies on social, political, and economic indicators.[4] Government compliance is measured as two processes: *policy harmonization* and *institutional adjustment*. Policy harmonization evaluates the compatibility of domestic laws with EU requirements on gender equality. Institutional adjustment measures the institutional capacity to enforce policies on gender equality and evaluates their compatibility with EU requirements.

To evaluate levels of state compliance, I develop original *Indexes of Policy Harmonization* and *Institutional Adjustment*. Both of these indexes represent an original measure of government action in the area of policy and institutional reforms on gender equality in ten EU Enragement states since 1995 to 2010. All measurement and coding errors are mine.

Policy harmonization[5] is broken down into three categories: the adoption of a blueprint policy on gender equality, the adoption of a national administrative strategy for policy enforcement, and the comprehensiveness of policy provisions in the five policy areas (maternity and parental leave; care and informal work; equal pay and gender pay gap; tax and benefit policies; and nondiscrimination and equal access to work). To compare state compliance with legislative requirements across time and across ten accession states, I develop a *Policy Harmonization Index*, which ranges from: "not compatible," "minimally compatible," "partly compatible," and "compatible" with the EU equality directives on the scale from 0 to 7. For the detailed operationalization and coding rules, review Appendix III. For review of surveyed laws and policies, please see Appendix I.

The second component of state compliance, *institutional adjustment*, measures the compatibility of state institutions on gender equality with EU requirements.[6] First, this measurement reflects the existence of such an institution, and second, it measures its capacity to enforce policies on gender equality. I identify three sets of criteria to capture institutional powers and the status of government offices on gender equality: the status of the institution, the legislative and policy influence capacity of the institutions, and the enforcement capacity of the institution. The scale is from 0 to 3. Appendix II lists the institutions created in EU Enlargement states from 1995 to 2010. Appendix III presents coding rules for this measurement in detail.

To enable a quantitative comparative analysis of this measure, I developed the *Institutional Adjustment Index*. The Index range is as follows: "compatible" with EU requirements and "strong" institutional capacity; "partly compatible" and "moderate" institutional capacity; "minimally compatible" and "weak" institutional capacity; and "non-compatible" and "no institution" or "extremely dysfunctional and weak" institution. The category of "extremely dysfunctional" institution can be applied to cases when institutions exist but do not advance gender equality policies; on the contrary, they advance conservative anti-feminist policies.

The *Policy Harmonization Index* focuses on the legal adjustment of domestic laws, and the *Institutional Adjustment Index* focuses on the institutional capacities to enforce policies. Conceptually, these two indices measure two aspects of the same process—state compliance with EU accession requirements. The differentiation of these two aspects, though, is important for identifying the relationship between them and assessing if there is a gap between policy adoption and policy enforcement. Many EU Enlargement commentators have voiced concerns that adopted laws would remain "dead letters," or "laws on the books" which would not be enforced (Falkner, Traub, and Holzleithner 2008a,b). Scholars argue that EU incentives and conditional pressures are not sufficient to stimulate change in behavior and practice at the domestic level, so the adoption of new laws is merely window dressing which does not generate changes in policy practices at the domestic level (Bretherton 2001; Roth 2008a,b; Sloat 2004b). With the enormous number of new laws that the accession states had to transpose in a very short time, there is a real risk that the states can fall short in allocating adequate administrative, financial, and human resources for enforcing these new laws. Through an analysis of policy adjustment and institutional capacities to enforce these policies, a measure of state compliance, thus, is evaluating the gap between the adoption and the enforcement of EU policies by national governments. I recognize that the measure of institutional capacity offered in this study is an imperfect shortcut for grasping the full picture of policy enforcement. With all its limitations, though, it is a useful analytical concept that helps us understand the relationship between the two processes, policy adoption and policy enforcement.

Comparative Analysis of Compliance in Ten Enlargement States

Below I review relative levels of compliance among ten accession states in their efforts to adjust their policies and institutions to fit the EU requirements on gender equality. I group states by their level and speed of compliance to sort out basic differences and similarities between them. As the description of policy change in Appendix I shows, most states amended their Labor Codes and other relevant laws to accommodate the provisions of the EU equality directives in the short period from 2000 to 2004, reaching a "partly compatible" level of compliance in the area of policy harmonization. Some states postponed the enactment of new laws until the day of accession. For instance, in the Czech Republic, which amended its Labor Code in 2001, new provisions went into force in 2004, the year of accession. Other states, including Estonia (2004), Latvia (2004, 2006), Poland (2001, 2004), and Slovakia (2003, 2007), enacted policy changes in the year of accession or even after accession. Most states had satisfactory levels of compliance with EU legislative requirements at the time of accession but were expected to further align their national laws with EU directives upon accession. As for specific policy areas, some EU requirements were less problematic than others. For instance, most states complied with maternity and parental leave requirements, the area of policy which did not require extensive adjustments in most CEE states (except for Romania, which had to institute paid parental leave). Other areas of policy were more problematic for state compliance. The protection of self-employed workers and informal workers was marginal and unsatisfactory in many EU Enlargement states. Procedures to combat discrimination on the grounds of sex were poorly specified and required attention in all countries after accession. This resulted in the EU Commission beginning infringement procedures against all EU Enlargement countries in 2008 (EC Commission 2008). All states were in violation of the EU directives on the protection against discrimination on the grounds of sex in social security and occupational payment schemes. Most states developed strategies of equalizing the retirement age for working men and women, but the process will occur over several steps with the final equalization to occur between 2022 and 2028 in each different state. The equal age of retirement was one of the most unpopular principles of the EU directives among the CEE governments, because it challenged the concept of the women's "privilege of early retirement," which was established in most communist regimes and granted to working women in recognition of their work as caregivers (Sloat 2004b). However, the early retirement of women violated principles of gender equality in social security and occupational pension calculations by putting retired women at a greater risk of poverty than retired men, and therefore, required policy reconsideration.

The EU required that all states adopt a blueprint policy on gender equality to take force no later than 2008. The Enlargement states responded differently to this requirement: while some states adopted a specific law on gender equality and the equal opportunity for men and women (Estonia, Hungary, Lithuania, Romania, and Slovenia), others chose to enact a general anti-discrimination law (the Czech Republic, Bulgaria, Poland, and Slovakia), which is generally considered a less effective instrument for enforcing gender equality. Latvia has not adopted a law against discrimination to this day. The timing of adoption also varied: Lithuania was the first to enforce a law in 1999. Most other states adopted such a law before the accession in 2002–2004. While Poland and the Czech Republic lagged behind considerably, they passed Anti-Discrimination

Acts in 2010 and 2009, respectively, after heated parliamentary debates, presidential vetoes, and multiple drafts rejected by parliament and governments since the early 2000s (see table 3.1).

I also observe some variation between states in compliance with institutional adjustment. Most states created gender equality institutions at the executive level quite early. In fact, many of them opened these units before they received an accession invitation from the European Union. Poland, Slovenia, Lithuania, Slovakia, and Romania established their offices on women's affairs or women's policies in response to the UN World Conferences on Women in 1985 (Poland and Slovenia) and 1995 (Lithuania, Slovakia, Czech Republic, and Romania). Other states opened these offices in response to EU requirements (Latvia, Estonia, and Bulgaria), which was reflected in the title of the office. For instance, in the Czech Republic and Latvia, the bureaus on gender equality were opened as parts of the Departments on EU Relations and EU Integration, which is indicative of their instrumental purpose—they lacked the power or the political will to advance the gender equality agenda set forth by the European Union. Table 3.2 presents the overview of offices on gender equality by their institutional status, showing that only two states had ministry-level offices in 2010 (Slovenia and Lithuania). Most states had departments within a relevant Ministry (most commonly Ministry of Labor and Social Affairs), and several had low-level units with inadequate resources and limited agendas included as part of a larger division inside a relevant Ministry.

By the time of accession, most candidate states reached a "partly compatible" level of compliance with EU institutional requirements on gender equality, and three states, Lithuania, Hungary, and Slovenia, were

Table 3.1. The Adoption of Law on Gender Equality (Blueprint Policy) by Country, 1999–2010

Early Adoption	Adoption before the Accession	Adoption Laggards (after deadline)	No Adoption
Lithuania (1999)	Romania (2002)	Czech Republic (2009)	Latvia
	Slovenia (2002)	Poland (2010)	
	Hungary (2003)		
	Bulgaria (2003)		
	Estonia (2004)		
	Slovakia (2004)		

Table 3.2. Status of Institutions on Gender Equality and Equal Opportunity for Women and Men, 2010

Ministry-Level *High Compliance*	Department within Ministry *Medium Compliance*	Unit within Department within Ministry *Low Compliance*
Lithuania (1999–present)	Estonia (2004–present)	Bulgaria (2004–present)
Slovenia (1992–present)	Hungary (2004–2006)	Czech Republic (1999–present)
Hungary (2003–2004)	Poland (2005–present)	Hungary (2006–present)
Poland (2001–2005)	Romania (2003–present)	Latvia (2003–present)
		Slovakia (1999–present)

in full compliance with this requirement. By 2010, as table 3.2 shows, states had a pronounced variation in the powers vested in institutions overseeing gender equality. Common trends in institutional diversity include most states establishing structures in executive and legislative branches, consultative bodies in the form of inter-ministerial councils, or ombudsperson's office. Some states created offices at municipal and regional levels, although these bodies are quite underdeveloped in the CEE countries.

Combining information for legislative and institutional compliance, I note consistently higher levels of compliance in Lithuania and Slovenia, average levels of compliance in Estonia, Romania, and Slovakia, periods of progressive compliance and policy reversals in Poland and Hungary, and consistently poor compliance in Bulgaria, the Czech Republic, and Latvia.

The Explanatory Variables: International and Domestic Dimensions of Compliance Conditionality, Normative Pressure, and Social Pressure

Conditionality is conceptualized as the process by which an international institution explicitly links compliant behavior with a conditional incentive, specifically, the incentive of gaining membership in the European Union (Kelley 2004). The conditionality period begins when the European Union and prospective candidate sign an agreement to initiate accession negotiations (for some states it was the Luxembourg Summit of 1997; for others it was the Helsinki Summit of 1999) and ends when the candidate state gains membership to the European Union (2004 or 2007). In quantitative analysis, the period of "conditionality" is presented by a dummy variable which is coded as "present" during 1998/2000–2004/2007 and "absent" in other periods. Detailed analysis of period coding is provided in the notes.[7]

I conceptualize "normative pressure" as an instance in which international institutions express concern about the status of policy and policy practices in a given state; provide recommendations for changing policies and practices; engage with governments and non-governmental organizations in dialogue about the issue in question; and run public awareness campaigns or provide funds for such campaigns or other programs of public outreach. But they do not link the change in state behavior to a conditional incentive (Kelley 2004). In both qualitative and quantitative analysis, I consider the pre-negotiation and the post-accession periods as a stage of exclusively "normative pressures," when membership conditionality was not yet used or was already abolished due to state accession to the European Union. Thus, conceptually I link the period in EU-Enlargement state relations with dummy variables for measuring the type of exerted international pressure: normative influence, conditionality, and post-accession normative pressure. In quantitative analysis, "normative pressure" is linked with pre-accession negotiations (1995–1997/1999) and post-accession period (2004/2007–2010). In qualitative analysis, I note that normative pressures accompanied conditionality and were present virtually throughout the course of the studied periods.

I conceptualize "social pressure" as an instance when international organizations place informal expectations about policy, practices, and institutions states that desire membership in the European Union. Such expectations, both real and perceived, influence the behavior of prospective candidates, states with candidate status, and member states. In qualitative analysis, I note that social pressures accompanied conditionality and were present all throughout the entire period being analyzed, 1995–2010. In quantitative analysis, the period dummy variable for social pressures coincides with the period dummy variable for "normative pressures" (see above). In the subsequent qualitative discussion in chapter 4, I provide a more dense description of "conditional pressures," "normative pressures," and "social pressures" and analyze the EU–candidate states interactions, including initial reaction to EU conditionality, their reform target and goals, and commitment to pursue them. In addition, I review strategies of normative engagement used by the European Union during and after conditionality to describe the types of EU programs targeting state governments, NGOs, and the public. Further, I assess their power to change the state elites' normative positions on gender equality. Finally, I present a detailed model of social pressure as a mechanism of international influence.

Domestic Political Actors and Control Variables

This study takes into account the impact of domestic political systems and actors. Among non-government actors, the study evaluates the impact of feminist non-governmental organizations that supported the gender equality agenda of the European Union. These organizations may include advocacy groups, resource centers, regional umbrella organizations, women's research groups affiliated with academia, and research institutions explicitly focused on advancing gender equality. Following Stetson and Mazur's approach, I evaluate the strength and organizational capacity of these organizations by analyzing the activity of women's movement actors

(2003). For the quantitative analysis, the operationalization of feminist NGOs is centered specifically on the activity of these groups in regard to government compliance with EU gender equality policies. Do these NGOs participate in policy drafting? Do they lobby the government to initiate and continue reforms? Do they protest against reluctant governments? In coding the activity of feminist women's groups, the scores range from "weak" (a fragmented activity; weak organizational structures; no cohesion; no issue focus; coded as 0.33) to "moderate" (some lobbying activity and protesting, but no organized targeted mobilization; moderate strength organizational structures; low cohesiveness, some focus on the issue; coded as 0.66) and "strong" (a history of lobbying and protesting activity, a strong advocacy voice; and ties with multiple women's organizations inside the country and within the region; broad organizational base; cohesive coordinated activity; issue focused activity; coded as 1). In the qualitative analysis, these questions are discussed in detail and specific examples of NGO activities and their level of mobilization will be illustrated.

Societal opposition includes various groups and non-governmental organizations not affiliated with the government and whose actions are targeted at halting state compliance with EU gender equality requirements. For the region, I did not find a massive opposition to gender equality principles, but an occasional organized effort to halt these reforms is reported in cases when religious organizations opposed the reforms on gender equality and when conservative trade unions did not support new policies. I code oppositional activity as: "weak," when efforts to oppose gender equality principles are not well articulated and when social groups are not well organized against this principle (0.33); "moderate," when there is some organization of oppositional forces occurring, but the actions are fragmented (0.66); and "strong," when the opposition uses broad-based organizational powers and structures in a targeted campaign against gender equality policies (1).

This study takes into account the degree of parliament support or opposition to gender equality policies. As discussed in chapter 2, political parties have often established positions on gender equality in the labor market. Left-wing parties are more likely to support such policies while right-wing parties, including nationalist and liberal parties, have historically situated themselves in opposition to these principles. I utilize a traditional ideological division between parties centered on their respective socioeconomic policy platforms. To capture the political influence of parties on policymaking, I identify the governing majority party, or a governing coalition, in national parliaments for each particular year. I code the governing majority as follows: right (0), center-right (1), center (2), center-left (3), and left (4). The qualitative analysis provides for a deeper account of party support or resistance to policy change and enforcement. It evaluates party platforms and official statements on the issue of gender equality and not only discusses the specific positions of individual parliamentarians but also evaluates the general course of parliamentary debates.

To understand the role of female politicians in the creation and advancement of gender equality policies and institutions, this study measures the proportion of women in national parliaments and in cabinets. I record this measure as a percentage of women's share in national parliaments (for each year) and cabinets (also, a yearly observation). Case studies are then used to evaluate the positions of female politicians on the issue of gender equality, their level of organization in support of this policy (in case this activity was significant), and in certain cases, expert evaluation of the role of female politicians in advancing this policy forward.

In addition, I include several control variables in the quantitative analysis. These factors include two variables that control the costs of compliance, such as the level of unemployment (percent of unemployed labor force) and the gender pay gap (difference in income between working women and working men), and one general control variable (the country's GDP per capita in real U.S. dollars) to control for economic development. The general purpose of these controls is to determine if the costs of compliance are prohibitive for those states which experience the largest discrepancy between their socioeconomic realities and the EU accession requirements. I do not include the level of democratization in my analysis because all candidate states made a concerted effort to democratize their political institutions. For instance, both non-democratic Slovakia and Romania could move forward with accession negotiations only after committing themselves to democratic restructuring and ridding themselves of the authoritarian leadership of Mečiar and Iliescu. Since only democratic states could be part of EU accession negotiations, the level of democratization could be a redundant control variable in my study; however, other research supports the hypothesis that democracy positively effects the level of state compliance with EU requirements (Kelley 2004; Schimmelfennig 2001). Table 3.3 provides an overview of the quantitative variables and Appendix IV presents coding rules for the independent variables.

Table 3.3. Overview of Variables

Variable	Coding
Policy Harmonization Index	"Compatible"/"partly compatible"/"minimally compatible"/"non-compatible"
Institutional Adjustment Index	"Compatible" and "strong"/"partly compatible" and "moderate"/"minimally compatible" and "weak"/"non-compatible" and "no institution" or "extremely dysfunctional"
Pre-Negotiation Period	"Present"/"absent"
Conditionality Period	"Present"/"absent"
Post-Accession Normative/Social Pressure Period	"Present"/"absent"
Women's NGO	"Absent"/"weak"/"moderate"/"strong"
Social Opposition	"Weak"/"strong"
Party Ideology	"Right"/"center-right"/"center"/"center-left"/"left"
Female MPs	Percent of all members
Female Cabinet Ministers	Percent of all members
Level of Unemployment	Percent of working force
Gender Pay Gap	Female to Male Income Ratio
GDP per capita	In real U.S. dollars

Statistical Analysis and Results

To test the effect of international pressures and domestic factors on state compliance with EU accession requirements on gender equality, I employ OLS models with panel corrected standard errors. The model uses random effects because the data has a relatively balanced number of countries and periods, whereas datasets with fewer countries and larger periods are suggested for fixed effects models.[8] This study does not use lagged variables.[9] With 160 observations, this study allows for the testing of additive models for the effect of domestic actors. I test for the interactive effects of governing parties in parliament and the strength of women's NGOs activism in order to test the hypotheses that political parties in power and women's NGOs produce a mediating effect on compliance (H8). In addition, I use the interaction between the year variables and the period variables to explore the role of conditionality both during the accession period and after its removal in the post-accession period (H1–4).

Results and Discussion

Table 3.4 presents the results of the statistical analysis for state compliance with policy harmonization requirements. Table 3.5 presents the results for the analysis of institutional adjustment. I will discuss each set of factors separately.

International Pressures and State Compliance with
Gender Equality Requirements

Several hypotheses on types of international involvement propose that international pressures are the driving force for state compliance (H1–4). I test the effect of conditional pressures during the accession conditionality period and normative and social pressures during the post-accession period. These two periods are coded as dummy variables on state compliance in policy harmonization and institutional adjustment. While the strength of the effects of conditionality and post-conditionality pressures varies across the two stages of compliance, their effects demonstrate similar patterns in the expected direction: states rapidly adopt new policies and establish institutions on gender equality in the accession conditionality period; however, the rate of policy harmonization and institutional adjustment slows down upon state accession to European Union. In the case of institutional adjustment, I observe marginalization of state offices

Table 3.4. State Compliance with Policy Harmonization, 1995–2010; Coefficients (PCSE), Linear Cross-Sectional Time-Series

Model	1	2	3	4
Accession Conditionality	-2.150** (0.327)		-1.820** (.280)	-1.860** (0.278)
Post-Accession Normative Pressure	3.490** (0.561)		3.220** (0.590)	3.240** (0.576)
Pre-Negotiation Period	0.090 (0.060)		0.150* (0.059)	0.120 (0.059)
Accession Conditionality Period	0.630** (.043)		0.570** (0.043)	0.560** (0.042)
Post-Accession Normative Period	0.072 (0.042)		0.090 (0.040)	0.090* (0.039)
Strong Activist Women's NGOs		3.880** (.655)	1.200** (0.300)	0.770* (0.325)
Ideology of Party in Power		0.230* (0.078)	0.160** (0.040)	0.030 (0.063)
Proportion of Female MPs		0.030 (0.026)	-0.034* (0.012)	-0.040* (0.012)

	Model 1	Model 2	Model 3	Model 4
Conservative Movement	0.001 (0.010)	0.002 (0.010)	-0.007 (0.020)	
Proportion of Female Cabinet Ministers	-0.001 (0.010)	0.001 (0.010)	0.060* (0.020)	
Interaction Women's NGOs and Ideology of Party in Power	0.290* (0.124)			
Gender Pay Gap	0.030** (0.005)	0.030** (0.005)		
Level of Unemployment	-0.020 (0.015)	-0.025 (0.014)		
GDP per capita	0.000* (0.000)	0.000 (0.000)		
Constant	0.590* (0.236)	0.380 (0.260)	-0.010 (0.677)	0.780** (0.123)
N	160	160	160	160
R2	0.880	0.870	0.430	0.830

*Significant at 0.05 level;
**Significant at 0.001 level.

Table 3.5. State Compliance with Institutional Adjustment, 1995–2010; Coefficients (PCSE), Linear Cross-Sectional Time-Series

Model	1	2	3	4
Accession Conditionality	-0.620* (0.222)		-0.470 (0.250)	-0.504* (0.220)
Post-Accession Normative/ Social Pressure	1.440** (0.389)		1.100* (0.500)	1.120* (0.440)
Pre-Negotiation Period	0.060 (0.030)		0.030 (0.050)	-0.008 (0.043)
Accession Conditionality Period	0.190** (0.030)		0.102* (0.040)	0.102* (0.040)
Post-Accession Period	-0.024 (0.030)		-0.035 (0.034)	-0.040 (0.030)
Strong Activist Women's NGOs		1.470** (0.178)	0.870** (0.230)	0.430 (0.255)
Ideology of Party in Power		0.090* (0.036)	0.080* (0.030)	-0.050 (0.045)
Proportion of Female MPs		-0.010 (0.010)	-0.020* (0.010)	-0.020 (0.010)

	(1)	(2)	(3)	(4)
Conservative Movement		0.010 (0.010)	0.010 (0.010)	0.010 (0.007)
Proportion of Female Cabinet Ministers		0.025* (0.008)	0.017* (0.010)	0.020* (0.008)
Interaction Women's NGOs and Ideology of Party in Power				0.289** (0.090)
Gender Pay Gap			-0.010* (0.010)	-0.001* (0.010)
Level of Unemployment			-0.004 (0.010)	0.001 (0.010)
GDP per capita			0.000 (0.000)	0.000 (0.000)
Constant	.4 (.076)**	-.22 (.183)	.59 (.16)**	.83 (.152)**
N	160	160	160	160
R2	0.340	0.330	0.440	0.470

*Significant at 0.05 level
**Significant at 0.01 level.

on gender equality in some states upon the accession. This generates a negative coefficient for post-accession period, but this trend is not statistically significant.

Models 1 and 4 present the effects of conditional pressures and normative and social pressures on policy harmonization (variable range 0 to 7) and institutional adjustment (variable range 0 to 3). As it was expected, in the period preceding the accession negotiations (1995–1997/1999), states did not engage in active reforms of policies and institutions on gender equality controlling for state economic performance and the composition of political actors inside and outside the government. We observe that the estimate of the slope for that period reported in Models 1 and 4 as the interaction effect between the year and pre-conditionality period is substantively and statistically insignificant from 0 (see the interaction term for the period preceding accession negotiations). The situation changes dramatically when the European Commission begins monitoring state compliance in the pre-accession phase (1998/2000–2004/2007). In this period states pursue rapid reforms of their policies and institutions on gender equality: we observe that EU conditionality is both substantively and statistically significant as a predictor of state compliance (in both models it is significant as part of the interaction term between the year and accession period). The results in Model 4 in both tables suggest that the estimate coefficient for this period is substantively and statistically larger than 0, controlling for other factors. In the post-accession period, the rate of policy adoption and institutional adjustment slows down, as we can see from the smaller coefficients on the interaction term for normative pressures for policy harmonization (table 3.4) and a negative coefficient for the estimation of the slope for post-accession period in case of institutional adjustment (table 3.5). None of these effects, however, are statistically significant. In other words, there is a pattern in the direction expected in hypothesis 2 (deterioration of compliance upon accession), but it does not meet the requirement of statistical significance. Overall, these results support the expectations in hypotheses 4, which states that social pressures force states into conformal behavior, meaning that states do not pursue high levels of compliance, rapid and comprehensive reforms, and may show policy and institutional stagnation, or some reversal of reforms.

To explore the effect of international influences in depth, I present the predicted probability of state compliance in EU accession states during three periods: pre-negotiations, accession conditionality (conditional requirement to comply applied), and post-accession (conditional requirement is lifted, normative and social pressures continues). Figures 3.1 and 3.2 present the predicted probability for policy harmonization and institutional adjustment, respectively, over three periods of accession. For policy adjustment (figure 3.1), we find that during the first period, before official negotiations, the states already had some policy provisions on the books (years 1 to 4 on both figures). The general rate of policy reform in this period is very small and statistically insignificant from 0. The coefficient of rate of policy adoption at this time is 0.085. The situation changes dramatically as states acquire candidate status and the European Union initiates monitoring compliance: the rate of policy change per year during the second period is 0.655 (year 5 to 10).[10] The slope coefficient increases seven times when the conditional monitoring begins! The highest rate of policy change per year is the last year of conditional requirement; the slope coefficient equals 0.698 indicating that states pursued last-minute policy adjustment and changes to meet the accession requirement. Bulgaria and Romania, accession 2007, had to meet their social policy requirements in 2004 as well as several other countries, whose accession was scheduled in May 2004). This confirms

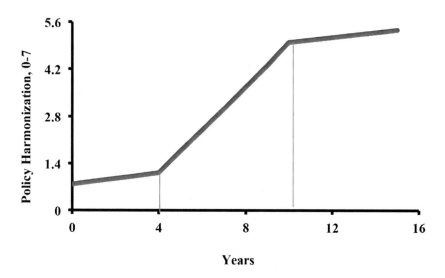

Figure 3.1. Predicted Probabilities for Policy Harmonization in EU Enlargement States, 1995–2010

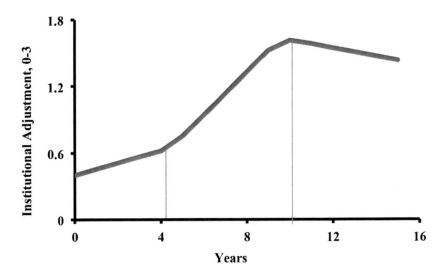

Figure 3.2. Predicted Probabilities for Institutional Adjustment in EU Enlargement States, 1995–2010

expectations proposed by the rationalist bargaining model and reviewed on pages 27–28. Once the conditional requirements are lifted (year 11 on both figures), the slope coefficient flattens reflecting a significant decrease in the speed and scope of reforms; on average, it equals 0.0725, falling at least nine times from the highest rate of policy reform at the year 11. But the slope is not negative, so some reforms are taking place in some countries even in the post-accession period (adoption of anti-discrimination acts in Poland and the Czech Republic and adoption of National Programs on equality and equal opportunity in several other states).

The graph of predicted probabilities for institutional adjustment reveals a similar pattern: some states already had institutions on gender equality before the accession negotiations started. This fact is reflected on the graph by the slope coefficient for period 1 (years 1–4) (see figure 3.2). The average rate of institutional adjustment per year in this period equals 0.055. The slope coefficient for institutional adjustment changes dramatically when accession monitoring begins: on average 0.1935 per year, almost 23 times faster! The rate of reforms already begins to slow down during the last year of the accession period (–0.0757 for the year 10), and falling dramatically, 0.002413 per year, after states gained membership. While the slope coefficient is negative, it is not statistically significant, so we can say that the rate of reforms slowed down and the powers of some institutions on gender equality were diminished, but we do not observe the disappearance of these institutions across the region. These findings confirm the expectations of the rationalist bargaining model about the effect of conditionality on state compliance and demonstrate the stagnation of policy and institutions on gender equality in the post-accession period predicted by the sociological model. Stagnation of policy and institutional reforms in the post-accession period suggests that no serious normative change occurred among state elites. If the governments of the new member states viewed gender equality policies as a priority, then we would expect to observe continual reform even after accession. On average, state compliance with institutional adjustment reached its highest point, 1.6 out of 3 points possible, so the states had enough room for improvement of their institutions (see also table 3.2 on institutional status to further illustrate this point). For policy adjustment, the states on average reached 5.2 points out of 7 possible points, but their rates of compliance slowed down upon the accession.

To sum up the analysis of state behavior in the post-accession period, I argue that while the rate of state reforms decreased after the EU accession, new member states did not dismantle their policies and institutions on gender equality, as many commentators feared. Overall, we observe three trends in state actions in the post-accession period: first, most states continued adjusting their policies and strengthening their institutions after their accession to European Union, see tables 3.1 and 3.2 near the beginning of this chapter. For instance, Poland and the Czech Republic passed their anti-discrimination laws in 2008 and 2011, respectively, long after their EU accession. Many other states adopted National Plans on Gender Equality to outline administrative orders for new policy enforcement. Second, some states made no concerted effort to improve their policies or institutions. For instance, Latvia never passed a long-overdue anti-discrimination law, and Slovakia and Estonia failed to improve the status of their gender equality institutions. Third, there is only slight evidence indicating reform reversal in the institutional stage of compliance. Although Poland and Hungary decreased the powers of their offices on gender equality in the post-accession period, many other states marginally improved the status and functions of these institutions or allowed them to remain at the same level. For instance, the Czech Republic established the position of Minister on Equal Opportunity in

2007 only to later abolish it in 2010. Taking these data into consideration, it is safe to conclude that there are no signs of regional reform reversals that could potentially result in gross incompliance with EU gender equality regulations.

To summarize the findings from the statistical models, I contend that accession conditionality was a powerful and effective mechanism for inducing compliance in the pre-accession stage, resulting in dramatic changes both in policy and institutional areas of compliance. A continued trend to preserve policies and institutions on gender equality after the removal of conditional pressures, however, demonstrates the failure of the rationalist bargaining framework to explain post-accession compliance. This is consistent with arguments put forward by several scholars who argue that conditionality is important for the initial stages of compliance, but it does not matter as much when compliance takes root in state practice and other mechanisms of enforcement become more important (Finnemore 1996; Keck and Sikkink 1998). In this analysis, I demonstrate that arguments of the sociological school support the findings about state conformal behavior upon the accession.

While the tested models demonstrate the independent effects of conditionality and social and normative pressures, I recognize that these processes occurred simultaneously, and therefore, could strengthen each other's effect. I, therefore, cannot make any definitive conclusions about whether social pressures would have been as effective if no conditionality was used, and whether conditionality would have been as effective if no socialization took place. In the subsequent qualitative chapters and analysis of a counterfactual case, I will clarify some of the hypotheses on the role of conditional and social pressures posited in chapter 2.

Political Actors Hypothesis

The results in tables 3.4 and 3.5 report that activist women's NGOs have a strong positive effect on both stages of compliance, policy and institutional adjustment (H5). All models where the effect of women's activism was tested show consistent statistical and substantive significance. Their effect does not fade even if we test their interaction with political parties, suggesting that strong NGOs influence reforms on policy harmonization under right-wing parties (table 3.4, model 4). This, however, is not true for institutional adjustment where parties seem to play a more powerful role and women's NGOs do not seem to influence the institutional status under right-wing parties, controlling for interaction effects between women's NGOs and parties in power and other factors. These findings are remarkably consistent with scholarly expectations about the role of social movement actors in ensuring government compliance with international agreements (Keck and Sikkink 1998, Weldon 2002, 2011).

The models show consistency in the role of governing party ideology in promoting institutional and policy compliance (H7). For both policy harmonization and institutional adjustment, we see that the ideology of the ruling party is statistically significant and substantively influential, with left-wing parties being more supportive of adopting policies on gender equality and establishing stronger institutions for their enforcement while right-wing parties prove less supportive of such policies and institutions. Moreover, we see the interaction effect between the strength of women's NGOs and the party in power being strong and statistically significant in models 4 (tables 3.4 and 3.5) (H8). The party effects on state compliance are illuminating because they reveal the debates and controversies about gender equality demonstrate that the issue is politically charged and divisive.

To explore the joint effect of women's NGOs and political parties on levels of state compliance, I estimate the marginal effects of these actors presented in figures 3.3 and 3.4. Considering the effects of this interaction at various levels of the constitutive variables provides more insight into the observed dynamics (Brambor, Clark and Golder 2006). For policy harmonization, when there is no women's NGO on gender equality, the party in power has a statistically significant positive effect, which increases from 1.059 (right parties) to 1.18 (left parties) keeping all variables constant (at 0 or at means). For institutional adjustment, however, parties seem to have a divergent effect on state compliance: when no women's NGOs are present, right-wing parties are more likely to establish gender equality institutions (or promote them) than the left-wing parties. When women's NGOs are the strongest, left-wing parties have strong positive influence: the effect of interaction increases substantially from 1.82 points (under right parties) to 3.10 points (under left parties). Similar dynamics of change were observed for institutional adjustment: the effect changes from .79 points (under right-wing parties) to 2 points (under left-wing parties, controlling for all other variables). The interaction effect suggests that strong activist women's NGOs are more likely to succeed in pushing their agenda on gender equality when leftist parties are in power. Thus, left-wing parties serve as a window of opportunity for activist women's NGOs in supporting the creation of strong institutions on gender equality. When there is no strong women's movement to influence them, left-wing parties are not likely to promote gender equality institutions. Right-wing parties might do it under pressure from the European Union; for example, Latvia's conservative government only established its gender equality institutions after Brussels stressed their importance. The qualitative analysis supports these findings and reveals that right-wing parties postpone policy reforms until the last possible moment to qualify for accession and pursue minimal steps to enforce these policies.

The results for the effects of female politicians reveal some differences in their powers to influence political decisions. Female cabinet ministers had statistically significant effect on both stages of compliance in models 2 and 3 (and in model 4 for institutional adjustment) in the expected direction: a larger number of female cabinet ministers are associated with stronger policy harmonization and institutional adjustment

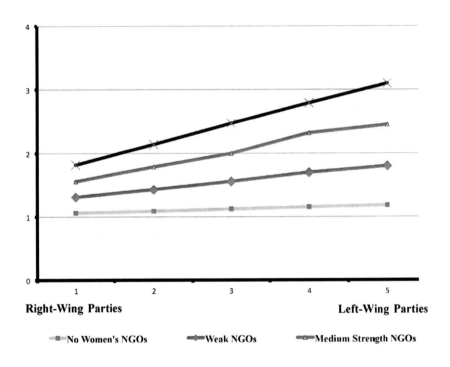

Figure 3.3. Marginal Effects of Political Parties and the Strength of Women's NGOs on Policy Harmonization in EU Enlargement States, 1995–2010

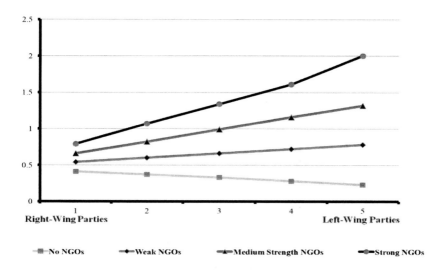

Figure 3.4. Marginal Effects of Political Parties and the Strength of Women's NGOs on Institutional Adjustment in EU Enlargement States, 1995–2010

after controlling for other international and domestic factors. Substantively, these statistical findings make sense (H10). Female cabinet ministers were often in charge of policies relating to "women's issues," like welfare, social assistance, and women's affairs. Being in charge of these policies, female cabinet ministers could have a positive effect on the degree of policy adoption and the creation of offices on gender equality. The effect of female cabinet ministers disappears when we include an interaction between political parties in power and women's NGOs for explaining policy harmonization (model 4). This shows that female members of cabinets had a less consistent impact on the process of policy adoption, but were instrumental for institutional adjustment. Such a finding reveals that the cabinet ministers can control the executive decision making (and institutional adaptation falls under executive power) but lacks mechanisms for influencing the legislative process (policy adoption).

The effect of female parliamentarians is contrary to our original expectations (H9). In the incomplete model for policy harmonization, female MPs had a small positive effect on policy adoption, but this effect becomes negative when we add international and domestic variables as well as an interaction term to model 4. For the institutional adjustment variable, female parliamentarians have a statistically significant, negative effect, which is consistent with their influence on policy harmonization. This finding suggest that a number of female MPs in national parliaments is not an important factor for promoting state compliance with gender equality regulations in the region overall. An in-depth analysis of cases sheds some light on this dilemma. We find that nationalist and conservative religious parties recruited and promoted a large number of female representatives to parliaments in several countries of the region. For instance, in Poland, the League of Polish Families, and in Bulgaria, the Movement of King Simeon, had the largest number of female representatives in parliament. It is important to note, however, that these women represented conservative parties and policy positions and supported traditionalist views, thus, marginalizing gender equality policies on the parliament agenda.

The existence and strength of the conservative countermovement did not produce a statistically significant effect either on policy harmonization, or on institutional adjustment (H6).

Control Variables

The gender pay gap is found to have a statistically significant effect on both stages of compliance, albeit in different directions. The gender pay gap is statistically significant with a small substantive effect in models 3 and 4 for policy harmonization. But contrary to conventional expectations, its effect is positive: a higher gender pay gap is associated with the creation of stronger compliance with policy harmonization. The direction of this relationship is unexpected and is hard to explain since gender pay gap is thought to be one of the major problems that the new legislation is meant to combat. Gender pay has a statistically significant, positive effect on institutional adjustment, which means that states with higher gender pay gap are more likely to establish weak institutions on gender equality. One way to think about this puzzling finding is to speculate that states with bad records on equal pay gap are aware of this fact and try to "appease" the Commission by changing their laws, while states with smaller gender gap do not feel as much pressure to do so. Since the enforcement of gender pay regulation is a cost, states with poor records tend to establish weaker institutions to avoid enforcing this law.

The effect of unemployment is not statistically significant for either stage of compliance. In both cases, its effect appears in the expected negative direction (higher levels of unemployment are associated with lower levels of compliance in policy and institutional adjustment). The GDP per capita in real U.S. dollars is found to have a negative effect on policy harmonization, suggesting that poorer states are more likely to comply with policy adjustment. To understand this finding I consider it from the perspective that poorer states are trying to work harder to qualify for accession and, therefore, change their policies quicker than richer states. While this explanation has some potential value and calls for further research into the question, I conclude that the costs of compliance, thought of as unemployment and GDP per capita in real U.S. dollars, did not produce consistent significant results, while other factors like international influences and domestic political actors overrode the costs of compliance.

Overall, I find that these models produced a high R-squared with results ranging from .47 to .88 in the models that included all independent variables. Thus, the models provide high explanatory leverage in confirming the role of international involvement, activist non-state actors and parliamentary parties for promoting policies and institutions on gender equality. The next chapter introduces case study analysis, presents in-depth discussion of compliance mechanisms invoked by EU conditionality, and provides empirical analysis from the countries of the region. The following three chapters present case studies on Poland, the Czech Republic, and Lithuania. Each chapter begins with a brief discussion on their respective gender equality situation and provides an overview of the political context during the course of the studied period. I then discuss individual policy cases by issue, choosing the most illustrative and rich examples of policy and institutional adjustment. This process allows analyzing several cases within a single state and drawing comparisons over time.

II

Case Studies

International and Domestic Dimensions

4

Introduction to Qualitative Analysis

The main goal of case study analysis is to discover if the chain of events, decisions, and policy changes develops in the manner predicted by the theory, and whether the actor behavior and actions fit our theory predictions (Van Evera 1997). Case studies go beyond arguments about correlations to reveal actor interests, motivations, and attitudes in a story of reconstructed decision making and detailed timeline-of-event sequence (Van Evera 1997; Underdal 1998). In the following chapters, I explore the findings from the quantitative study with the goal to reveal the events of the decision-making process and to demonstrate the involvement of various political actors in relevant policy debates, their motivations and strategies, their relative positions of power and influence, and their impact on the policy outcome. The systematization of the data, the attention to details, and the examination of how events unfolded complement the quantitative analysis and make the inferences sounder and stronger. In addition, detailed examination of how decisions about policy and institutional changes took place in individual countries inevitably reveals new factors and actors in a process of policy formation. Case studies, therefore, not only reveal if the theory works, but also expand our original theoretical propositions with new hypotheses and new causal links (George and Bennett 2005).

In the following chapters, I will employ qualitative analysis to explore the causal relationship between different types of international institutional engagement (preconditionality, conditionality, and post-conditionality), the configuration of domestic political actors in support of and in opposition to gender equality norms, and state compliance with EU gender equality requirements. Furthermore, case study analysis will help to resolve the puzzles which statistical analysis could illuminate only tentatively. For instance, careful qualitative inquiry will allow disentangling the effects of simultaneous processes, such as international socialization and social pressures, and evaluating the outcomes of these forms of international engagement. Thus, qualitative investigation will enhance the validity of our findings in the quantitative analysis. In addition, the examination of an outlier case, Lithuania, will allow evaluation of the strength of the tested theoretical model and provide new theoretical explanations for state compliance in this area of women's rights. In the remaining part of this section, I will introduce the design of the case study analysis, discuss the logic of case selection, provide an overview of qualitative methods (structured, focused comparison and process tracing) used in the study, and present an outline of the case study chapters.

In chapter 4, I evaluate the effects of international institutional engagement on state compliance referring to data from the entire EU Enlargement region. The goal in this chapter is to unravel the effects of conditionality, normative pressures, and social pressures on the levels of state compliance with EU requirements on gender equality in the workplace. I engage in careful examination of secondary archival data, scholarly and expert evaluation of compliance, normative change, and reputational pressures, as well as original interview data collected during my fieldwork in Poland and the Czech Republic. To systematize the comparative analysis, I employ structured, focused comparison and process tracing. Structured, focused comparison defines and classifies the data of the case studies by standardizing the criteria of examination for each case (George and McKeown 1985). Specifically, in evaluating state responses to international institutional engagement, I concentrate on the effects which I categorize in three ways according to my theoretical expectations: conditional compliance, normative change, and reputational pressures. In particular, I am interested in answering several questions. First, I explore whether conditionality produced compliance on paper, characterized by formalistic, window-dressing adoption of policies, or full-scale compliance with required directives. I also investigate if post-conditional compliance is likely to decrease over time. Second, I investigate if the public and elites changed their understanding and normative positions on gender equality in the workplace. To answer this question, I explore survey data and official government statements on the issue, as well as expert evaluations and assessments of normative change. Finally, I evaluate expert assessments of whether reputational concerns are at play as regard to compliance with EU gender equality requirements. To answer these questions, I refer to published materials and original interviews. I use the method of process tracing to explore causation by analyzing the original data from interviews, government statements, and secondary assessments with the goal to reveal the motivations of the main actors and establish the connections between various events.

Chapter 4 concludes with an examination of an alternative policy case—state compliance with international requirements on violence against women (VAW). This case represents counterfactual analysis, in which one major factor, international conditionality, was absent. While the European Union provided financial and technical support to candidate states in the area of violence against women, this area of women's rights was not part of conditional accession requirements. The European Union does not have binding directives on combating violence against women, thereby relying exclusively on soft law. In addition, other international players, most notably the UN, have developed and promoted recommendations on policy and practice to combat VAW globally. The case of VAW, therefore, presents a unique opportunity to evaluate policy change and state compliance with international recommendations in ten EU Enlargement states in the absence of strict international conditional pressures. In the area of VAW, therefore, we expect that normative pressures and social reputational pressures, as well as the dynamic of domestic policy support and opposition, will play the most important role in explaining state compliance with international recommendations. This case will help to disentangle the effects of simultaneously occurring events, such as conditional, normative, and social pressures, a problem that I confronted in the case of gender equality requirements. Careful examination and comparison of state compliance in two gendered policy areas will significantly strengthen my conclusions about the role of each individual mechanism of international engagement.

To enable meaningful analysis and evaluation, I rely on the method of structured, focused comparison in my examination of state compliance in the areas of VAW and gender equality in ten EU Enlargement states. In my assessment of compliance, I use the same criteria: legislative adjustment and institutional adjustment. For legislative adjustment on VAW, I present data on the adoption of a separate law on violence against women and changes to penal codes that are recommended by international organizations. I also evaluate policy practice by presenting data on police training, government-sponsored campaigns on VAW, government support for shelters for battered women, and state-sponsored trainings for government officials and judges. To evaluate institutional adjustment, I present data on state institutions designed to implement state policy on VAW. I note the status of this institution and its capacity to enforce policy on VAW. This data is presented and discussed for all ten EU Enlargement states.

In addition, I explore one case, Lithuania, in depth, as a case study of government reforms in the area of VAW with the goal to explore causal relationships between policy change and international engagement and domestic actors. The choice of Lithuania as a single country case study is not random. Lithuania is an interesting outlier case in both policy areas, albeit with opposing modalities of compliance: it is a front runner, a model state, in the area of gender equality and a stubborn laggard in the area of violence against women. Careful process tracing of events and policy debates in both policy areas allows us to reconstruct a causal story of government decision making in these two areas of gender equality and to enrich our understanding of how domestic policy reforms occur (or do not occur) in the face of international pressures.

The following chapters 5, 6, and 7 present three country case studies. The goal of the country case studies is to explain variation in state compliance with EU requirements. It is important to explore in detail countries with significant differences and rich within-case variation in their responses to EU conditionality. I chose three countries, Poland, the Czech Republic, and Lithuania, to demonstrate the complexity of a domestic political environment, its interactions with international institutions, and their consequences for state compliance with international requirements on gender equality. The case selection is motivated by several considerations: important variations on the dependent and independent variables, rich within-case variation, and an extreme outlier case, which helps to illuminate additional factors that propelled state reforms on gender equality. Below, I briefly introduce each of these cases and discuss the logic for their selection.

The first country study is Poland, a state that traveled a troubled path to compliance with EU gender equality requirements. Poland has been through periods of strong political will to harmonize policies and establish strong institutions on gender equality, but it has also seen times of political neglect and the complete abolishment of gender equality principles as the state endorsed a conservative, pro-family doctrine. It is also the state of many battles lost and won by strong feminist organizations in their effort to restore the gender equality agenda at the state level. Poland represents a case of interesting within-case variation, thus, enriching my investigation with important causal explanations and providing opportunity for their test in a changing political environment of a single state.

The second case study focuses on the Czech Republic, known to be the most economically advanced and developed among other CEE states and to have a more secular, more highly educated population than citizens of other EU Enlargement states. While these preconditions suggest the Czech Republic would be better at harmonizing and enforcing policies on gender equality, the data show that the Czech government consistently lagged behind the other states in adjusting their policies and institutions. This was so even though the EU Commissioner on Equal Opportunities, Vladimir Špidla, was the former minister of the Czech Ministry of Labor and Social Affairs who regularly confronted the Czech government with criticism about their inaction in the area of gender equality. What explains this paradox of negligent compliance? The detailed discussion of the Czech case will attempt to shed light on this question. The case of Czech compliance with EU requirements on gender equality is in stark contrast to the Polish path of reforms, characterized by periods of policy advancement and periods of reform reversal; it is also very different from the case of Lithuania, which took the path of early comprehensive reforms.

Lithuania is the third country case study. It is the state that was on the early track to compliance, beginning policy reforms in the late 1990s. Lithuania was ahead of all other candidate states, pursuing comprehensive reforms and complementing its "laws on the books" with strong institutions on gender equality having a broad range of responsibilities and powers. Lithuania was a model state for other democratizing post-communist states: the UNDP used Lithuanian human rights institutions as a model for emulation in Mongolia and Moldova. Different independent international agencies place Lithuania in top ranked positions on gender equality in society.[1] Lithuania is a clear outlier among the rest of the post-communist states and their compliance with international requirements on gender equality. Careful case study of an outlier case reveals new factors and actors at play in this country, which enriches my original theoretical model with novel detail and insight and expands our theoretical understanding of factors facilitating compliance with international gender equality norms.

The case studies are organized along major policy debates and government decisions with the goal to reveal the motivations of political actors. Each case study is situated in a broader political, socioeconomic, and cultural context that helps to understand the motivations and positions of the actors. This provides the reader with detailed insights about the situation in each country. All case study chapters begin with a brief overview of the major events of state transition from a communist system to a market economy and the early efforts at democratization. Since political parties in power are found to be crucial mediators of state reforms on gender equality, each country case study has a section on party politics with a focus on party competition, party ideology, and party positions on gender equality. This section creates a context for understanding the role of parties in power and policy debates on gender equality. The following section discusses the development of women's NGOs in each state. It presents information about the major activity of these organizations, and discusses their interconnectedness and level of cooperation in the area of gender equality. This discussion is important for understanding the success or failure of these organizations in influencing the government agenda on gender equality. Policy events and policy debates are presented in two sections organized along the two components of state compliance with gender equality requirements: legislative and institutional compliance. The study explores the specific policy events in individual countries central for understanding the debates on the issues of gender equality and the subsequent actions of the governments either to accommodate the required changes in national law and to establish state institutions on gender equality, or to ignore international pressures and take no government action. A single policy issue, policy debate, and a government decision following the debate is a unit of analysis in the case study. The analysis investigates the impact and interaction of international incentives and domestic actors for the outcome of state reforms on gender equality. In a concluding section for each case study, I will evaluate the interaction of international and domestic factors and discuss their joint impact on the level of state compliance with international requirements gender equality in these three EU Enlargement states.

Evaluation of International Engagement

The process of EU Enlargement has had a profound effect on government policies and institutions in candidate states. Many scholars view the EU's power over candidate states in the enlargement process as "unprecedented" and "pervasive" (Grabbe 1999; Schimmelfennig and Sedelmeier 2005). My analysis confirms this argument: EU conditionality compelled state compliance with EU gender equality directives, thereby forcing states to both transpose the legal language of directives into national laws and to establish institutions on gender equality. In this chapter I will explain how compliance took place and examine the implications that imposed compliance had on policy enforcement and reform stability upon accession.

Gender equality directives are only one of the areas in a vast range of policies that candidate states had to calibrate with EU standards to qualify for membership. In total, state governments had to harmonize national laws with the thirty-five chapters of the *acquis communautaire*, an immense body of legal regulations, commonly cited to have over 80,000 pages (Weiner 2009). As a result, the legislative process in candidate states was dominated by the enormous volume of policy change required for EU accession. Schimmelfennig and Sedelmeier, for instance, cite the case of Hungary where, in June 1999, the parliament passed 180 laws, of which 152, "were not subject to any debate because they were part of the *acquis*" (2005, 2).

The process of policy harmonization and institutional adjustment was streamlined by the European Commission (EC) during the accession period. The EC carefully monitored the processes, evaluating state progress in annual reports with guidelines for further alignment. The main feature of EU conditionality was the enforcement of rapid state reforms. Since the start of accession negotiations, candidate states had approximately seven years to undergo dramatic policy and institutional changes within the various spheres of economic, political, and social regulations. Despite the fact that negotiations for the alignment of social requirements began later than those in the economic and political policy areas, the final negotiations on social policy for the first wave of Eastern Enlargement (Czech Republic, Poland, Hungary, Estonia, and Slovenia) occurred in 2002. Most states met these requirements, with the exceptions of Poland, which received a warning from the European Commission in 2002 to hasten its reforms, and Estonia, which received an extension until 2004 on the adjustment of their social requirements (including gender equality laws). For states in the second wave (Latvia, Lithuania, and Slovakia) and the third wave (Romania and Bulgaria), the European Council set a different timetable for adjusting their social legislation and institutions. These states were required to fulfill these reforms by 2004. For these states too, conditional pressures generated compliance, albeit with some variation in the levels of compatibility with EU requirements. What incentives did rapid reforms create in these candidate states? Furthermore, what implications does EU conditionality have for state compliance, policy enforcement, and reform stability in the future?

Some commentary about conditionality and EU Enlargement embraces the idea of "rapid reforms" and "rapid rewards" (Schimmelfennig and Sedelmeier 2005). For instance, Schimmelfennig states that the success of EU conditionality is explained by a credible promise of EU membership (2007; Schimmelfennig et al. 2003; Schimmelfennig and Sedelmeier 2005).[2] Among other characteristics, the credible promise of membership includes a relatively short period of accession negotiations leading to membership in the European Union. If the accession negotiation period is too long and the rewards are distant or uncertain (as in the case of Turkey), then state elites have less incentive to under-take dramatic transformations and, consequently, they avoid engaging in costly and often unpopular reforms.[3] Sedelmeier argues that condition-ality "locked in" compliance during the negotiation period and did not allow for reform reversal following accession (2011). His research on gender equality reforms in four enlargement states demonstrates that, after gaining EU membership, countries maintained the same levels of compliance as during the conditionality period; furthermore, states with better compliance as candidate states also demonstrated higher levels of compliance when they became members. Likewise, none of the states included in his study dismantled their policies or institutions after acces-sion (Sedelmeier 2011).

Other commentators view rapid reforms as an incentive for the formal adoption of policies and institutions that do not generate high levels of policy enforcement (Bretherton 2001; Falkner et al. 2008; Miroiu 2006; Weiner 2009).[4] In addition, scholars question the legitimacy of forced policy reforms that effectively establish the European Union as a "new paternalist" power for newly independent states, many of which only recently moved away from the influence of another regional power, the Soviet Union (Miroiu 2006).

In my analysis, I examine the incentives for states within the given framework of conditionality, reveal the processes of strategic compliance with accession requirements, and analyze its impact on a state's com-mitment to new policy enforcement. It is necessary to note that the enforcement of gender equality most significantly concerns domestic labor markets and, therefore, relies on the capacity and commitment of the state to facilitate and administer its implementation. This is different from some of the economic policies in which enforcement can be facili-tated by external actors or agencies, including foreign states and compa-nies. The domestic locus of implementation of gender equality policies dramatically weakens the capacity of the European Union to influence the enforcement of these policies upon state accession and, consequently, it forces Brussels to rely on domestic elites to do so. Taking this fact into consideration, it is important to analyze the conditions which will lead to greater cooperation between the European Union and local elites.

Conditional Compliance

The impact of EU conditionality on policy and institutional development in the area of gender equality in the workplace cannot be underestimated: by their accession date, all enlargement states adopted policies and established institutions for gender equality. However, in the absence of public demand for the enforcement of gender equality and a lack of political interest in such reforms, EU conditionality created government-initiated reforms. Many experts hoped that EU conditionality would create an opportunity for local NGOs to participate in the policymaking process. The evidence from most states, however, suggests that civic actors were marginalized during the process of policy formulation. In many states they did not participate in the drafting of laws. In other states, local NGOs were not even invited to consult governments, despite their demands to be included in this process. Most legislative changes were initiated and carried out by governments with only mixed cooperation between the executive and legislative branches.

This is widely confirmed by patterns of policy transposition observed in CEE candidate states. Experts from Latvia, Bulgaria, Hungary, Romania, and the Czech Republic indicate that legal adjustment in these states occurred with very little debate in national parliaments and without consulting NGOs or other civic actors.[5] Governments initiated and promulgated these legislative and institutional changes which resulted in half-hearted, formalistic compliance with EU regulations. Hana Hašková and Alena Křížková characterize "the attitude of the Czech government towards the creation of legislation relating to the equality of men and women . . . as ambivalent" and "marked by a sense of disinterest" (2008, 160). In their words, the government "mechanistically" transposed all necessary requirements to guarantee Czech accession to European Union; there was no attempt to discuss the applicability of the new legislation to the Czech context or to make it more pertinent to the Czech public (2008, 160). Hungarian scholars Noémi Kakusc and Andrea Petö report that while the Hungarian government satisfied EU requirements and achieved *de jure* compliance with all equality directives, the government did not adopt "any strategic policy document to introduce gender mainstreaming" or administrative orders for enforcing new laws (2008, 183). Iona Borza writes that the main issue discussed during the debate on the draft of the *Law on Equal Opportunities between Women and Men* in the Romanian Chamber of Deputies was the proper translation of the term "gender equality" into Romanian (2010, 50). On the grounds that there was "no serious opposition to the bill's adoption" and that "there was general agreement that the bill had to be adopted, because it would help Romanian society to modernize and become more European," no other substantive issues pertinent to the passing of the law were discussed or addressed, (Borza 2010, 51). At the same time, the government bill did not name "*a single independent* body responsible for implementing and monitoring the application of the provision" (italics by Borza 2010, 50).

Slovenia was one of the few states where social partners, trade unions, and employees' associations, had an active role in the promulgation of changes to national employment laws on gender equality. Despite the fact that more actors were involved in policy transposition, the process was not controversial. Petra Furtlehner writes that the introduction of the Equal Treatment Directive and Employment Equality Directive "created no problems and therefore caused no conflicts among the actors involved" (2008, 142). She quotes one of the representatives of an employees' association regarding the introduction of Article 6 on the equal treatment between men and women in the Employment Relationships Act as saying: it ". . . did not touch us so much. It is just one article. There were more than 200 other articles. Some of them were very important for the price of the labor force. Equal treatment does not raise the price of the labor force. So it was nothing to be negotiated" (Furtlehner 2008, 142). At the same time, the commentator raised concerns about public awareness of new anti-discrimination laws and government efforts to change the court system that would allow victims of discrimination to seek redress (Furtlehner 2008).

Accession governments recognize the weaknesses of gender equality reforms in candidate states. Stanislav Drapal, Vice-President of the Czech Statistical Office and member of the Government Council on Gender Equality, stated that, despite the fact that the Czech Republic created several institutions on gender equality, the main function of these institutions was to inform the government about gender equality issues (2005). Two main Czech institutions on gender equality, the Unit on Gender Equality within the Ministry of Labor and Social Affairs and the Government Council on Gender Equality, do not have the power to enforce new labor regulations. Mr. Drapal recognized the general disinterest of government officials in the meetings of the Council, noting that "it is typical for ministers, members of the Council, to send low-level officials as their substitutes to the meetings" (2005). The Council meetings also should be attended by representatives from regional administrations, "but out of fourteen regions, only two regions send their representatives regularly" (Drapal 2005). Mr. Drapal explains this as being a result of low interest in the questions of gender equality, gender discrimination, and the policy of voluntary attendance of the Council meetings among government officials and regions.

The principle of rapid rewards for rapid compliance at the core of EU accession conditionality, therefore, created an incentive for formalistic compliance, emphasizing *de jure* observance of EU equal opportunity directives, which effectively eliminated the costs of *de facto* enforcement of gender equality directives and encouraged CEE governments to take this shortcut to compliance. All parties to these negotiations were well aware that accession requirements most importantly referred to formal compliance: the monitoring of state progress toward compliance by the European Union reviewed only the formal transposition of directives into domestic laws and the formal creation of institutional mechanisms for enforcement. Lack of political need or public demand for these policies generated what Weiner terms a "negligible import; that is, EU gender equality directives went largely unsupported by domestic enforcement mechanisms (2009, 307). In the words of Mihaela Miroiu, the transposition of EU equality directives represents only a "costless room-service state feminism" that is pursued by all states in the region in exchange for EU membership (2006, 90). Driven by requirements for rapid formal reforms, EU conditionality distorted the incentives to pursue meaningful compliance with gender equality principles. State elites tried to maximize their interests at the least possible cost, pursuing *de jure* transposition and ignoring or postponing *de facto* compliance. A general attitude of the national elites toward conditional compliance with EU requirements can be best summarized in the words of the Bulgarian Prime Minister Ivan Kostov: "The West really does not interest me. . . . With all my respect for the West, I am watching there only the opinion of the structures, which finance Bulgaria. All the others, whatever they say, are of no importance" (Reuters 2000).

Were EU observers aware of this formalistic compliance with gender equality directives, and what were their reasons for carrying out rapid reforms? Most scholars agree that the very intent of EU-driven conditional reforms on gender equality was to satisfy formal requirements of legal harmonization and institutional adjustment (Bretherton 2001; Chołuj and Neusüß 2004; Pollert 2003; Weiner 2009). The enlargement process was driven by the logos of "rapid reforms and rapid rewards," and formal compliance was one of the "externalities" of this rapid transition. Moreover, the legal power of directives that structure compliance in the area of gender equality in the labor market has limited binding capacity; all member states should have the same provisions and this process is monitored by the Commission, but the implementation of these provisions is left to the states (Warleigh-Lack and Drachenberg 2010). Similarly, the power of the European Commission to inspect policy implementation is also limited. The Commission has a wide range of monitoring capacities during the accession period, but it does not have such powers for member states, except in the competition and agriculture policies. In reality, it is the task of citizens and interest groups to report problems to the Commission. Then the EC reviews these complaints, evaluates violations, and decides whether the evidence of noncompliance is sufficient and the climate for policy enforcement is conducive to impose sanctions on violating states. In order to impose sanctions, the Commission can file cases against violating states to the European Court of Justice for review and judgment (Alter 2001).[6] According to this enforcement structure, formal incorporation of policies into national legislatures creates legal avenues for policy enforcement. Many experts in accession countries share this optimism and hope that positive results will derive from the new laws in the future. Anita Seibert of the Karat Coalition in Poland stated that "the gender equality policies transposed in to the Polish legislation are more than symbolic policies. They became the law. At the moment it is a poorly enforced law and there are several reasons for that: low gender equality awareness, lack of enforcement mechanisms, lack of training among labor inspectors, and high unemployment rates" (2005). But public attitudes will change in the future and the government will become responsive to these laws with time. Marianne Schulze states that all of the representatives from the Slovak NGOs who she interviewed about the impact of the Slovak Anti-Discrimination Act agreed that the Act was a "major achievement" and a "necessity" for the "gradual reduction of discrimination" in Slovakia (2008, 112).

The EU application of conditionality to gender equality and equal treatment was not always consistent. For instance, the European Union introduced gender equality requirements into the accession negotiation much later than many other aspects (Chołuj and Neusüß 2004; Morgan 2008). The European Commission put greater emphasis on the ability of states to introduce neoliberal economic and social reforms which in many ways was contradictory to the idea of equal treatment in the labor market (Roth 2008). In addition, the European Union used different standards in evaluating state compliance with gender equality norms: some states got away with major violations, while other states were held accountable for less severe inconsistencies (Pollert 2003). For instance, the European Union allowed Latvia, Poland, and the Czech Republic to adopt their anti-discrimination acts after their accession and beyond 2008 (the deadline for the adoption of the bill). This critique is also consistent with the evaluation of EU anti-discrimination initiatives inside EU institutions, such as the highly unsuccessful EU program on gender mainstreaming

(Hafner-Burton and Pollack 2009)[7]. The marginalization of gender equality policies at the EU level and its weak position in the accession negotiations contributed to formal state adoption of gender equality directives and negatively impacted the capacity of states to enforce these policies.

Did EU Socialization Efforts
Bring about Normative Change?

The European Union applied a wide range of socialization strategies to stimulate state compliance. In the area of gender equality, the European Union developed a broad array of soft laws that complement the equality directives, including the European Employment Strategy and the Lisbon Strategy, recommended for the transposition and implementation for member states. The European Union supported new laws by extending financial and technical help through the EU's Technical Assistance Information Exchange Office (TAIEX). For example, the TAIEX ran exchange programs between "new" and "old" member states, known as "twinning programs," which placed policy experts from the "old" EU members directly into relevant governmental structures of candidate states to encourage policy and institutional emulation, learning, and exchange. During the accession period, all CEE candidate states participated in "twinning programs" with Western counterparts in the area of gender equality. Most commonly, Western experts provided assistance in the development of training programs on gender equality and gender discrimination for government officials, gave recommendations for the improvement of functions of national offices on gender equality, provided technical advice for the collection of gender statistics and the development of gender budgeting, and shared their experience on the models of cooperation between governmental and non-governmental actors.

The European Union channeled financial resources to support educational and public advocacy campaigns on gender equality. The European Social Fund provided financial support for programs and campaigns focused on gender equality and nondiscrimination, assistance to victims of discrimination in courts, educational initiatives, and training seminars. Additional EU funding was available through PHARE, SOCRATES, and INTERREG. Overall, the spectrum of EU socialization efforts included raising awareness about gender equality and gender discrimination among government officials, NGOs and social partners, such as labor unions and employer organizations, and the public in general. Did these efforts ensure "normative change?" Reasonable evaluation of elite and public attitudes suggests that little was achieved by the EU's socialization programs. In the words of Stana Buchowska, a National Coordinator of the La Strada Foundation in Poland, "attitudes and awareness [about gender equality and gender discrimination] are the last to change" (2005).

The 2005–2006 wave of the World Values Survey demonstrated that people in CEE states generally support the concept of gender equality and recognize equal rights between women and men as "an essential characteristic of democracy." Sixty-five percent of respondents in Poland, 62.5 percent of respondents in Slovenia, 57.2 percent of respondents in Bulgaria, and 73.5 percent of respondents in Romania chose "10" on the scale from 1 ("Not an essential characteristic of democracy") to 10 ("Essential characteristic of democracy") when answering the question "Do women have the same rights as men?"[8] In addition, 32.1 percent in Poland, 26.3 percent in Slovenia, 28.9 percent in Bulgaria, and 21.1 percent in Romania chose "7," "8," or "9" on the same scale indicating that this is an important characteristic of democracy. However, taking gender equality from the abstract level of values to a concrete evaluation of problems in the countries demonstrates that the public places low priority on gender discrimination. Cumulatively, 2.5 percent of the respondents in Poland (2005), Slovenia (2005), Bulgaria (2006), and Romania (2005) thought that "discrimination against girls and women," "is the most serious problem in your own country" (in the list of five other problems, including poverty, poor sanitation and infectious diseases, inadequate education, and environmental pollution).[9] The range of answers across the countries is quite narrow, with 1.8 percent choosing this problem as most serious in Bulgaria and 4.0 percent of respondents choosing it in Slovenia.

These findings resonate with the expert evaluations of attitudinal changes in CEE states. Marianne Schulze succinctly describes public attitudes toward nondiscrimination in Slovakia as a struggle: "People are increasingly aware of their rights and gradually appreciate the benefits of diversity and tolerance. However, people seem to maintain an abstract knowledge of these ideas, which they find hard to apply, or which they cannot transform into action at the individual or personal level" (2008, 112–113). She reveals a generational gap in the public perception of the prevalence of gender discrimination. In her survey, she finds that "younger, more affluent women are very aware and also outspoken about gender-based discrimination," while older women, educated during socialist eras, tend to deny the severity of this problem, referring to it as "a luxury problem" and "a caviar concern," and maintaining that there are many other more important issues on the agenda (Schulze 2008, 116). For instance, some respondents in her survey indicate that anti-discrimination policies are not relevant, unless Slovakia reaches more appropriate levels of unemployment of "7 to 8 percent" (Schulze 2008, 113). With unemployment rates close to 15 percent, people feel that they may jeopardize their working status if they stand up for themselves "against abusive employment conditions" (Schulze 2008, 116). Similarly, the 2001 surveys in Latvia and Lithuania found that respondents tend to value stability and job security as one of the key characteristics of a good job, regardless of pay and discriminatory practices (Sloat 2004). It is clear that public awareness about gender discrimination and the individual rights of workers is increasing, especially among the young and educated population, but gender equality and gender discrimination is not perceived as a critical issue that requires immediate attention by the state and society.

Negative elite attitudes toward gender equality and low support for anti-discrimination policies challenge the prospects of public empowerment against discrimination and discourage victims from fighting for their rights on the labor market. Country experts describe government attitudes toward gender discrimination at best as "negligible" and at worst as "extremely negative" (Ciocoiu 2011). Liliana Pagu, a coordinator of women's NGOs in Romania, stated in an interview with the *Southeast European Times*: "The public authorities approached the topic [of gender equality] only during the negotiations prior to EU accession" (Ciocoiu 2011). Once Romania gained membership in the European Union, the concept of gender equality disappeared from the public agenda, including party politics, electoral campaigns, and government statements (Ciocoiu 2011). No parties included gender equality in their electoral platforms during the last elections in Bulgaria, the Czech Republic, Hungary, Estonia, Latvia, or Romania. When gender equality appears in government statements, it is not always cast in a positive light. The former Prime Minister of the Czech Republic, Mirek Topolánek, shared his essentialist views on gender equality and women's role on the labor market during his opening speech at the European Year of Equal Opportunities for All on April 2, 2007. He asserted:

> In the case of women—who are not, in my view, a disadvantaged minority people usually consider them to be—we also cannot speak of equal opportunities. Pregnancy and maternity are women's privileges and these privileges make

them different from men. It is natural, it is logical, and it is sound. A woman can decide not to have children and in this case I am convinced she has the same opportunities as a man. The law should take this into account and should not force protection on women, which women do not care for to begin with and which paradoxically causes their discrimination on the labor market. If a woman decides to dedicate herself to the role entrusted to her by nature, then she does not need the law that tries to make her equal to a man.[10]

While this speech was booed with anger and indignation by many proponents of gender equality, Mr. Topolánek's views on gender equality are widely shared by many other top ranking officials in newly admitted states. The current Czech Prime Minister, Petr Nečas, is less vocal about his conservative views than his predecessor, but his actions speak more loudly than words. For example, as soon as he assumed the position of the Prime Minister, he eliminated the position of Minister on Human Rights and Minorities. In explaining his decision, the Prime Minister was very clear: "The ministry is a luxury the country cannot afford" (cited in Albert, 2010). In Czech political debates, the Civic Democrats (ODS), a center-right, neoliberal party, strongly endorse a position that links biological determinism with neoliberal arguments regarding policy interventionism into economic freedoms. For instance, Czech President Václav Klaus (ODS) referred to gender equality policies as a "freedom-impeding form of 'political correctness'" (cited in Weiner 2010). These views are very similar to those of top politicians in other states. Late President of Poland Lech Kaczynski was a vocal proponent of traditionalist conservative values, including his reactionary position on abortions and reproductive rights, rights of homosexual people, rights of minorities, and capital punishment. Among his many notorious bills, the law that demands chemical castration for men convicted for pedophilia ranks highest. It is not surprising that once his party, Law and Justice, came to power in 2005, one of its first changes was the elimination of the Office of Government Plenipotentiary on Gender Equality and Equal Opportunity. The Polish political scene was always divided on the issues of gender equality, where conservative and nationalist parties had been stalling the adoption of the anti-discrimination law since 1997 (the law was finally adopted in 2009). In one of her speeches, late Deputy Prime Minister of Poland, Izabella Jaruga-Nowacka, compared debates in the Polish Sejm between the late 1990s and early 2000s to debates in 1911:

Members of nationalist parties always denied women the right to participate in public life. In 1911 nationalists argued: "The discussion of women's rights is not a national issue. Women do not have the political awareness men possess." To tell you the truth, when I listen to current debates on the Act on Equal Status of Women and Men in parliament, I know that similar views not only can be found in some party platforms, but that they actually get articulated! (Jaruga-Nowacka 2003)

The dramatic conservative turn in national parliaments across all CEE states that took place in the last round of elections brought right-wing parties into power in seven out of the ten studied countries. This leaves little room for aspirations about "normative change" among government elites. While we do not see dramatic dismantling of the state gender equality institutions and policies adopted during the accession period, we do observe the marginalization of these policies and offices under the rise of neoliberal, traditionalist, nationalist, and, at times, dangerously extremist rhetoric (e.g., the radical nationalist Jobbik party in Hungary).

From Conditional Compliance to Post-Accession Conformity

What happens when conditional requirements are lifted? If conditional compliance were a function of pure cost-benefit calculations, we would expect to see governments dismantling policy and institutional reforms after accession. If, on the other hand, it were a function of socialization, then we would expect to observe a move from formal conformity to enforced compliance. In cases of unsuccessful socialization, we would have observed institutional dismantling. But in the case of ten EU Enlargement states, we observe the stagnation of policies and institutions on gender equality with no definitive signs of their dismantling or development. Thus, the conditional reforms turned out to be "sticky." What explains their persistence?

Conventional explanations of institutional and policy stability often cite the well-known arguments of Paul Pierson, which refer to the "increasing returns" of the institutions. Once established, policies and institutions create their own constituency and a circle of shareholders who will oppose policy and institutional annulation (Pierson 2000a,b). While "increasing returns" apply remarkably well to welfare policies and welfare regimes, the primary subject of Pierson's study, its application to gender equality institutions and policies in the context of EU Enlargement states, is problematic. The shareholders of welfare policies are well-known. It is also established that welfare policies are very important for party politics in Europe. On the contrary, we can hardly contemplate the role of gender equality policies and institutions in East European party politics or clearly identify the "shareholders" of these policies who would oppose their shutdown domestically. The arguments about institutional inertia are also problematic because these policies and institutions are too new and ill-connected to the general apparatus of policy and decision making in these states to cause institutional inertia.

Rationalist explanations would propose that the costs of dismantling might prevent any radical reform reversals. For many states, however, these institutions are not "too costly" in the form that they currently take. Thus, the transaction costs of reversal are not prohibitively high. For instance, gender equality units in the Czech Republic, Hungary, Bulgaria, and Latvia employ approximately two to eight people. Employees of gender equality focal points in ministries and advisory councils work part-time, sharing these responsibilities with other duties. Thus, states would not save much by abolishing these institutions; nor would they spend a lot to maintain these offices and policies in the form that they now exist. So why do they maintain these offices even under conservative and neoliberal governments who often publicly oppose the very idea of such institutions?

The stability of conditional reform can be explained by reputational pressures. If states abolish gender equality policies and institutions in their states, they will signal to other members that they are openly "sexist" and "not civilized." This message is too strong and undesirable to communicate to other members of the European Union, and states prefer to follow the "logic of appropriateness," or shared behavioral rules of the group (March and Olsen 1989). The abolition of these institutions would also mean breaking their accession promise, when the European Union has fulfilled its promise by granting them membership. This situation invokes "positive reciprocity," or using game theoretic language, the desire to fulfill promises made to partners who have demonstrated trust in a social transaction (Camerer and Fehr 2004; Henrich et al. 2004; Ostrom, Gardner, and Valkner 1994). This is confirmed by some of the interviewees in enlargement states. Agnieszka Grzybek, from the OSKA Coalition in Poland, thought that "governments have to maintain equality institutions in one or another form, because this is what they have committed to when they applied to EU," despite the fact that 2005 elections brought the right-wing parties to power (2005). She considered the possibility of dramatic changes to the institutional agenda, as well as to personnel reshuffling once ultra-conservative parties came to power, but she did not think "governments would dare to permanently shut down such offices" (2005). "We might see the same scenario as we have observed in 1997: they closed down the office on gender equality and reopened it as an office for women and family affairs" (2005). This assessment was prescient. Once the newly elected right-wing parliament came to power and formed the government, the office of Plenipotentiary on Gender Equality was abolished, only to be reopened later at a lower status with a different conservative agenda.

Stanislav Drapal of the Czech Statistical Service assessed the situation similarly. He thought that, despite the fact that the offices on gender equality are not popularly supported and do not occupy a top priority on the government agenda, these institutions would remain after accession, "because it was a conditional requirement and we committed to this policy. Abolishing these institutions would compromise our reputation and demonstrate to the European Union that we do not keep our promises" (Drapal 2005). Alena Králiková from Gender Studies in Prague also does not think that the offices and the advisory council created during the accession period are going to be dismantled after the accession. "At a minimum, they have to write and submit reports to the European Commission. It is not in the interest of the government to abolish these institutions" (2005).

The European Commission can punish noncomplying member states, but it rarely initiates the monitoring of policy enforcement. The case against state violations often must be filed by a third party (e.g., NGOs or interest groups) and only then will the Commission initiate an investigation. Of course, the EC investigation will expose a noncomplying state as a violator to other members and ruin its reputation more than its pocketbook, the fines for violations in the area of gender equality being insignificant. The Commission began several infringement procedures against member states in violation of gender equality directives. For instance, in 2008, the European Commission initiated infringement procedures against seven Eastern European states because their definition of gender-based discrimination was incompatible with EU requirements. The infringement process sped up the passage of Anti-Discrimination Acts in Poland and the Czech Republic and, consequently, they avoided fines. Thus, there is a structure of punishment embedded in the framework of such procedures for noncomplying member states. However, states respond to the EC warnings, and the system of warnings applies social pressure, rather than serious financial penalties, thus confirming the argument that states are more worried about reputational concerns than pecuniary punishments.

Social pressure is a "soft" punishment. It lacks enforcement powers yet pushes states toward conformal behavior and formalistic compliance. Conformal behavior is an adjustment strategy by which new states in a group become formally assimilated. If we observe state compliance in all EU member states, we will find a remarkable variation in the degree of gender equality enforcement. If "old EU members" like Italy and Greece can get away with poor enforcement of gender equality directives, then why should Bulgaria and Latvia pursue meaningful enforcement? This variation in compliance signals to EU Enlargement states that EU requirements are merely formal. Thus, if there is no demand from the domestic public, states can forgo meaningful compliance. This gives rise to conformal behavior driven by symbolic, reputational concerns rather than by the threat of significant punishment or normative congruence.

In summary, conditional compliance driven by the formula of "rapid rewards for rapid reforms" generated formal compliance with EU Equality Directives. This continued in the post-accession period, leading to conformity, or formal recognition of EU laws and maintenance of EU-like institutions in new member states in response to "soft" pressures from the European Union. State reforms achieved during the conditionality period are not likely to be easily reversed as long as group pressures (in our case, the European Union) continue to maintain gender equality policies and institutions. Even in cases where states significantly reduce their input in this policy area, we do not observe the radical dismantling of these policies and institutions because reform reversal is considered inappropriate state conduct.

"Soft powers" eventually can lead to compliance, but as the structure of EU Directives implies, the enforcement mechanisms must be generated from within the state, aided by interest groups and the public charged with monitoring state noncompliance in this policy area. Governments will respond to those pressures because they will create substantial threats to state legitimacy. In this context, I conceptualize legitimacy as a state perception of its own status in the group of other states and its perception of what other states think about it. In other words, legitimacy is thought of as a state's perception of its appropriate and congruent status in the national and international arenas. Thus, conformal behavior is generated by a desire to normalize a state's position in a group of other states in response to pressures that challenge state legitimacy (or congruence with group standards) rather than a change in the belief systems of actors (normative congruence) or substantial material punishments (coercion). In the next section, I will explore the question of whether social pressures alone can bring states to compliance or conformity with international requirements, or if conditionality is always a necessary condition for initiating state reforms. To answer this question, I will review the case of violence against women and state compliance with this policy in ten EU Enlargement states. Violence against women was not part of the EU's accession requirements, but it became an important area for international socialization and "soft law" enforcement.

Alternative Policy Case of Violence against Women

Can international social and normative pressures alone generate compliance with international women's rights norms or is international conditionality the most efficient strategy for promoting women's rights globally? In the following case of violence against women, I will explore the effectiveness of non-coercive international mechanisms of policy promotion to influence domestic policies and practices in a gendered policy area. The choice of violence against women as a counterfactual analysis is straightforward: (1) It is a major women's rights policy area promoted and supported by international organizations and international law. (2) All post-communist EU Enlargement states signed the Convention on the Elimination of All Forms of Discrimination against Women (CEDAW), the major international legal instrument of promoting action against VAW; thus, all of these states are subjects to compliance with CEDAW requirements. (3) State compliance with CEDAW can be measured along the same set of criteria, *legislative adjustment* and *institutional adjustment* as my main dependent variable. Thus, I will be able to make meaningful comparison of state compliance in these two gendered policy areas. (4) Globally, policies on violence against women are promoted solely by "soft law," or nonbinding agreements, which allows exploring the effectiveness of noncoercive international strategies for generating state compliance.

To measure state compliance in the area of VAW, I develop criteria similar to my main measures of state compliance, using the method of structured, focused comparison. I conceptualize state compliance with CEDAW as a double-fold process: legislative adjustment and institutional adjustment. CEDAW recommends that all states, as signatories to the convention, adopt a separate law on violence against women and change their penal codes to introduce and enforce legal clause on combating violence against women (known in the CEE region mostly as domestic violence). The governments are also expected to create institutions responsible for enforcing these policies. Thus, I will investigate and evaluate legislative and institutional changes. In addition to these aspects of compliance, I will explore the enforcement of certain policy practices recommended by CEDAW, such as police training, training of judges, state support to shelters for battered women, and awareness-raising campaigns on VAW, among other policy practices. Based on this information, I will evaluate state compliance as adequate, poor, or no compliance with CEDAW. To explore the causal links between international pressures and state compliance, I will investigate the case of Lithuania, known as a noncomplying state in the area of VAW, to reveal the factors that impeded state engagement in policy reform in the course of fifteen years and to explore which actors enabled these reforms in 2011. The case of Lithuania is an illustrative example of a country that succeeded to enforce comprehensive early reforms in one policy area (gender equality), while resisting the reforms in another pivotal women's rights policy, violence against women. The exploration of these two policy cases demonstrate which factors activated state compliance in one policy area and whether these factors were absent in another policy area. Data for the analysis derives primarily from the research on primary documents, such as country laws on violence against women, government reports on state compliance with CEDAW submitted to Division for the Advancement of Women (DAW), and secondary analyses of policies and institutions on gender equality published in Avdeyeva (2007), Minnesota Advocates for Human Rights, and independent scholarly evaluations.

In the following, I will, first, discuss the problem of gendered violence in Central and Eastern Europe; second, I will briefly discuss international legal instruments for combating VAW. Then I will present data on compliance with these requirements in ten EU Enlargement states. Finally, I will explore the case of Lithuania in depth to reveal why reforms were stalled for so long and what lead to the adoption of law against VAW in this country.

Violence against Women in Central and Eastern Europe

Violence against women, and especially domestic violence (or violence faced by women in private family settings and personal relations), has astonishingly high rates in the post-communist region of Central and

Eastern Europe. For instance, according to the 2002 UNIFEM survey, "Life Free of Violence," in Lithuania, 82 percent of respondents ages 16 and over had experienced psychological violence or coercion in the family and 35 percent of respondents experienced physical abuse. Eighty-seven percent of respondents in this survey recognized the existence of violence against women in Lithuania and agreed that it was a serious social problem. The research from other CEE states reveal similarly high rates of sexual assault, stalking, trafficking, violence in intimate relationships, and other violations of women's bodies and psyches (Fábián 2010; Martinez 2006; Minnesota Advocates for Human Rights 2008). The data on violence against women is mostly generated by surveys. The CEE states lack a clear system of data registration of instances of gender-based violence and violence in the family. Domestic violence is viewed as a private matter by governments and society alike, rather than a crime against a person (Fábián 2010). Such privatization of violence against women makes it difficult to reveal the scale of actual crime occurrence, because in many cases victims of violence do not report this crime to the police, nongovernmental organizations, or social workers. For instance, in Lithuania, in 2006, 283 women filed cases against their husbands and 142 women filed cases against their co-habiting partners, reporting cases of physical and sexual abuse (IT and Communications Department under the Ministry of Interior, cited in the Government of the Republic of Lithuania 2007). At the same time, the official estimated rate of domestic violence in Lithuania is 36 percent and, considering that the total female population in Lithuania is 5 million, this suggests that most victims prefer to privatize the social problem and do not seek legal redress (Mecajeva and Kisieliene 2008). The most commonly cited reasons for such silence is "low trust in the ability of police to effectively solve the problem," "shame and social stigma," and "fear of negative reaction from the perpetrator" (Mecajeva and Kisieliene 2008). These outcomes are well explained by the gendered social order established in post-communist CEE states which are characterized by a weak civil society and a strong patriarchal tradition.

The social order in CEE states is based on two distinct trajectories of their history: inherited traditions from a patriarchal pre-communist past and the communist social legacies of female "emancipation" in the work sphere (Fábián 2010). Traditionally, partner violence against women has been socially accepted and seen as a private matter. A patriarchal power dynamic normalizes and legitimates male violence against women. In this context gender violence serves as a vehicle for claiming and defending privilege in relationships and women assume the subordinate

position without realizing it. Gender inequality and the socially con-
structed division between the public and private spheres have shielded
domestic violence in all societies where this social order has not been
challenged (Weldon 2004; Htun and Weldon 2012).

Communist societies did not dismantle traditional gendered hierarchies within the family or in intimate relations. Women entered the
labor market in large numbers and achieved high visibility in public and
political institutions, but traditional relations in private settings, including family and relations between intimate partners, did not change. On
the contrary, the patriarchal heritage of the communist period not only
survived but was often transformed and strengthened upon the post-
communist transition (Einhorn 1993; Gal and Kligman 2000; Johnson
and Robinson 2006). Violence against women in family and partner relations increased in the 1990s as states experienced a collapse of political,
economic, and social institutions. Such uncertainty and tension in public
and private relations resulted in escalating rates of domestic abuse and
violence.

International observers expressed numerous concerns about the
rates of gender violence in post-communist states (Coomaraswamy 2000).
After the fall of the communist system, a broad human rights framework
and policy agenda—most notably the Austrian framework of criminal-
izing domestic violence—appeared in Eastern and Central Europe and
the newly independent, former Soviet republics (Minnesota Advocates for
Human Rights 2008). Transnational and international actors alarmed the
governments in CEE states about the catastrophic scale of the crime in
the region. International governmental and non-governmental organizations framed women's rights as human rights and helped raise public
awareness about the scale of the crime, increasing the political salience
of violence against women in the region.

The Impact of International Actors on National Policy on Combating Violence against Women

Since the early 1980s, violence against women has been a prime subject in
international human rights discourse (Coomaraswamy 2000). International and transnational organizations had a large impact on state responses
to violence against women at the national level. For EU Enlargement
states, three international organizations were especially instrumental for
putting violence against women on the state agenda: the United Nations,
the Council of Europe, and the European Union. All of these interna-

tional organizations, however, rely on states' voluntary participation in international treaties against gender violence. The international law on violence against women lacks an enforcement mechanism, provides no clear structure of incentives for nonviolating states, and does not enumerate sizable material punishments for violating states.

The UN Fourth World Conference on Women (Beijing 1995) developed a comprehensive set of measures to combat violence against women on local, national, and international levels thereby setting the stage for all other international organizations to join this effort. According to the Women's Platform for Action adopted in Beijing, national governments assume primary responsibility for developing and implementing policies against gender violence, including domestic violence. A broad set of measures contains strengthening and expanding domestic legislation, including penal, civil, labor, and administrative codes, as well as the adoption of separate legislation to combat violence against women and create avenues for legal redress. The Platform for Action requires states to create, establish, and fund training programs for judicial, legal, police, medical, immigration, and social work services to raise awareness about violence against women among professionals and to develop a concerted institutional plan for combating it. It introduces an integrated approach for eliminating and preventing violence against women by encouraging governments to develop training programs for the prevention of domestic abuse and to establish rehabilitation and counseling services for victims of violence. National, regional, and local governments are encouraged to establish and financially support shelters for victims of violence and run periodic public awareness-raising campaigns about this crime and the services to prevent it. In response to these requirements, all states, as signatories of the CEDAW and the Women's Platform for Action, are required to develop National Action Plans to combat violence against women (VAW) and to submit periodic reports to the UN Commission on the Status of Women (Avdeyeva 2007). In addition, in 2000 the UN issued the Optional Protocol to clarify and strengthen the measures against VAW articulated in the CEDAW and the Women's Platform for Action.

Regional international organizations, including the Council of Europe and the European Union, supported the UN efforts in combating violence against women but maintained a similar "soft law" approach to enforcement. In 2002 the Council of Europe adopted a framework document entitled the "Recommendation on the Protection of Women against Violence." The framework endorsed definitions and policy measures articulated in the CEDAW and Optional Protocol and provided an additional monitoring mechanism, which required member states to submit progress reports on the enforcement of these measures to a Group of Specialists (Montoya 2012). The European Union, however, refrained from any monitoring or binding mechanisms for enforcing laws against VAW. While its power as a supranational entity implies that it could use levers to impose conditions on its member states, candidates, affiliates, and numerous trading partners so that they would introduce laws against violence against women to promote human rights and enhance democracy, it has generally avoided doing so. It did not develop enforceable rules or explicit conditional expectations of member states in the field of gender violence. Instead, the European Union uses implicit value expectations ("good practices" and recommendations, or what is known as "soft law") to steer member states and to persuade candidates to consider violence against women as a crime and to adopt laws against it. In addition, the European Union actively funds the operations of regional and local NGOs working in the area of violence against women through its Daphne Project, which aids in building local capacity and non-governmental effort in combating this problem (Montoya 2009, 2012).

State Responses to International "Soft Law" Initiatives

In response to international calls to address violence against women at the national and local level, ten EU Enlargement states pursued some policy changes which I will evaluate below. Policy reforms are assessed along the following set of criteria: *legislative adjustment,* including amendments to penal codes and the adoption of a separate bill on combating VAW; *institutional adjustment,* encompassing the creation of a specific institution charged with the enforcement of policies against gender violence or domestic violence; in addition, I evaluate general government effort to enforce policies and *policy practices* to combat VAW, including police and judicial training, support to shelters, services for victims of violence, and state campaigns on raising public awareness about domestic violence. Such reform evaluation uses similar criteria to those employed in the analysis of state compliance with EU gender equality requirements, largely concentrating on legislative and institutional changes. This choice is justified for several reasons: (1) It is conceptually consistent with reform evaluation across the two policy areas, and therefore, allows for cross-sectional comparative analysis of state compliance. (2) It focuses on government input into reform, rather than reform effectiveness, which may depend on many factors and is not always the best measure of policy reform and compliance (Htun and Weldon 2012). Government input, on the other hand, is a solid measure for evaluating compliance. (3) Finally, it provides clear criteria of assessment. In this project, I evaluate policies on violence against women and, more specifically, domestic violence.

All candidate states ratified the UN Convention on the Elimination of All Forms of Discrimination in the 1990s. All states sent their governmental and non-governmental delegates to the World Conference on Women in Beijing and signed the UN Platform for Action on Violence against Women. By 2010 eight Enlargement states signed the CEDAW Optional Protocol (OP); Latvia and Estonia did not sign the OP (table 4.1). Non-ratification of the OP allowed these two states to lag behind in adopting policies and establishing institutions of the VAW.

Since the Beijing conference, several states adopted specific laws on combating violence against women, or against domestic violence in other states (table 4.2). By 2011 we see an even split between ten states: those which adopted a specific law (five states) and those that did not (another five states). But all states amended their existing penal codes to accommodate at least some of the provisions to combat VAW, such as providing definitions for crimes like domestic violence, marital rape, and violence against children and dependent family members (Slovenia, Slovakia, Latvia, Hungary, and Estonia). Amendments in some cases also enhanced the punishment for rape and severe cruelty (the Czech Republic, Slovakia, and Slovenia), removed the requirements to file a consent form at different stages of investigation (Slovakia), and removed the repertory clause in cases of rape if the victim consents to marry a perpetrator (Romania). Some amendments introduced restraining orders, but generally experts recognize that restraining orders and victim protection clauses are the

Table 4.1. Ratification of the CEDAW Optional Protocol

Ratified	*No Ratification*
Hungary (2000); Slovakia (2000)	Estonia
Czech Republic (2001)	Latvia
Poland (2003); Romania (2003)	
Lithuania (2004); Slovenia (2004)	
Bulgaria (2006)	

Table 4.2. Law on Violence against Women/Domestic Violence, 2011

Adopted Law	No Adopted Law	Amendments to Existing Penal Codes
Romania (2003)	Estonia	All states
Bulgaria (2005)	Hungary*	
Poland (2005)	Latvia	
Czech Republic (2007)	Slovakia	
Lithuania (2011)	Slovenia	

*Hungary adopted a Law on Restraining Order (2009) partially addressing international requirements against VAW.

least developed provisions in amended penal codes (Coomaraswamy 2003). Victim protection and the removal of the offender from a shared household are articulated in states which adopted specific laws to combat VAW (Bulgaria, Romania, the Czech Republic, Poland, Hungary, and Lithuania). Thus, overall we note uneven compliance with international requirements to adopt policies on combating violence against women. In some states the adoption of such laws was relatively uncontroversial (Romania and Bulgaria); in most other states governments have seen several drafts of such laws in a recent decade and could not pass them (Hungary, Slovakia, and Slovenia); in other states after many drafts were reviewed, bill passage followed after a new ruling coalition came to power (Poland, the Czech Republic, and Lithuania). In Latvia and Estonia parliamentarians refrained from serious consideration and development of a draft bill, and the drafts from NGOs were also rejected.

A similar pattern of uneven compliance was observed in the area of institutional supervision of policies against VAW. Only three states created specific offices to address the issue and coordinate policy enforcement (Poland, Romania, and the Czech Republic). In other states, the government charged a general ministry, usually the Ministry of Interior, with developing measures and enforcing National Action Plans on VAW (Bulgaria, Hungary, Lithuania, and Slovenia) (table 4.3). No institution is mentioned in Latvia, Estonia, or Slovakia in government reports to the UN Commission on the Status of Women. The existence of a permanent office or working group that deals specifically with combating VAW and coordinating the enforcement of this policy between different units suggests that there is a better chance that these policies will be enforced. The recognition of responsibilities for policy enforcement by a general institution, like the Ministry of Interior, but where no permanent office is created, suggests that the government pursues "window reforms" by creating a temporary office solely for the task of writing a report for the UN, and thus reflects poor, if any, policy enforcement. It also indicates that the state does not pursue consistent training of personnel, including judges and police, and does not have substantial capacity to assist and protect victims of violence. Overall, policy enforcement in such states is considerably lower than in states with permanent offices on VAW.

The analysis of policy enforcement suggests that the CEE states demonstrate poor efforts to provide protection and safety to women and girls. All across the region, states take minimal, nonsystematic steps in securing the well-being of women. In states where governments take part in assisting victims of violence, shelters and centers are run by NGOs. In Poland, Romania, and Lithuania, governments provide minimal financial support to such shelters. State support to shelters is systematic and comprehensive in only two states: Slovenia and the Czech Republic. The government of the Czech Republic succeeded in expanding the network of supported shelters and crisis centers to 107 in 2004, the goal stated in the government document *Priorities and Procedures of the Government in*

Table 4.3. Institutions on Violence against Women/Domestic Violence, 2011

Specific Institution	*General Institution*	*No institution*
Romania: Center for Family Consulting and Information (1996)	*Bulgaria:* Ministry of Interior	Estonia Latvia Slovakia
Poland: The State Agency for Solving Alcoholic Problems (1998)	*Slovenia:* Ministry of Interior and Ministry of Health	
Czech Republic: Inter-ministerial working group for healthcare, social, legal, and police coordination (2001)	*Hungary:* Ministry of Interior*	
	Lithuania: Ministry of Interior**	

*To coordinate the enforcement of restraining orders.
**The Law in Lithuania does not mention institution responsible for law enforcement.

Promoting the Equality of Men and Women (Gender Equality Unit 2000). For a country of this size with total population of 10 million people, this is a commendable achievement. In most states, governments did not organize systematic police training to improve their efficiency in combating violence against women and domestic violence. In Poland a well-known program, "Blue Card," provided systematic training and technical support to police officers (Avdeyeva 2007). The Czech Republic is another case of systematic police training. The Czech Republic also ran several seminars for judicial training. Other states did not demonstrate regular efforts in addressing police or judicial training.

Table 4.4 presents classification of state efforts to enforce policies against VAW. No state demonstrates high levels of compliance with international provisions; however, Poland and the Czech Republic have exhibited significant effort in addressing the problem. Both of these states adopted laws on VAW and established permanent institutions for combating it. They also pursued systematic action in police training. Most states, however, have demonstrated poor compliance. In Romania, Hungary, Bulgaria, Slovenia, and Slovakia, governments pursued some action to create legislative avenues for redress and unsystematic actions in enforcing policies against VAW. In Estonia, Latvia, and Lithuania, there was no policy enforcement in the studied period. With the Lithuanian law against domestic violence in force since November 2011, we can expect that Lithuania will pursue some policy enforcement in the future. Delayed policy reform and enforcement in these countries can be explained by weak efforts of women's organizing, low salience of the problem of VAW in public discourse, and strong conservative opposition to VAW policy among top governmental officials. These factors allowed

Table 4.4. Enforcement of Policies on Violence against Women/Domestic Violence, 2010s

Some/Adequate	Poor	No Enforcement
Czech Republic	Romania	Estonia
Poland	Hungary	Latvia
	Bulgaria	Lithuania
	Slovakia	
	Slovenia	

the governments to stall the reforms despite pressures from international organizations. Below I discuss these factors in the case of Lithuania.

Lithuania: Stalled Reforms on Violence against Women

The Government of Lithuania ratified the UN Convention on the Elimination of All Forms of Discrimination against Women on January 18, 1994, without reservations. The Convention came into force in February of that year. In 2000, Lithuania signed the Optional Protocol of the CEDAW, which detailed definitions and additional measures for combating violence against women. Despite the treaty ratification, the government of Lithuania did not initiate legal reforms to comply with the CEDAW requirements on combating VAW until 2004, when the Human Rights Commissar of the Council of Europe issued a communique on its noncompliance with recommendations by the European Council. In response to this warning, the Ministry of Justice amended articles 120 and 132 of the Criminal Code to provide definitions for domestic violence and to introduce measures for restraining orders against perpetrators. While these amendments were endorsed by the Parliamentary Women's Group, they were opposed by strong conservative forces in parliament and in the Ministry of Justice. As a result of fierce debate and opposition to the amendments in parliament and in the government, the state failed to provide administrative orders and legal provisions on how to implement the removal of perpetrators from the house (Mecajeva and Kisieliene 2008). The introduction of amendments to the bill, therefore, resulted in only a symbolic reform of the law because neither police nor social workers received any administrative orders regarding how to enforce these new amendments (Minnesota Advocates of Human Rights 2008).

The Criminal Code of the Republic of Lithuania stipulates punishments for different acts of violence against persons in various spheres of life, including murder, bodily damage, rape, and other types of physical abuse. Before the 2004 amendments, the Criminal Code did not provide definitions of psychological, physical, and sexual abuse and norms of responsibilities for violence in families. The 2004 amendments added these definitions, but did not introduce the requirement of a public prosecutor in the consideration of domestic violence cases (2008). This means that new amendments did not change the general attitude about family violence as a private matter that was traditionally solved through private negotiations. In addition, Lithuania did not have specialized family courts and did not have specialization or training on family cases for judges.

Among other detrimental consequences deriving from a symbolic legal reform to the Criminal Code of Lithuania is the fact that the code did not consider physical abuse of a wife as an aggravated circumstance. The Criminal Code specifies that aggravating circumstances include only "crimes against father, mother, and child"; crimes against wives are not included in this list (Mecajeva and Kisieliene 2008, 5)! Two amendments introduced in 2004 failed to change these legal provisions.

Lithuania lacks comprehensive programs and highly skilled, professional personnel with the ability to detect and prevent domestic violence, assist victims of violence, provide counseling to perpetrators of violence, and raise public awareness about the issue. In the last ten years, there were several campaigns and training seminars organized by international and domestic NGOs for judges, attorneys, prosecutors, and police officials with the goal to raise awareness about domestic violence and to share strategies for violence detection and prevention. These efforts, however, were not sufficient to change existing practices or to establish coordinated police response to domestic violence. In addition, these campaigns were not endorsed by the Lithuanian government. Many of the senior officials in the Ministry of Interior, the coordinating state institution for this policy, vehemently opposed the enforcement of the new amendments. In general, lack of political will, insufficient legal provisions, absence of clear administrative guidelines and institutional responsibilities inhibited the NGOs' efforts to raise the profile of domestic violence in the professional legal and law enforcement community. Until 2007, no comprehensive government program was adopted on training professionals to address the problem of domestic violence.

The government returned to the topic of violence against women in 2007, when the National Program of Equal Opportunities for Women and Men compelled some state officials to enact a strategy to combat violence against women (Minnesota Advocates for Human Rights, 2008). The Program outlined three measures for combating violence in the family: improvements to existing law; measures to support victims of domestic violence; and suggested procedures to help perpetrators change their aggressive behavior. In addition, the program outlined the necessary changes to the legal code which would allow state officials, including police and social workers, to initiate an investigation of domestic violence without requiring that the victim to file a formal complaint with police. In 2008 there was another attempt to introduce a bill on violence in the private sphere. However, several top-ranking officials, including Minister of Justice, Minister of Interior, and Minister of Health, were very critical of it and the bill did not pass (Fábián 2013).

It all changed in 2010 when the push for the adoption of a bill came from an unexpected, but powerful actor, the U.S. Embassy. The U.S. Embassy announced that domestic violence became an "important foreign policy consideration for the Obama administration" and pressured the Lithuanian government to adopt a bill against domestic violence (Fábián 2013, 15). While these pressures were nonconditional, the authority of the endorsing institution ensured a quick response from the Lithuanian government and the bill hastily passed the Lithuanian parliament in May 2011.

The bill came into force on November 26, 2011. The Law on the Protection against Domestic Violence provides broader definitions of domestic violence and the domestic environment, specifying types of assistance to victims of violence. It defines principles of protection against domestic violence, emphasizing cooperation, comprehensiveness, accessibility, humanity, impartiality, and solidarity. The responsibilities for preventing domestic violence are shared between state, municipal, and non-governmental organizations, which have to prepare and implement measures meant to prevent domestic violence. These measures are to be implemented in accordance with the national program developed by the Government of Lithuania. The budget for these programs is shared by the state, municipal and international donor funds. The prevention measures include: public awareness raising; in-service and general training for judges, prosecutors, police offices, and other personnel working in the area of domestic violence; the collection of statistical data on VAW; and public education on violence prevention. Chapter two of the law defines measures for the protection of a victim of violence, including the enforcement of restraining orders, rules for pre-trial investigation and punishment, rules for the initiation of the pre-trial investigation, and types of cases that must be heard at the district court. Article 7 defines the responsibilities and duties of police officers, including their cooperation with specialized shelters for victim protection. Chapter three defines management and organization of assistance to victims of violence which emphasizes cooperation between municipal authorities, police, and non-governmental organizations. The law defines the rights of victims of domestic violence and institutes criminal liability for domestic violence. The government is obliged to submit draft programs on the implementation of this law to the Parliament of the Republic of Lithuania within a three-month period following the publication of the law. This law, however, does not specify a concrete government institution responsible for promulgation of this program.

The law demonstrates a state commitment to initiate a comprehensive campaign of multifaceted dimension to address the problem of domestic violence in the Republic of Lithuania. Since the law requires the participation of three partners—the central government, the municipalities, and non-governmental organizations—we can expect uneven implementation of this law, at least in the initial stage of its enforcement. While the law specifies state support for the enforcement of this policy, it is not clear if the budget of state support will increase. In 2007, state support to NGOs working in the area of domestic violence constituted U.S. $130,000 per year, shared between all NGOs in the country—an insufficient amount to complete any programs. At this point, it is very early to assess the impact of this law on the prevention of domestic violence and the protection of victims against domestic violence since the law only recently went into force. As with many other laws concerning human rights protection, it may take time for the state to train legal and law enforcement personnel to efficiently respond to domestic violence and to protect victims. It may take even longer to change general public attitudes and remove the social stigma of domestic violence for it to be considered a crime against a person, rather than a private family affair.

In Conclusion

The case of compliance with international laws on violence against women demonstrates that, in the absence of conditional pressures, or coercive mechanisms for enforcement, soft international pressures generated uneven state reforms and non-systematic enforcement of the policy reforms across ten EU enlargement states. In most cases we observe conformity with international requirements: all states ratified the CEDAW, eight states ratified the Optional Protocol, and almost all states pursued some action, albeit minimal and insufficient, in addressing the problem of violence against women at the domestic level. If we compare compliance patterns across two policy areas—gender equality in the labor market and violence against women—among ten EU enlargement states, we will observe that conditionality generated rapid policy and institutional reforms in the case of the former. The absence of conditionality in the latter policy area allowed for delaying policy and institutional reforms and produced greater decoupling between formal international commitments and domestic policy enforcement.

Did soft law generate social pressures or normative change among the CEE states? A pattern of uneven, nonsystematic compliance with violence against women requirements suggests that most states responded to social pressures to conform to group requirements. The analysis reveals low change in normative positions of the public and elites. Conformity generated by social pressures is different from normative change generated by persuasion in several important ways. First, it does not require active debate and deliberation whereby actors change each other's normative position. Second, it does not involve actors (state elites in this case) in the critical evaluation of content. Third, and most importantly, social pressures do not require either the acceptance of new norms or change in actual state behavior (or domestic practices)—that is, how social pressures permit behavioral deviation (nonenforcement of a norm) from a norm in question. Social pressures are driven by cognitive pressures to adopt socially legitimated beliefs, ideas, and behaviors. As these new norms are imposed on actors by the international community, actors do not normatively accept them and do not act upon them immediately. This consideration explains why states choose to ratify international human rights treaties, even if they do not intend to enforce them.

But social pressures also explain why and how states become vulnerable to pressures from monitoring bodies and non-governmental organizations after they ratify a treaty. By ratifying a treaty, states open themselves to criticism in regard to their formal recognition of treaty norms; if openly shamed, or otherwise socially sanctioned, they will try to bring their behavior into congruence with their formal commitments to avoid negative evaluation of their behavior, threats to their status in a group and group reputation, or to avoid sociopsychological dissonance that can arise in response to shaming. Soft social pressures from monitoring bodies, such as shaming, shunning, and exclusion, can serve as strategies to bring states into compliance with their formal commitments to international human rights treaties. The level of state responsiveness, however, will depend on the degree of state association with the group that exerts this pressure and the state's desire to elevate their group social status and reputation (Avdeyeva 2012).

The next three chapters will present case study evidence to demonstrate the importance of the interaction between the international pressures and the domestic political actors on reform initiation, development, and stability. First, the chapters will present an overview of the basic political environment and identify key actors in the reform process; then, they will engage in analysis of policy and institutional development.

5

Poland

Political Swings and Challenged Compliance

Poland was one of the first post-communist states of Central and Eastern Europe to express strong interest in joining the European Union.[1] In 1994, the Polish government officially applied for EU membership. Poland was granted candidate status at the Luxembourg Summit in December 1997. Accession negotiations began in 1998 and were closed in 2002. In May 2004, Poland became a member of the European Union.

Following the dramatic collapse of communist economic and political systems in the late-1980s, Poland took a resolute path toward democratization and market liberalization. It was one of the first post-communist states to dismantle its state-planned economy and to introduce rapid "shock therapy" policies in order to pursue macroeconomic stabilization and privatization. As in many other transition states, "shock therapy" proved to be "all shock and no therapy,"[2] as the country experienced a precipitous decline in economic growth, skyrocketing inflation, rampant unemployment, and severe austerity in state spending intended to fight the inflationary pressures. "Shock therapy" produced a dramatic rise in social inequality. Women were particularly disadvantaged by the economic transition, as they experienced higher rates of unemployment and earned lower wages, on average, than men.

This dramatic social and economic instability had a detrimental effect on the fertility rates of Polish women, and lead to negative natural population growth for the first time in Polish history (Kotowska 2002). Fears of population decline fueled public debates about the place of women in society. The Polish Catholic Church took an assertive position against the emancipation of women by linking gender equality policies to depopulation of the Polish nation. The Church's demanded a highly restrictive abortion policy which resulted in the adoption of the anti-abortion law in 1992. In the early 1990s, the influence of the Church extended beyond the Polish government. In order to pursue its interest in joining the European Union, the Polish government had to reach an agreement with the Catholic Church in exchange for Church support of Polish membership in the European Union (Lohmann and Seibert 2003). The blessing of the Church, however, put the Polish government in a peculiar position regarding its obligations to transpose and enforce policies on gender equality as part of its accession agreement. This conflict of interests is reflected in the troubled Polish path toward compliance with EU gender equality requirements.

Any analysis of gender policy formation in Poland since the early 1990s should be situated within the social and political debate on the role of men and women in the labor market and in the family, the degree of institutionalization of Catholic doctrine by the conservative right, party politics and parliamentary majority, and the activity of women's NGOs (Anderson 2006; Avdeyeva 2009). While reproductive and gender equality issues were contested by many social actors, most importantly liberal and conservative women's groups, this controversy is only partially reflected in party contestation. For instance, Polish leftist parties traditionally sided with liberal women's groups, but leftist governments did not challenge a restrictive abortion law, even when they had an opportunity to overturn it. In regard to gender equality policies, however, left-wing governments responded to international pressures and demands by domestic women's groups: every change in the government's composition following parliamentary elections has led to major changes in the direction of reform concerning gender equality policies and institutions. The alliances of autonomous liberal women's groups and leftist parties in power help one to understand progress in compliance with EU gender equality requirements in Poland. But for all policy experts it is clear that international conditional and nonconditional pressures created a pivotal opportunity to introduce and promote international gender equality norms and institutions. In the following sections, I will review how the changes in Polish governments and the tactics of Polish women's NGOs influenced the direction of reforms on equality policies and institutions.

Political Swings:
The Composition of Polish Government, 1995–2010

Most political scientists assume that political divisions in post-communist states revolve around key economic views between pro-market and anti-market parties. In Poland, however, this division was accompanied by a variety of cultural divides, including religion versus secularism, liberalism versus cosmopolitanism, and traditionalism versus libertarianism, all of which debated the difference between individualist and collectivist conceptions of society (Kostelecky 2002). This division of values was evident even from the earliest stages of Polish post-communist transition. A group of liberal democratic parties advocated individual rights and neoliberal reforms (Democratic Union and the Liberal Democratic Congress), the social democratic left supported civic and socioeconomic rights (Democratic Left Alliance and the Labor Union), and the conservative-nationalist right advocated socioeconomic rights, but demanded the primacy of the family and the nation over the individual (e.g., the Christian-National Union) (Stanley 2011). These debates reflect the substantial currents in attitudes about the Polish identity, national self-assertion, and the role of history. Espoused by politicians of different political camps and the public, this controversy had an impact on the direction of government policies and on the promulgation of the Polish Constitution, which was only adopted in 1997 after prolonged debates, heated disagreements, and substantial concessions. The Church demanded that the preamble of the Constitution appeal to God and the principles of "natural law," reject the separation of the state and the Church, and protect life "from conception to natural death" (Stanley 2011, 256). The final text of the Constitution attempted to soften these postulates by mixing them with values of civic nationalism and universalism.

These controversies and divisions had a long-lasting impact on Polish party politics. By determining the outcomes of elections and party factions in parliament and reflecting the unstable and vulnerable nature of the Polish government, these divides contributed to the inability of parties to form long-lasting coalitions in parliament, especially in times of social discontent. Consequently, this led to high government turnover. In the first semi-democratic elections of June 1989, pro-reform, anti-communist Solidarity politicians won 160 of the 161 parliamentary seats for which they were allowed to compete in the Sejm and 99 of the 100 contested seats in the Senat. In September 1989, Solidarity leader Tadeusz Mazowiecki became prime minister of the new Grand Coalition, which included ministers from all parties, but was dominated by Solidarity (Curry 2011). In this advantageous situation, the leaders of the liberal, pro-reform center-right saw their chance to initiate a full-fledged transformation of the economic system and thus moved rapidly to adopt the "Balcerowicz Plan," a program of economic transition and microeconomic stabilization, also known as "shock theory," which came into force on January 1, 1990. The Minister of Finance, Leszek Balcerowicz, emphasized the importance of acting quickly to pass these reforms since he feared losing the political opportunity through interest group opposition, cooptation, and distortion of reforms (Balcerowicz 1995). As he predicted, the reforms quickly became a focal point of resentment for radical opposition groups which destroyed the unity of Solidarity in the bitter election campaign of November 1990 and ultimately accelerated the government's collapse. New parliamentary elections took place in October 1991. With twenty-nine parties represented in the lower house (the Sejm), the parliament was incoherent and highly dysfunctional. Two major parties were the Liberal Democratic Union (UD), a major successor of the Solidarity movement, and the Democratic Left Alliance (SLD), built on the remnants of the Polish communist party. Neither of these major parties could build a coalition with the minor parties in parliament: the former due to its link to highly unpopular economic reforms, the latter due to its connection to communism. Three governments were formed on the basis of this parliament, but each was short-lived due to an inability to assemble a governing coalition that could manage the growing social discontent, which arose from the painful effects of the economic reforms (Bugajski 2002).

Early elections in September 1993 brought left-wing parties to power, resulting in a coalition of the SLD with the Polish People's Party (PSL), both of which strongly opposed and criticized liberal economic reforms. Although the SLD-PSL government of 1993–1997 made more concessions to trade union demands than the previous right-wing governments, it did not radically change the path of economic reforms. References to social rights, including full employment, gender equality in the labor market, and universal health care were included in the Constitution of 1997 at the insistence of the SLD, but these rights had a declarative, rather than substantive, status. To review changes in Polish governments since 1995, see table 5.1.

By the 1997 election, the Solidarity trade union created a common opposition against former communist parties, Solidarity Election Action (AWS), which united around forty parties largely composed of conservative nationalists and Christian Democrats. Liberal parties of UD and KLD also banded together and formed the Freedom House (UW). Following the elections, the AWS and UW formed a post-Solidarity coalition under the leadership of Prime Minister Jerzy Buzek. The Buzek

Table 5.1. Governments in Poland, 1995–2010

Government	Parties	Seats in Sejm	Seats in Senate	Total Seats of Coalition Sejm; Government Ideology
Josef Oleksy, 1995–1996	**SLD***	**171**	**37**	**303/460**
	PSL	**132**	**36**	**Left-Wing**
Włodzimierz Cimoszewicz, 1996–1997	UD	74	4	
	UP	41	0	
	AWS	**201**	**51**	**261/460**
	UW	**60**	**8**	(until June 2000);
Jerzy Buzek, 1997–2001	SLD	164	28	**201/460**
	PSL	27	3	(after June 2000)
	ROP	6	5	**Right-Wing**
Leszek Miller, 2001–2004	**SLD-UP**	**216**	**75**	**291/460**
	PSL	**42**	**4**	**Left-Wing**
Marek Belka, 2004–2005	PO	65	—	
	SRP	53	2	
	PiS	44	—	
	LPR	38	2	
	Senate 2001	—	15	

continued on next page

Table 5.1. *Continued.*

Government	Parties	Seats in Sejm	Seats in Senate	Total Seats of Coalition Sejm; Government Ideology
Kazimierz Marcinkiewicz, 2005–2006	**PiS**	**155**	**49**	**244/460**
	PO	133	34	**Right-Wing**
Jarosław Kaczyński, 2006–2007	**SRP**	**55**	**3**	
	SLD	55	7	
	LRP	**34**	**2**	
	PSL	28	0	
Donald Tusk, 2007–present	**PO**	**209**	**60**	**240/460**
	PiS	166	39	**Right-Wing**
	LiD	53	—	
	PSL	**31**	—	

*Party of a Government Coalition in Bold

Acronyms: SLD: Democratic Left Alliance, PSL: Polish People's Party, UD: Democratic Union, UP: Labor Union, AWS: Solidarity Electoral Action, UW: Freedom Union, ROP: Movement for Reconstruction of Poland, PO: Civic Platform, SRP: Self Defense of the Republic of Poland, PiS: Law and Justice, and LRP: League of Polish Families.

government faced serious challenges in the economic and social sphere. While privatization of small scale businesses was growing, a significant portion of large scale enterprises, including such sensitive areas as mining and energy, remained under state control. In the social sphere, the Buzek government was forced to address unpopular government cuts to unemployment and housing benefits while also introducing caps to pensions and reduced subsidies for prescription drugs. In addition, the government attempted to reform the health care, education, and social security systems at the same time that it introduced administrative reforms to local government. Public reactions to health care and social security reforms reflected a growing sense of apprehension and discontent, which outweighed the sense of personal economic improvement and gains brought by deeper liberalization and privatization of the economic system. A weak coalition between the liberal and conservative-nationalist camps was shaken by public disapproval, forcing the liberal UW to leave the coalition in 2000. The collapse of the right-wing coalition ensured the victory of left-wing parties in the 2001 elections.

The victory of SLD-UP electoral campaign was predicted before the elections. The post-communist parties formed a coalition with the PSL under the leadership of Prime Minister Leszek Miller. The collapse of the right-wing coalition brought new parties to parliament. The liberal Civic Platform (PO) united liberals from the former UW. The leadership of another large party, Law and Justice (PiS), came from the core of the AWS coalition parties, including PiS leader Lech Kaczyński. The populist nationalist party Self-Defense (SRP), in existence since the early 1990s, was unsuccessful in winning any seats before 2001. The League of Polish Families (LRP) is a descendent of the Christian National Movement (ZChN), a radical Catholic nationalist party. It asserted clerical views and supported moral traditionalism (Curry 2011). For more information on party ideology, review table 5.2.

The electoral success of two radical parties, the LRP and the SO, once again reflected uncertainty about the outcomes of transition and pro-market reforms among a large segment of Polish society. Both parties campaigned on a ballot that severely criticized the politics of transition, bashing both the liberals and the postcommunists alike. The LRP brought the fundamentalist Catholic views to parliament and actively promoted by ultra conservative Radio Maryja and its appealing speaker and activist Father Tadeusz Rydzyk. The SO, originally a grassroots movement of small farmers who protested the effects of the early transition, significant-

Table 5.2. Ideology of Major Polish Parties

Party	Ideology
Democratic Left Alliance	Social Democratic, Left-Wing
Polish People's Party	Agrarianism, Social Conservatism, Left-Wing Populism; 2005– on: Centrist
Civic Platform	Liberal Conservatism, Christian Democracy, Pro-Europeanism, Center-Right
Law and Justice	National Conservatism, Mild Euroskepticism, Social Conservatism, Christian Right
League of Polish Families	National Conservatism, Catholic Nationalism, Social Conservatism, Right-Wing Populism
Freedom Union	Liberalism, Conservative Liberalism, Christian Democracy, Center-Right
Democratic Union	Liberal, Christian Democracy, Center
Solidarity Electoral Action	Conservatism, Christian Democracy, Right-Wing
Self-Defense of the Republic of Poland	Polish Nationalism, Social Conservatism, Agrarianism, Statism, Euroskepticism, Left-Wing Nationalism, Left-Wing Populism
Labor Union	Social Democracy, Center-Left

ly widened its electorate by appealing to urban citizens disadvantaged by the reforms. Together these parties were persistent opponents of Poland's accession to the European Union. They attacked the process of accession, the EU's intrusion on Polish sovereignty, and the humiliating monitoring of compliance. They capitalized on fears about the effects that accession might have on Polish agricultural and industrial sectors, especially mining and shipbuilding, and criticized the SLD-UP-PSL government for taking weak stances in negotiations on farmer subsidies and land use by foreign investors (Stanley 2011).

But the popularity of the left-wing government coalition was plummeting due to internal disagreements and scandalous cases of corruption that shattered the Miller government and led to his resignation. The SLD lost public support and its ties with coalition parties resulting in their defeat in the 2005 elections. The conservative Law and Justice (PiS) party, led by Lech Kaczyński, won the 2005 parliamentary elections. After his narrow victory over PO's Donald Tusk in the presidential elections in 2005, PiS formed a minority government. Thus, it proved challenging to find the support of the parliament with a minority government. In 2006, PiS established a new coalition with SO and LPR and appointed a new Prime Minister, Jarosław Kaczyński. This radical, three-party union terrified Polish liberals, as the government took a stern nationalist and populist stance toward both the international and domestic arenas. The PiS rhetoric became increasingly radical and populist, thereby reflecting the character of new policies, most notorious of which were laws on lustration, anti-corruption, the media, and the policy of "patriotic instruction," which introduced moral traditionalism into the public school curriculum. In addition, PiS President Lech Kaczyński vetoed reforms of the PO-PSL government on health care and public media (Stanley 2011).

The resurgence of radical politicians divided the country's electorate into clear groups of supporters and opponents of liberals and right-wing populists. The Smolensk tragedy that took the life of President Lech Kaczyński, and many other key political figures of the Polish government, further consolidated these divisions and resulted in the victory of liberals in the 2010 presidential elections. While liberal reforms proved to be bitter and painful, the government of Donald Tusk pursued a persistent course toward greater liberalization and privatization. These reforms helped Poland to withstand the trying times of the global financial crises, marking Poland's positive GDP growth during the crises and a quick recovery of its economy by 2010.

Contested Terrain: Polish Women's NGOs

Polish women's organizations have a rich history dating back to nine-teenth-century activism around a broad array of issues including Polish political independence, nationalism, education and literacy, social justice, and community support.[3] However, the "Solidarity" movement was the impetus and template for contemporary women's organizing during the mid-1980s (Fuszara 2004; Fuszara and Zielińska 1995; Regulska and Grabowska 2011). The collapse of the communist system in 1989 opened up new spaces for democratic civic activism in various spheres of social and political life.[4] Women's mobilization played a distinct role in Polish civic activism. Women were active participants of the Solidarity move-ment; in the post-1989 period, women's grassroots organizations took various forms. The first feminist organization, the Polish Feminist Asso-ciation, appeared in 1989, signaling the transformation of civic activity into a structured, institutionalized organization. Most of the first women's organizations emerged from grassroots informal networks in support of, or in opposition to, a specific political or social cause. For early women's organizations in Poland, public debates around reproductive rights pro-vided the impetus for civic activism. Women in various parts of the coun-try mobilized in protest against restrictive abortion policy: pro-choice demonstrations took place in Warsaw, Kraków, Poznań, and Wrocław, just to name a few cities. These civic initiatives grew into Poland's first pro-choice organizations, including the Pro-Femina Association and the Federation for Women and Family Planning. Their pro-life oppo-nents included many women's organizations associated with the Catholic Church. This division represents the deepest controversy in contemporary Polish women's movements. It manifested itself most notably in 1995 when pro-life and pro-choice women's NGOs submitted two independent "shadow reports" to the UN Commission on Women as a follow-up to the UN Conference on Women in Beijing (Fuszara 2005a).

The challenges of transition reflected a great diversity of needs and concerns which the Polish state could no longer address. Non-govern-mental organizations sprang up across the country in response to the dire situation many Polish women faced, offering programs on retraining and job search, programs for disabled and elderly people, business women, single mothers, students, and women politicians or those interested in running for political office. Violence against women is another area of social concern which was ignored by the Polish state until the early 2000s. Numerous women's NGOs across the country organized to provide services for battered women and to lobby local governments, police, and the medical community to help combat this social ill. Not all of these organizations restricted their target audience to women. Many addressed issues of families, including alcohol and drug abuse, psychological help, and services to children and teenagers.

The arrival of Western organizations and funds in the mid-1990s re-introduced principles of gender equality and equal opportunity for men and women to the public debate. In Poland, like in many other CEE states, the principles of gender equality are largely perceived to be a communist legacy associated with planned economy and full employment. The challenges of transition, loss of employment, and the collapse of the welfare system, however, revealed dire inequality between the sexes in public and private life, including the labor market, inequality of wages, the male-dominated political leadership, and the traditional division of labor within families. At the local level, several organizations emerged to disseminate information and improve public and government awareness about gender inequality, for example, the Organization of Women's Initiative (OŠKa) and the Center of Women's Rights in Warsaw, Konsola in Poznań, and the Women's Foundation (eFKa) in Krakow. At the supranational level, women and feminist groups sought cooperation and collective action in support of international gender equality initiatives with specific focus on economic rights (KARAT Coalition), legal rights (Network of East-West Women), and reproductive rights (ASTRA). These NGOs functioned as umbrella organizations that connected multiple Polish women's NGOs with women's NGOs in other CEE states and European organizations. These NGO networks also strengthened the connections between Polish women's organizations and helped to coordinate and publicize their activities, such as through the monthly publication of *Kalendarium* (1997–2005) by OŠKa and periodic national reports overviewing the impact of EU accession on women's status in the labor market by KARAT Coalition (for Bulgaria, Czech Republic, Hungary, and Poland).

International organizations played a pivotal role in boosting the activity of women's organizations in the region. They strengthened the legitimacy of women's NGOs in the eyes of the governments which ultimately transformed women's NGOs into mediators between international organizations and state governments. They also provided financial and technical assistance, and reinforced the capacity, expertise, and connections of women's NGOs with other women's organizations at local, state, and international level. For instance, the 1995 UN Conference on

Women in Beijing created avenues for collaboration between the state and non-state actors in Poland, resulting in the first effort to establish a permanent consulting body, the Forum for Cooperation, between the Government Plenipotentiary for Family and Women and women's NGOs (Nowakowska 2000). The Forum's most notable achievement was their collaborative work on the *National Action Plan for Women*, which allowed substantial input from women's NGOs on state policy proposals and initiatives concerning women and gender equality. The work of the Forum was suspended after the 1997 elections. The European Union was another organization that shaped and transformed the legitimacy, strength, and capacity of women's NGOs in Poland. Polish-EU accession negotiations set the agenda for multiple NGOs around the anti-discrimination clause outlined in Chapter 13, "Social Policy and Employment." Taking a pragmatic approach to accession negotiations, women's NGOs sought to push forward the anti-discrimination agenda, mediating disputes and conflicts between the European Union and the national government. Many NGOs strategically employed the frame of the EU accession requirement in their negotiations with states concerning policy and institutional change in the area of gender justice (Hašková and Křížková 2008).

Based on the analysis of women's NGO activities published in *Kalendarium* from 1997 to 2004, Joanna Regulska and Magda Grabowska identify three stages of NGO activity in Poland: (1) *Introducing* (January 1997-September 1999); (2) *Informing* (October 1999–December 2001); and (3) *Engaging and Creating Partnership* (January 2002–December 2004) (2008, p. 142, italics by Regulska and Grabowska). There was no mention of any NGO activities related to the EU Enlargement process prior to mid-1997, when the first meeting regarding EU accession and EU gender equality requirements was organized. The first collective action took place in December 1997, when many women's NGOs petitioned the Parliament and the Prime Minister in a collective letter outlining their demands for policy and institutional change. In this period, conferences and seminars were a form of collective action commonly employed by NGOs to raise public awareness about the EU gender equality clause that attempted to translate and adapt EU equality *acquis* to a Polish policy context (Regulska and Grabowska 2008). The second stage in NGO activity, informing, is characterized by the increased "flow of information between the EU and women's NGOs, and the greater propensity of women's groups to generate new information" (Regulska and Grabowska 2008, 144). This was the period of EU-Polish negotiations in the area of social policy and employment. The NGOs used this opportunity to disseminate information about the equality *aquis* to inform the public about the actions of the state in these negotiations, mediate the conflict between the reluctant state (governed by conservative right-wing parties) and the European Union, and demand greater compliance from the Polish state. Women's groups repeatedly tried to confront state resistance to reforms in the area of gender equality; mobilization, petitioning, and lobbying, as seen in the case of two attempts to introduce draft law on gender equality though the Women's Parliamentary Group, were all used as a means to influence political decisions.

Starting in 2000, Polish women's NGOs became eligible to compete for EU funds. The additional financial support boosted the activity of women's groups resulting in a growing number of conferences and seminars on gender-related issues, including gender equality in the market and EU accession requirements. Using EU funds, Polish women's NGOs carried out at least three major awareness-raising initiatives concerning equal rights: campaigns by the Women's Rights Center, 2006; *EU Manual for Women* (OŠKa 2001); and the Polish translation of the EU manual, *100 Words about Equality Between Men and Women* (KARAT Coalition 2006). While the relations between women's NGOs and the government were difficult and distant due to the right-wing government's denying them access to policy agenda setting power, during this period women's groups grew stronger, more informed, and better connected to regional and international state and non-state actors. When left-wing parties came to power in November 2001 women's NGOs seized their opportunity.

Lobbying and protesting against government inaction became a ubiquitous strategy for demanding state compliance with EU legislation, which resulted in the reestablishment of the Office of Government Plenipotentiary for the Equal Status of Women and Men on November 27, 2001, at the level of State Secretary in the Chancellery of the Prime Minister (Lohmann and Seibert 2003). This period is characterized by a successful collaboration between the state office on gender equality and women's groups. It is clear that left-wing governments in Poland are more responsive to the demands of women's NGOs, who they view as political partners and supporters. During this period women's NGOs received an opportunity to engage in institutionalized politics by collaborating and advising the staff in the Office of Plenipotentiary and Women's Parliamentary Group. The appointment of two prominent feminist activists, Izabella Jaruga-Nowacka (2001–2004) and Magdalena Środa (2004–2005), to the position of Government Plenipotentiary strengthened the connections between the government and women's NGOs. Following the fall 2005 elections, we observe another dramatic shift in the state's agenda: the office of the Plenipotentiary for the Equal Status of Women and Men was closed down and reestablished at a much lower level with a conservative agenda that suited the conservative right-wing parties in the Polish parliament. The stage of engaging collaboration shifted to a period of political marginalization and contestation.

Besides the political challenges, the post-accession period brought financial difficulties to many Polish NGOs as they became ineligible for many EU grants targeted toward Enlargement countries. As EU funds moved eastward and the financial crises hit the European Union, the struggle for survival became real for many Polish women's NGOs. Many prominent women's organizations closed, including the KARAT Coalition and OŠKa. But their efforts were not completely in vain: they left a strong legacy of political engagement and activism adapted by many other women's groups.

Governing parties in parliament and activist women's NGOs mediated Polish compliance with EU gender equality requirements. In the following sections, I will review paths of policy and institutional reforms in Poland from 1995 to 2010, paying particular attention to the role of governing coalitions and activism in women's NGOs.

Paths to Compliance: Policy Adoption

The UN Conference on Women in Beijing (1995) and the application of the Republic of Poland for membership in the European Union (1994) created an impetus for reforms of national social policy to address international requirements on gender equality. The Polish government initiated work on policy harmonization with international standards on gender equality as early as 1994. In 1995 the office of the Government Plenipotentiary on Family and Women Affairs prepared the *Government Report on the Situation of Women in Poland* and *Report on the Situation of Polish Families*. These two documents were debated in Parliament in 1996, along with a draft of *Government Family Policy* prepared by the Parliamentary Committee on Social Policy. Prepared by left-wing politicians, these reports recognized the basic premises of gender equality in the labor market and in the family, although they did not fully encompass all aspects of gender discrimination.

International pressures inspired women's NGOs to cooperate with the Parliamentary Women's Group on proposals to include the gender equality clause in the new draft of the Polish Constitution. Representatives from several women's NGOs participated in the parliamentary debate criticizing the lack of both gender equality guarantees and protection against gender discrimination (e.g., Women's Rights Center). The final version of the Constitution adopted in February 1997 included basic guarantees of gender equality, but it did not explicitly address protection in cases of discrimination on the grounds of sex (Article 32, 33 (1,2)). Women's groups recognized that the Constitutional guarantees offered only minimal protection, but they were content with these changes. The heated debate and strong opposition from social groups and members of parliament affiliated with the Catholic Church could have potentially led to a less progressive overall outcome. A softening of Constitutional protections reflected a compromise with the opposition.

In the aftermath of Beijing the Government Plenipotentiary, in active cooperation with multiple women's NGOs, started the work on the *National Action Plan for Women*. The first stage of the implementation of the National Plan was adopted in April 1997. The Forum for Cooperation, a partnership between the office of the Plenipotentiary and several women's groups, was indispensable for elaborating the plan and guiding it through the parliamentary procedure. It was the first comprehensive government program on the advancement of women's rights. The Plan followed the recommendations of the Beijing Platform for Action. It proposed to establish institutional mechanisms for women's advancement, including responsibilities of individual ministers, a campaign on raising public awareness about gender equality and various forms of gender discrimination in public and private spheres, and a timetable for program enforcement. The election of a right-wing government in November 1997 halted the implementation of the National Action Plan, as well as many other programs for women including a UNDP program against domestic violence, a government program, entitled "Against Violence–For Equal Opportunities," and a draft of the Law on Equal Status of Women and Men (Nowakowska 2000).

The *Government Opinion on the Law on Equal Status of Women and Men* issued in February 1998 was highly negative, stirring discontent among women's groups who petitioned the Speaker of the Parliament and Prime Minister Jerzy Buzek demanding the adoption of the Law of Equal Status. Following the Conference on the Situation of Women in Poland (organized by women's NGOs), women's groups wrote a collective letter with their recommendation to the government on policy toward women. Since their petitions elicited no reasoned response, women's NGOs issued a statement criticizing government policies toward women, which they addressed and sent to the Presidium of the Sejm and the Prime Minister (April 1998). In addition, women's NGOs sent a collective letter to Francoise Gaudenzi, the EU Commissioner who led accession negotiations with Poland. In this letter, women activists criticized the backlash against women's rights and expressed their protest against the direction of policies under new Plenipotentiary Kazimierz Kapera, a right-wing conservative notoriously known for his homophobic and sexist statements. Eventually, Kapera had to resign from the position of Government Plenipotentiary for Family (the name of the equality mechanism under the right government) because of pressure from both women's groups and the European Union (Nowakowska 2000*b*). Meanwhile the government pursued an explicit policy to support traditional family values. Several parliamentary debates held throughout 1998 and into 1999 resulted in the adoption of the Government Program on Pro-Family Policy (1998) and the rejection of a draft of the Law on Equal Status of Women and Men (1999) (Dąbrowska 2007).

The confrontation between right-wing governments and feminist women's groups resulted in greater mobilization of NGO activity. From 1997 to 2001 women's NGOs organized at least thirteen conferences and seminars on gender equality and women's rights in Poland (Regulska and Grabowska 2008). They became active advocates for institutional and policy change, reaching out to central and local governments, the European Union Commission, and transnational women's NGOs. The Polish right-wing did not realize that the European Union was serious about their requirements on gender equality until an official warning from the European Commission threatened to close negotiations and to terminate the accession process (Zielińska 2002). Following this warning, the right-wing government initiated debates on the amendments to the Polish Labor Code. However, the amendments came into force on January 2002, only after the left-wing parties came back into power. The 2002 amendments added a new chapter to the Labor Code entitled "Equal Treatment of Men and Women," which provided definitions for direct and indirect discrimination, shifted burden of proof to the employers in cases of labor disputes, stipulated the principle of equal pay for equal work, set the standards for working hours, and guaranteed parental leave in accordance with EU requirements. In addition, the list of jobs prohibited for women was modified and two protection policies were adopted to regulate the work of pregnant women: the Government Ordinance on Safe Working Conditions (July 2002) and the Directive of the Ministry on Labor and Social Affairs from July 30, 2002, on the list of work prohibited to women (127/1092). These changes allowed the European Commission to complete negotiations with Poland regarding Chapter 13 in June 2001. Additional amendments to the Polish Labor Code guaranteeing safety in the workplace and extending the definition of discrimination on the grounds of sex were adopted in January 2004 (Šmiszek 2005). New stipulations regarding parental leave were added to the Law on Family Allowances in 2006. The laws concerning gender equality in statutory and occupational social security schemes were addressed after the accession in Government Regulation on the Coordination of Social Security Schemes with EU Requirements (May 2010). The enforcement of these rules, however, will not start until 2022. For more information on amendments, see Appendix III.[5]

While these amendments addressed the major discrepancies between the Polish laws and EU Directives on gender equality, they did not fully meet the EU requirements and standards. The law on gender equality was not passed by the right-wing or the left-wing government. Below, I will discuss the debates surrounding this Act.

Act on the Implementation of Certain Provisions of the European Union in the Field of Equal Treatment (2011)

The work on drafting the Law on Equal Status of Women and Men started in 1996 with the goal of creating an all-encompassing blueprint policy for the protection against direct and indirect gender-based discrimination. Professors Eleonora Zielińska and Małgorzata Fuszara prepared the first draft at the request of the Women's Parliamentary Group (Dąbrowska 2007). The draft provided definitions and mechanisms for protecting people against discrimination within several spheres: the labor market, political participation, and social protection. It provided clear definitions of direct and indirect discrimination, sexual harassment, and equal pay for equal work. It outlined specific provisions for protecting women in the labor market by recognizing their equal right to employment, education, training, promotion, equal pay, and protection against sexual harassment in the workplace. It also recognized the vulnerability of women to discrimination in cases of pregnancy, breastfeeding, and child caring, outlining specific mechanisms for their protection. In the area of social protection, the draft law stipulated equal access for women and men to social insurance, health care, education, and legal protection. Stressing inequalities in political participation, the draft proposed a 40 percent quota for all appointed and elected public positions. To enforce these provisions, the draft law established the government office of Plenipotentiary for Equal Status and established regional and local branches across the country.

This draft law was presented to the Sejm in the fall of 1996, but it was not debated. With small changes, it was proposed again in February 1997. After the first reading of the draft law, it was sent to the parliamentary commissions for further consideration and revision. However, the election of a right-wing government discontinued this work. Women's NGOs continued their work on a draft law and submitted their recommendations and proposals to the Speaker of Parliament and the Prime Minister. The right-wing parties criticized the draft. The major issue was the quota system and the introduction of neutral gender roles in school textbooks. The draft law was finally debated in Parliament in 1999 and was rejected in its first reading (Dąbrowska 2007). Women's NGOs attempted to reintroduce new versions of the law to parliament several times; but their efforts were unsuccessful until July 2002, when the left-wing parties came to power. A new draft of the Law on Equal Status of Women and Men was finally submitted to the Senat. In the Senat, the draft Law went through debates and revisions in two commissions and was supported in the third reading in December 2002. With the Senat's support, the draft law was debated in the Sejm and was sent for further work and consideration in two Sejm commissions. After long-standing debates, the draft Law on Equal Status of Women and Men was rejected by the Sejm in July 2005.

The work on the law came to a halt as the right-wing parties came back into power in November 2005. However, to fulfill the EU requirement on instituting a blueprint policy against discrimination by August 2008, the government commissioned the Department for Women, Family, and Counteracting Discrimination to propose a new draft of the Anti-Discrimination Act. In preparation of this document, the Department consulted with several trade unions and employers' organizations. None of the women's groups were invited to participate in drafting this Act. A final document, a watered-down version of a generic anti-discrimination act, which addressed all forms of discrimination rather than a specific policy aimed at preventing gender-based discrimination, was adopted in 2011, after the 2008 deadline set by the European Union. The title of the Act suggests its symbolic nature, reflecting the lack of specific mechanisms of protection against gender-based discrimination: *Act on the Implementation of Certain Provisions of the European Union in the Field of Equal*

Treatment. This document once again demonstrated the dependence of the Polish reform trajectory on the governing coalition in power.

Polish Institutions on Gender Equality

The first Polish Government Plenipotentiary for Women was established in 1986 under the communist government. The Council of Ministers introduced government mechanisms for the advancement of women in response to the UN Conference on Women in Nairobi in 1985 and this office operated until the collapse of the communist regime in October 1989 (Nowakowska 2000). In April 1991, a right-wing government, whose leaders were closely associated with the Catholic Church, reorganized the office on women's affairs into the Government Plenipotentiary for Family and Women, reflecting the importance of the family component for policymakers. Troubled by the rising social controversy around the anti-abortion law of 1991, the government closed down the office on the grounds that there was no gender discrimination in Poland and, therefore, there was no need for such office (Nowakowska 2000). Ironically, it was Poland's first female Prime Minister, Ms. Hanna Suchocka, who proposed shutting down the Government Plenipotentiary for Women and Family.

In 1993, new elections brought a reformed, ex-communist party back to the Polish Sejm. Liberal women's organizations mobilized in hopes of changing the highly restrictive anti-abortion law and demanded that the government reestablish the Office on Women and Family. It was re-opened in 1994 before the Beijing Conference on Women. The office became quite active in establishing connections with international and domestic women's organizations in preparation for the Beijing Conference and follow-up strategies and plans (Nowakowska 2000). As detailed earlier, the office drafted and adopted the National Plan of Action in response to the Beijing Platform for Action and established the Forum for the Cooperation of the Government Plenipotentiary for the Family and Women's Affairs and of women's NGOs.

But this office did not last long; in the 1997 election, the right-wing parties returned to power. A new government terminated all programs of the Plenipotentiary office, abolished government cooperation with NGOs, and changed its title to the Office on Family Affairs. New people replaced most of its staff. Kazimierz Kapera, a conservative right-wing politician from the Christian-National Union, became the Plenipotentiary. Kapera shut down most of the programs initiated under the leftist government and attempted to stop the cooperation between the government and women's NGOs by asking central and local government officials to ignore questionnaires sent out by women's NGOs in regard to the fulfillment of the National Action Plan (Zielińska 2002). This was the government's response to the rising activism and protests of women's organizations against the conservative turn in Polish policymaking. At the time, the Government Plenipotentiary for Family presented a socially conservative program in support of traditional family values, ignoring women's groups and the European Commission's demands to continue reforming the gender equality policy area.

The situation changed only when the left-wing parties won the elections in November 2001. Multiple women's organizations excluded from the policymaking process by the right parties seized this opportunity and pressured the left-government for comprehensive reform. The activism of women's organizations, however, was indispensable for the advancement of policies and institutions on gender equality even under the left parties in power. Without a strong lobby for women's NGOs, the left government would have pursued only marginal reforms. For example, although the left parties had plans to reestablish the Office on Gender Equality, initially they wanted to place it within the Ministry of Labor and Social Affairs as a marginal office with restricted powers and functions. But women's organizations protested this marginalization. They wrote letters of concern to government officials and international organizations, including the European Commission and the European Women's Lobby, organized protests at the government building, and used their political influence on high-end politicians within the government. As a result of these political debates, the Council of Ministers established the Plenipotentiary on the Equal Status of Women and Men in the rank of the Secretary of State, placed within the Chancellery of the Prime Minister, which became one of the highest ranked offices in the region (Wilkowska 2003).

Policy experts, however, recognize the feeble institutional foundation of the Government Plenipotentiary office. Established by the Prime Minister Ordinance (not by Parliament decision), the office is highly dependent on the government for its power, as it can be easily restructured or closed down by government decree (Stadejek 2005). After the collapse of the Miller government in 2004, there was an attempt to move the Office of Plenipotentiary to the Ministry of Social Policy in the competence of a new Minister, Izabela Jaruga-Nowacka, who was Government Plenipotentiary until this appointment. At the insistence

of women's NGOs and the Women's Parliamentary Group, the Plenipotentiary remained in the Chancellery of the Prime Minister, although its
status has been downgraded to Under-Secretary of State.

Although this office was one of the highly ranked gender equality
mechanisms in the CEE region at the time,[6] its competencies were limited to monitoring, education, awareness-raising, advising, and consulting
different branches of the government on the inclusion of gender equality
principles in various domains of policymaking. The Plenipotentiary did
not have powers of decision making, but it could influence the policy
process by submitting recommendations and drafts of governmental documents related to gender equality and discrimination, including ethnic
and religious, age, and sexual orientation (Stadejek 2005). Training of
government personnel and the development of a consistent program of
action to introduce gender equality into government decision making
was one of the most important priorities of the Plenipotentiary Office.
In cooperation with Austrian and Dutch partners, the office conducted
multiple three-day seminars for government employees at the national,
regional, and local levels, including judges, trade union activists, lawyers,
journalists, and women's NGOs. This twinning program with Austrian
and Dutch governments started in August 2003 and finished in the fall
of 2005 (Šmiszek 2005).

The office of Plenipotentiary was used as an example for the
regional and municipal levels. By 2005, regional offices on family and
women (their titles differ widely) were opened in sixteen voivodeships
and at least ten municipalities (Jawor 2005). As Anna Jawor, Plenipotentiary on the Equal Status of Women and Men in the Mazoviecky
Voivodeship explains, the main responsibility of this new office is to
build contacts with women's NGOs and to disseminate information about
government policy on gender equality in urban and rural areas (2005).
Not all regional-level plenipotentiaries cooperate with each other. Often
their ideological disagreements prevent cooperation. For instance, despite
both being located in Warsaw, the Office on Equal Status of Women and
Men of the Mazoviecky Voivodeship and the Warsaw Plenipotentiary
for Families and Women do not cooperate because the former supports
the agenda of gender equality and the latter espouses traditional family
support and runs programs for families with children.

After the elections of 2005 in which right-wing parties came to
power, the Office of Plenipotentiary for Equal Status of Women and
Men was closed down, but due to national and international protests
it was re-opened as part of the Ministry of Labor and Social Policy

in the rank of Under-Secretary of State. The title of the Office was changed to Plenipotentiary for Women and Family reflecting its focus on family related issues. The Department of Women, Family and Counteracting Discrimination, which directly reports to the Plenipotentiary, is responsible for developing national programs to combat discrimination on various grounds, including gender-based discrimination. The Department maintains connections with trade unions and conservative NGOs, including women's groups affiliated with the Catholic Church. The Plenipotentiary consulted these organizations in 2007, when the office prepared the "Program on Government Family Policy." None of the feminist women's organizations were invited to take part in the preparation of this program (Dąbrowska 2007).

While this office lost its prominence and status in 2005, it is responsible for maintaining all programs related to gender equality and communicating with international organizations on behalf of the Polish government in regard to gender equality policies and programs. It is clear that even the right-wing government does not intend to fully disentangle policies and institutions created under conditional pressures of EU accession. However, they adjust the functions and the agenda of these offices to suit their policy frame.

Reviewing the Role of International Organizations

International organizations were pivotal for shaping institutional and policy reforms on gender equality in Poland. These reforms, however, were not initiated under international conditionality. Poland is one of the early reformers of its institutions and policies. The first position of the Government Plenipotentiary for Women was established by the communist government in 1986 in the aftermath of the UN Conference on Women in Nairobi. It is evident that noncoercive influence of international organizations created a strong impetus for institutional reforms in communist Poland. The first non-communist government maintained the position of the plenipotentiary, albeit with a new conservative agenda. But the institution itself continued to exist and submit periodic reports to the UN Division for the Advancement of Women.

International socialization and international group (social) pressure also created an opportunity for the first policy reforms in Poland. The UN Conference on Women in Beijing (1995) was a catalyst for legislative work on the status of women, resulting in the preparation of at least three important documents, the *Government Report on the Situation of Women in Poland* (1995), *Report on the Situation of Polish Families* (1995), and a draft of the *Government Family Policy* (1996). All of these documents recognized the main principles of gender equality on the labor market and provided avenues for government action to combat gender inequality. These documents served as a foundation for a conceptual policy program, the *National Action Plan for Women*, adopted in 1997, and the first draft of the Law on Equal Status of Women and Men (1997–1998). While international noncoercive measures have given momentum for these reforms, they could not withstand fierce government opposition, when conservative parties came to power. As a result, the Law was not adopted.

Major policy reforms, including changes to Labor Code, were carried out under conditional pressures from the European Union when Poland received a warning from the EC threatening to put an accession process to a halt until gender equality directives were transposed into Polish law (2002 and 2004 amendments). This conditional threat weakened the resistance of the conservative government and ensured partial compliance with accession requirements on policy adjustment. But conditional pressures did not guarantee the adoption of the bill on gender equality; neither right-wing, nor left-wing government could pass this act before the deadline. In addition, the EU conditionality marginally affected the agenda of the government plenipotentiary: the office maintained an equal treatment and equal opportunity agenda under the left-wing governments and a conservative pro-family agenda under the right-wing government. Similarly, conditional pressures did not affect agendas of regional offices on women and family. The agenda of these offices depended on the party affiliation of the regional administration.

In the post-accession stage, the Polish government largely maintained the level of reforms achieved by 2004. However, under pressures from the European Commission it adopted a watered-down version of the anti-discrimination law. It is important to note that the EC pressures were mainly social: Poland was recognized as a noncompliant state, the EC threatened with initiation of infringement procedures against Poland and eight other EU Enlargement states in 2008. Poland was not singled out for not adopting this law; it was mentioned as a noncompliant state along with several other states-violators. This punishment is considered a social shaming, rather than a mechanism of coercive material punishment. In response to this threat, Poland adopted a rather symbolic generic act on anti-discrimination in 2011. The main goal of this act is to signal to the European Union that Poland formally has a law on anti-discrimination and, thus, is in compliance with EU requirements. At the same time, the law does not elaborate any mechanisms of protection against gender-based discrimination, provides no avenues for redress, and remains largely unenforced. The post-accession period characterizes Poland as a state conforming to EU rules and requirements in the area of gender equality that pursues formal legal changes, but does not establish solid mechanisms for policy enforcement.

Conclusion

International pressures shaped and guided Polish reforms on gender equality. Its first equality mechanisms at the executive level were created in response to UN World Conference on Women in Nairobi (1985). In addition, Poland opened the position of the Commissioner for Civil Rights Protection in 1989, mimicking the ombudsperson in some Western European states. Major changes to the Polish Labor Code were achieved under conditional pressures from the European Union. In the post-conditionality period, Poland has maintained its policies and institutions, but changed the official agenda of the government plenipotentiary to conservative family-friendly focus. Neither international conditionality, nor post-conditional membership provided enough power to the European Commission to control the agenda of Polish institutions on women, which is reflected in the policy shifts with each change in the Polish government. While accession conditionality strengthened levels of compliance with EU requirements, we do not see dramatic reform reversal in the post-accession period. The conservative government, which came to power in 2005 following Poland's accession to the European Union, had the opportunity to dismantle policies and institutions. Yet, not only did it maintain the adopted policies but it also passed an anti-discrimination act indicating its intention to comply with EU requirements despite heated parliamentary debates and low parliamentary support for this policy. Thus, we observe a continuing trend in compliance with EU accession requirements in post-conditionality period, albeit with modifications that suit the ideological views of the government. The government chose not to challenge the European Union openly by dismantling policies and institutions. They followed a more subtle way of noncompliance—by changing the agenda of gender equality institutions to support family-oriented policies and by adopting National Action Plans that suit their policy frame. This trend in policymaking continues the policy trajectory we observed in the earlier periods of Polish accession: shift in the government cause changes in policy agenda.

Thus, political parties in power are important for policy direction, as the case of gender equality policies in Poland demonstrates. However, political parties are only part of the story. Even if left parties are more likely to support gender equality policies and institutions, they would have pursued marginal reforms if not challenged by activist autonomous women's NGOs. Women's organizations were able to achieve remarkable changes, especially in regard to institutional reforms and gaining access to government offices on gender equality when left governments were in power. These achievements of women's NGOs in Poland demonstrate that the EU's policy enforcement strategy, built around the notion of compliance, monitoring, and mediation by NGOs, turns out to be a powerful tool in countries where these organizations develop sufficient capacity and expertise to challenge government inaction.

The Polish case also revealed that women in politics matters, but their party affiliation may affect their policy position on gender equality. A dedicated feminist, Izabella Jaruga-Nowacka was a passionate supporter of policies and programs on combating gender discrimination on the labor market as a member of Polish Sejm (1993–1997, 2001–2005, and 2005–2007) and as a Deputy Prime Minister in Marek Belka's government (2004–2005), who personally oversaw the adoption of 2004 amendments to the Polish Labor Code. Ms. Jaruga-Nowacka represented the Democratic Left Alliance and the Labor Union Party. At the same time, women who came on the ballot of the League of Polish Families openly supported an ultra-conservative position on the role of women in society and demanded that the role of women be restricted to the private family sphere. Thus, party affiliation can be a better predictor of a policy decision than the gender of a politician in this particular policy case.

6

Czech Republic

State Cooptation of Reforms and Marginal Compliance

The government of the Czech Republic officially applied for EU membership in 1996 and received candidate status at the Luxembourg Summit in December 1997. Accession negotiations started in 1998 and were concluded in 2002. The Czech Republic became a member of the European Union in May 2004, following years of accession monitoring, structural adjustments and reforms.

Gender equality and equal treatment never featured high on the agenda of either the Czech public or the government. The Czech Republic did not experience the same type of heated public debates around reproductive rights and the role of women and men in society as we have seen in Poland. Marked by low awareness of the issues, the public perception of gender equality in the Czech Republic rested on a common belief that Czech society had already achieved high levels of gender equality; dating from the communist era, women already had access to education, to the labor market, and to social benefits. Many believed that gender equality was a communist legacy and a potentially dangerous and useless policy in the context of a free market economy. President Václav Klaus, for instance, called gender equality policies "a freedom impeding form of political correctness" (cited in Weiner 2010). Other right-wing politicians including two recent prime ministers, Mirek Topolánek and Petr Nečas, shared these views as well. Left-wing politicians of social democratic and communist ideologies are more supportive of women's rights and, in general, recognize the value of gender equality in the labor market.[1] However, their understanding of gender equality is different from the one espoused by liberal women's groups and from the EU's conceptualization of gender equality as an individual right. Instead, they embrace a statist approach to guaranteeing gender equality by extending state protectionism to a vulnerable group, in this case women, as was once practiced under the communist state. But even for left-wing politicians, gender equality in the labor market and in social security calculations did not constitute an urgent policy priority.

Two factors drove the reforms on gender equality in the Czech Republic: the UN World Conference on Women in Beijing and accession to the European Union. Policy and institutional reforms were initiated as part of government preparation of reports for the UN Division for the Advancement of Women. Major changes to the Czech Labor Act occurred under conditional pressures from European Union. In response to the EC criticism of Czech equality institutions, the Czech government established an inter-governmental advisory body on gender equality; however, none of Czech equality institutions developed substantial policy-making and enforcement capacity and were largely ignored by mainstream bureaucracy. Following the accession, the Czech government maintained the existing institutions and policies on gender equality. Czech equality institutions remained marginalized in the bureaucratic hierarchy of the government.

One of the major reasons for this marginalization is the structural weaknesses of women's groups and their inability to create working relationships and ties with Czech political parties. This weakness allowed the Czech government to sideline women's NGOs during the accession process, excluding them from key policy decisions and, consequently, co-opting the reforms. State cooptation of legislative and institutional adjustment in the area of gender equality during the EU accession negotiation process resulted in low compliance with EU accession requirements, fragmented legislation, weak and incoherent institutions, and the delayed adoption of a generic anti-discrimination act.

Below, I discuss the process of policy and institutional transformation in the Czech Republic in detail. But first, I briefly review the Czech political environment concentrating on the key aspects that determined the course of reforms—party politics and women's NGOs. This discussion will create the context for understanding the debates on gender equality and the role of women in Czech political institutions; it will review the structure and relations between various women's groups and their ties with political parties; and finally, it will reveal their effect on gender equality reforms. The chapter will begin with a brief discussion of Czech post-communist transition and governmental changes since 1995.

Transition from Communism

Czechoslovakia started a broad process of changes designed to re-institute democracy, recreate a market economy, and reclaim the nation's rightful place in Europe following the collapse of the communist regime in November 1989. Mass demonstrations in Prague and Bratislava, also known as the "Velvet Revolution," were preceded by twenty years of stagnation and low civil activity. Czechoslovakia had been a "model satellite state" received after the notorious Soviet suppression of reforms aimed to create "Socialism with a Human Face" in the summer of 1968 (Wolchik 2011). But the fall of the Berlin Wall and regime changes in Hungary and Poland encouraged underground opposition movements, including Charter 77 in Prague and Public against Violence in Bratislava. Within twenty-one days mass demonstrations and protests brought the rigid and repressive communist system down. The opposition leader and former dissident playwright Václav Havel became president of Czechoslovakia, symbolizing the victory of the Velvet Revolution. Parliamentary elections in 1992 brought new leaders to Slovak and Czech parliaments. Soon it became apparent that the perspectives and ambitions of political leaders in the Czech Lands and Slovakia differed dramatically, and they were not able to find a compromise on many critical issues, including the painful question of Slovak autonomy. The Velvet Divorce took place in January 1993, splitting the federal state into the two independent states of Slovakia and the Czech Republic. After that, these two states followed different paths until 1998, when the quasi-authoritarian government of Vladimir Mečiar was voted out and Slovakia took a resolute path toward liberalization and democratization.

Since the early 1990s the Czech Republic had to address the same challenges as many other post-communist states in the region: political restructuring, economic transformation, and deteriorating social conditions. The Czech Constitution of 1993 established the Czech Republic as a parliamentary democracy and a unitary state where the supreme legislative authority is vested within the Parliament and the supreme executive power is given to a government led by the Prime Minister. The President is the formal Head of State with powers to approve the decisions of the government. The first Czech parliamentary elections of 1993 brought anti-communist, pro-market, reform-oriented parties to power, forming a right-wing government under the leadership of Prime Minister Václav Klaus (the Civic Democratic Party, OSD) (Mansfeldová 2004).

Following heated debates about the route of economic restructuring, the government pursued gradual economic reforms and liberalization in order to avoid the shocks of dramatic economic restructuring. Until 1996 the Czech Republic was believed to be the most successful transition economy in Eastern and Central Europe. Its gradual reforms produced minimal negative effects, no hyperinflation and low unemployment rates (World Bank 1999). The situation, however, started to deteriorate in 1997, resulting in a three-year recession, uneven employment rates across the country, and growing budget imbalances. The economy crumbled, and the newly elected left-wing parties had to take measures to improve economic performance and high structural unemployment which was especially troubling in regions traditionally dominated by heavy industry, coal mining, and steel work (Vidovic 2002). The government placed the emphasis of economic reforms on changing the investment climate and attracting foreign direct investment. These measures proved to be successful in stimulating economic growth, diversifying the Czech industrial sector, lowering high unemployment rates, and making the Czech economy less vulnerable to internal and external economic shocks.

From Right to Left: Czech Government, 1995–2010

After the end of communism the one-party system was replaced by a plethora of political parties. The most prominent of these parties came together to form a protest movement, the Civic Forum. The Civic Forum was the foundation for a new post-communist government. After 1990 the number of new political parties that fielded candidates increased dramatically. However, few of these parties were able to seat their members in parliament. In the 1990 elections, thirteen parties competed and four gained access to parliament; in 1992, ten parties competed and six of them were successful in gaining seats in parliament. Furthermore, the number of Czech parties grew from one election to another: in 1996 the ratio of new parties to parties represented in parliament was 17:6; in 1998 the ratio was 13:5; in 2002 it was 17:4; in 2006 it was 26:5; and in 2010 it was 26:5 (Wolchik 2011, 198). This trend suggests that the Czech party system is still highly unstable and that newly formed or reincarnated parties contest the political space. Political commentators provided different analyses of party volatility in the Czech Republic. Some argued that, although party labels continued to change, emerging parties fell into the same clearly identifiable ideological spectrum of left-right divisions observable in most European polities (Kostelecký 2002). Others argued that party volatility is linked to fluid voter support and the general tendency of Czech voters to punish incumbent governments (Mansfeldová 2004). Table 6.1 illustrates this trend: it was quite unusual for Social Democrats to win elections twice in a row—in 1998 and again in 2002. In 2006 they lost to right-wing parties. Right-wing parties came to power again in 2010, albeit with a new coalition.

While it is still debated whether a stable party system has become established or not in the Czech Republic, table 6.1 demonstrates that several parties have been able to gain seats in parliament since the early 1990s. (See also Table 6.2) The disintegration of the right-wing, anti-communist Civic Forum in 1991 gave rise to three political parties: the liberal-oriented Civic Movement (OH), the neoliberal-oriented Civic Democratic Party (ODS), and the conservative-neoliberal Civic Demo-cratic Alliance (ODA) (Mansfeldová 2004). The ODS is the most suc-cessful of these three right-wing parties. It gained seats in parliament in all elections since 1992 and was the dominant party in 1992 and 1996, forming the government under the leadership of Prime Minister Vačlav Klaus and again in the 2006 and 2010 elections. The Czech Social Demo-cratic Party (ČSSD) is the most successful left-wing party. Similarly to ODS, since 1992 it has always been represented in parliament. After a rough start in early elections, it finally received a majority of votes in the 1998 and 2002 elections. The inability to create a stable coalition, however, allowed the ČSSD to rule only as a minority government in 1998–2002 (with 94 votes in a 200-member parliament) resulting in the Opposition Agreement with ODS, which significantly decreased the ČSSD impact on policy formation. In the 2002 elections it managed to create a stable coalition with the Christian Democrats and the Freedom Union-Democratic Union, a right-wing party focused on a liberal agenda. This was a peculiar alliance for Social Democrats, but it proved to be a functional governing strategy. Finally, the unreformed Communist Party of Bohemia and Moravia (KSBM) had enjoyed stable support from its electorate throughout all elections in the post-communist period, but it confined itself to opposition because it was unable to create alliances with other parties in parliament, including left-wing Social Democrats.

Government stability is another problem that besets post-commu-nist governments. The second government of Vačlav Klaus, a minority government with 99 out of 200 votes in parliament, had to resign in January 1998 to be replaced by a caretaker government of Josef Tošovský. The resignation of the Prime Minister Vladimir Špidla in 2004 shook the

Table 6.1. Governments in Czech Republic, 1995–2010

Government	Parties	Seats in the Chamber of Deputies	Total Seats in the Chamber of Deputies, Government Ideology
	ODS-KDU*	**76**	**105/200**
	KSBM	35	**Right-Wing**
	CSSD	16	
	LSNS	16	
Václav Klaus, 1993–1996	**KDU-ČSL**	**15**	
	SPR-RSČ	14	
	ODA	**14**	
	HSD-SMS	14	
	ODS	**68**	**99/200**
	CSSD	61	Minority government
	KSBM	22	**Right-Wing**
Václav Klaus, 1996–1998	**KDU-ČSL**	**18**	
	SPR-RSČ	18	
	ODA	**13**	
	68		
Josef Tošovský, January 1998–July 1998	**Different parties and independents**		**200** Caretaker government
	CSSD	74	94/200

	Party	Seats	Notes
Miloš Zeman, 1998–2002	ODS	63	Minority government, Opposition Agreement with ODS.
	KSBM	24	
	KDU-ČSL	**20**	**Left-Wing**
	US	19	
Vladimír Špidla, 2002–2004	**CSSD**	**70**	101/200
	ODS	58	
	KSBM	41	**Left-Wing**
Stanislav Gross, 2004–2006	**KDU-ČSL-US-DEU**	**31**	
Mirek-Topolánek, 2006–2009	**ODS**	**81**	100/200
	CSSD	74	
	KSBM	26	**Right-Wing**
Jan Fischer, 2009–2010 (interim PM)	**KDU-ČSL**	**13**	
	SZ	6]	
Petr Nečas, 2010–present	CSSD	56	118/200
	ODS	**53**	
	TOP09	**41**	**Right-Wing**
	KSBM	26	
	VV	**24**	

*Party of a Government Coalition in Bold

Acronyms: ODS: Civic Democratic Party, KDU: Christian Democratic Party, KSBM: Communist Party of Bohemia and Moravia, CSSD: Czech Social Democratic Party, LSNS: Liberal National Social Party, KDU-ČSL: Christian Democratic Union—Czechoslovak People's Party, SPR-RSČ: Coalition for Republic—Republic Party of Czechoslovakia, ODA: Civic Democratic Alliance, HSD-SMS: Movement for Autonomous Democracy—Party for Moravia and Silesia, US - DEU: Freedom Union—Democratic Union, SZ: Green Party, TOP09: Tradition, Responsibility, Prosperity 09, VV: Public Affairs.

Table 6.2. Ideology of Major Czech Parties

Party	Ideology
Civic Democratic Party	Anti-communist, neoliberalism, conservatism, right-wing.
Christian Democratic Party	Christian democracy, social conservatism, right-wing.
Czech Social Democratic Party	Social democracy, Keynesianism, center-left.
Communist Party of Bohemia and Moravia	Communism, left-wing.
Liberal National Social Party	Liberal nationalism, progressivism, center-left.
Christian Democratic Union–Czechoslovak People's Party	Christian democracy, social conservatism, regionalism, center.
Coalition for Republic–Republic Party of Czechoslovakia	Nationalism, Euroskepticism, populism, extreme right-wing.
Civic Democratic Alliance	Anti-communist, neo-liberalism, conservatism, center-right
HSD-SMS	Nationalist, regionalism, secessionist movement, center-right.
Freedom Union–Democratic Union	Social liberalism, liberalism, libertarianism, European integration, center-right.
Green Party	Green politics, environmentalism, center-left.
Tradition, Responsibility, Prosperity 09	Fiscal conservatism, liberal conservatism, pro-European integration, center-right.
Public Affairs	Conservative liberalism, anti-corruption, direct democracy, center-right.

popularity of Social Democrats. The unpopular government of Stanislav Gross succeeded the government of Špidla, but he also resigned in 2005 and was replaced by the government of Jiří Paroubek. At that time a strong conservative right-wing turn all across Europe brought left-wing parties down, resulting in a right-wing coalition victory in the Czech elections of 2006.

The Czech political environment, however, is different from political environments of many other European countries, both new and old EU states, in one important way. It is characterized by strong Euroskepticism, mostly associated with Vačlav Klaus (Prime Minister 1992–1998, President 2003–present) and two parties—a right-wing ODS and the non-reformed KSBM.[2] Vačlav Klaus is the only Head of State in Europe who opposes the deepening of European integration. In April 2005 he started a campaign against the Constitutional Treaty of the EU, which created conflict with the European Parliament (Wiedermann 2008). In October 2009 Vačlav Klaus impeded the Czech ratification of the Lisbon Treaty by refusing to sign it without certain concessions from the European Union. He finally signed the Treaty on November 3, 2009, after the Constitutional Court rejected a challenge from the ODS. The Czech Republic was the last EU member state to sign the Treaty of Lisbon (Wolchik 2011). In recent years the ODS has softened its position toward the European Union and become more supportive of the EU integration processes. This led to the split between the ODS and its founding father and honorary chairman Vačlav Klaus, who left the party to form a new Euroskeptic party, the Party of Free Citizens, which unsuccessfully competed in the 2009 European Parliamentary elections.

Strong Euroskepticism among Czech elites is also a sign of a widespread suspicion toward the European Union among the general public (Linden and Pohlman 2003). It is unclear whether the Czech Republic would have met EU accession requirements if right wing parties, most importantly the ODS, had dominated the parliament during the EU conditionality period. However, at the time of *acquis* transposition, pro-European parties led by Social Democrats dominated the parliament (1998–2006). Social Democrats were also responsive to EU and women's NGO pressures to align Czech legislation with EU requirements on gender equality. Most of the changes to Czech laws on gender equality were introduced by amendments to the Labor Code and Administrative Act by 2002. The failure of leftist governments to adopt the Anti-Discrimination Act, however, resulted in its delayed adoption under enormous pressures from the European Union in 2009 when right-wing parties were in power.

Overall, we observe a weak party system, typical for the post-communist states of Central and Eastern Europe. Parties do not enjoy strong public support and are characterized by low membership. Even such broad-based parties with historically large organizational bases, such as the non-reformed Communist Party of Bohemia and Moravia, KSBM, and the Christian Democratic parties (KDU-ČSL and KDU), have relatively small membership, are poorly staffed, and have a fragmented regional base. Levels of party identification among voters also remain very low. Many citizens in post-communist states are skeptical that political parties and their leaders are genuine. Rather they see political parties as vehicles for competition between politicians driven by goals of personal advancement and personal benefits. These trends in public perception reflect the legacies of the communist period and the negative experiences from parties' inability to live up to their electoral promises and politicians' involvement in scandalous corruption during the post-communist era.

Divided Terrain: Fragmented Women's Movement

Political liberalization in 1989 inspired the creation of various civic and political initiatives, groups, and organizations all across the former communist states of Central and Eastern Europe. According to Potůček, approximately 20,000 civic organizations appeared by 1992 in the Czech Lands (1997). About 70 women's organizations appeared in the early 1990s (Čermáková, Hašková, Křižková, Linková, Maříková and Musilová 2000). As in many other CEE states, women's participation in formal politics declined precipitously following the collapse of the communist system, with women gaining only 10 percent of the seats in the lower chamber of the Czechoslovak Parliament (Saxonberg 2003). Excluded from formal political institutions, women took an active part in civic organizing, starting and joining non-governmental organizations. These new women's organizations addressed multiple issues neglected by the state, such as social care, health care, unemployment, domestic abuse, and human/sex trafficking. Many of the first women's NGOs represented professional associations, networks for the political empowerment of women, branches of international organizations, and groups connected to other formal organizations, such as political parties, churches, civic movements, academia, and trade unions (Čermáková et al. 2000). The focus of their interest included various spheres: training, employment, advancement of women in the labor market, political participation and empowerment of female candidates, violence against women and trafficking in women, health, social care for children, elderly and disabled individuals, single mothers, minority women (most visibly the Roma), sexual minority, awareness about women's rights, gender equality, gender sensitivity, and gender discrimination (Hašková and Křižková 2003; Sloat 2004a). There was a clear division among these new organizations into two categories: service-oriented groups, concerned with providing social services and support to vulnerable population groups, and advocacy groups, involved in education, training, lobbying, and awareness-raising about women's rights and women's rights violations in various spheres of public and private life. These organizations drew on various sources for support, but mostly relied on international donors and foundations. Funding from the local and national governments in the early 1990s was insignificant. Lack of charity and civic engagement in the post-communist region, coupled with significant financial struggles of the general population, resulted in the NGOs' reliance upon international donors, rather than on community-based support. Competition for funding and the lack of a strong umbrella organization that could unite multiple women's groups, produced fragmented activity within these organizations (Hašková and Křižková 2008; Röder 2009).

Some Czech women's activists recognized the disjointed character of multiple organizations and attempted to unite them through regional cooperation. Several Czech women's organizations joined the Network of East-West Women, a regional alliance and advocacy organization that supported women's NGOs in the post-communist region. In 1997 several Czech NGOs co-created the Karat Coalition, a regional umbrella organization and advocacy group for teaching lobbying strategies to women's NGOs in order to advance the adoption and enactment of gender equality in post-communist EU Enlargement states (Hašková and Křižková 2008). Other organizations established contacts with the European Women's Lobby (EWL), although Czech NGOs became eligible for joining the EWL only in 2002.

While all these efforts were remarkable and did initiate cooperation among different women's groups, the structural and ideological differences between Czech NGOs impeded greater integration and mobilization of women's organizations, particularly in the area of gender equality and gender discrimination. In the Czech Republic, women's advocacy groups focused on gender equality are divided into two camps: old communist-era organizations, including the largest (the Czech Women's Union), and new organizations affiliated with academia and academic research

(Hašková and Kořálová 2003). These two sets of organizations are distinct in their voice and position on gender equality, they draw upon different financial resources, and they also align themselves with the government in different ways. The Czech Women's Union (ČSŽ) was officially founded in 1990 after the Velvet Revolution, but it was created on the foundation of the communist mass women's organization established in 1967. It enjoys the largest membership among all women's NGOs, claiming some 20,000 members across all regions of the Czech Republic, and it maintains a network of some 1,600 local offices (Hajna 2005). The ČSŽ was the largest and the only legitimate women's organization during the communist era due to the fact that it enjoyed large state support and high status. After its reincarnation as a civic organization in 1990, the ČSŽ lost most of its state-provided funding but became eligible for competitive state funding for specific programs. The ČSŽ's large presence in the regions, its connections with the government, and its structural strengths, provided a clear advantage over other new and smaller organizations when competing both for state and foreign funding. The ČSŽ is also a successful fundraiser, having obtained the largest grant ever given to a Czech women's NGO in 2003 (Linková 2005). About half of the government members of the Council for Equal Opportunities of the Czech Republic, a consultative body between the Czech government and Czech NGOs, are members of the ČSŽ, which allows this organization to enjoy insider access to some government officials, which other organizations do not have (Forest 2007).

New women's organizations were established in the early 1990s. The Center for Gender Studies and Pro-fem are the largest of these organizations. The Center for Gender Studies focused on education and public awareness campaigns about gender equality and gender discrimination, while Pro-fem provided training and legal consultations for women victims of domestic violence. In 1997, both organizations were recognized by Czech governments and received the title of advocacy and lobbying organizations eligible for public support. The Center for Gender Studies was founded by the sociologist, Jirina Šiklová, an active promoter of feminist ideas and founder of the Gender Studies program at Charles University (opened in 1998 in the Department of Social Work). The goal of the program was to train social workers and public servants in a gender sensitive program and to assist victims of gender discrimination. The foreign funding and local supporters allowed the Center to open a gender studies library and create connections with research centers at Charles University and the Czech Academy of Sciences. Together with these research centers, Pro-Fem and the Center for Gender Studies took an active part in analyzing the impact of socioeconomic reforms on men and women in the Czech Republic as well as other CEE states. They provided evaluations of existing laws and institutions and issued reports on Czech compliance with EU requirements on gender equality. These organizations were successful at securing international funding, especially through the EU PHARE program (Forest 2007).

The two camps of women's organizations, the ČSŽ and the new women's groups, are not connected by a single umbrella organization, which could help generate an activist agenda for cooperative action.[3] Each branch has its own agenda and its own voice. Moreover, activists in these organizations are mistrustful of each other; suspicion creates room for competition between the branches and leaves very little opportunity for strategic, collective action. Ideological differences are one of the reasons for mutual distrust between Czech women's organizations. Some activists believe that they have different understandings of the principles of equality. For instance, NGOs affiliated with the Charles University and the Czech Academy of Sciences embrace equality principles as being individual rights that must be exercised in a free market economy. The old communist-time organizations understand social protectionism and state paternalism as guarantors of equality. Others say that this is a conflict between two generations: old-timers and new political leaders.[4]

Understanding these differences among multiple women's NGOs, EU funding encouraged greater partnership and collaboration between the groups by attaching "cooperation of multiple women's groups" as a requirement for project funding. One such multi-year project, sponsored by PHARE, was coordinated by the ČSŽ on work and life balance. As a winner of the grant, the ČSŽ was required to contract with a large number of partner organizations across the country. The partner NGOs that worked on this project included such diverse groups as advocacy and academic organizations, service providing NGOs, trade unions, business organizations, and state institutions. This project created an opportunity for cooperation between different organizations that were sometimes resentful of each other. However, while praising these efforts and goals toward encouraging greater partnership, some experts remained skeptical about the ability of such temporary projects to create a solid foundation for cooperation in the future (Linková 2005). Others expressed concerns that, if such cooperative projects fail to foster mutual understanding between different groups, it could inadvertently instill implicit hierarchies in relations between NGOs (Hašková and Křižková 2008).

In comparison to Polish NGOs, which achieved higher levels of strategic cooperation, fragmentation of women's groups in the Czech Republic was exacerbated by several factors. First, there was an absence of a salient politically charged issue, like the struggle for reproductive rights in Poland in the early 1990s, that could focus the energies of the disparate groups on a single concern. In Poland, political contestation of highly restrictive abortion laws provided a fertile ground for uniting the efforts of many pro-choice, liberal women's organizations and fostered strategic cooperation, collective action, and trust between them, even when they disagreed on other issues. Liberal pro-gender equality organizations in the Czech Republic did not have such a contested issue which could foster their strategic cooperation. Thus, they did not have an opportunity to overcome suspicion and distrust toward each other. Second, this organizational weakness to act as a collective front allowed the Czech state to assume that they are dealing with weak organizations, and they could easily forgo the demands of women's groups to be included in policy process. Moreover, the differentiated access to state bodies by women's NGOs discussed above encouraged further fragmentation of women's groups. As in many other countries, the Czech women's organizations are close to the political left, but due to their organizational weaknesses, they did not persuade the Social Democratic government (1998 to 2006) to strengthen policy and institutional reforms. In the next section I will discuss the relations between the state and women's NGOs in greater detail and analyze their consequences for policy and institutional reform.

Missed Opportunities: Policy Reforms on Gender Equality

As in many other post-communist states, legal recognition of gender equality was instituted in the Czech Constitution. Article 3 of the Constitution guaranteed equality of women and men before the Czech law. The Charter of Fundamental Rights of 1993 provided that men and women have equal rights and guaranteed these rights as inherent, inalienable, unlimited, and un-appealable. The Czech Labor Code of 1965 also recognized gender equality in the labor market as a binding principle for labor regulation. None of these documents, however, went beyond formal recognition of equality principles. They did not provide clear definitions for what were and were not violations of gender equality or discrimination, and they provided no avenues for redress when these rights were breached. But the Czech Constitution recognized the binding character of ratified international treaties on human rights and established these international treaties as superior to the Czech laws (Maksová-Tominová 2003). The legal obligations of ratified international treaties created avenues for reforming domestic laws in accordance with international requirements. Czech obligations toward the CEDAW (signed and ratified in 1982) and the ratification of the Beijing Declaration in 1995 required the state to submit their first periodic report to CEDAW in 1994 and a second follow-up report in 1999. In the second report to CEDAW, the government had to address recommendations received in 1998 from the UN Commission on the Status of Women and enlist changes achieved since the initial report (1995 to 1999). The strongest criticism of the first periodic report concerned a tendency to "conceive women as mothers and within the context of the family, rather than as individuals and independent actors in the public sphere" (cited in Maksová-Tominová 2003). The Commission expressed concern about the flawed interpretations of gender equality, gender roles, and gender discrimination, and it urged the Czech government to undertake fundamental, legal reforms to define these terms more clearly and to provide guarantees of gender equality. The reforms of Czech laws to address all international requirements on gender equality were further influenced by the Czech Republic's application to the European Union and the initiation of accession monitoring in 1998. Czech experts agree that major legislative reforms on gender equality laws occurred under international pressures from the European Union and the UN (Hašková and Kořálová 2003; Hašková and Křižková 2008; Havelková 2006; Maksová-Tominová 2003; Röder 2007). In 1998 the Czech government adopted the National Action Plan "Priorities and Procedures of the Government for the Enforcement of the Equality between Men and Women." This document analyzed Czech policies in seven areas outlined in the *Questionnaire to Governments on Implementation of the Beijing Platform for Action* published by the Division for the Advancement of Women (DAW). The "Summary Report on the Fulfillment of the Government Priorities and Procedures for the Enforcement of Equality between Men and Women" was then distributed to all ministries and NGOs for comments and suggestions (Pavlik 2004). After 2001 all ministries were required to develop their own Action Plans to ensure gender equality in their institutions. Under the conservative government that took office in 2006, however, the deadline for developing the Priorities was postponed (Röder 2007).

Major changes to Czech laws took place on January 2001 with the amendments to the 1965 Labor Code. The "Harmonization Amendment of 2001" included definitions for direct and indirect discrimination, defined some principles of equality in access to employment, training, and promotion, prohibited gender-specific job advertising, and harmonized the provisions of parental leave with EU directives. In addition, the 2001 amendments to the Act on Civil Procedures align Czech legislation with EU requirements on establishing the burden of proof in cases of gender-based discrimination. The amended Wages Act and the Salary and Bonus Act explicitly defined the principles of equal pay. In 2004 additional amendments were introduced to the Czech Labor Code, the State Service Act, and the Military Act; and a new Employment Act was adopted. The 2004 amendments of the Labor Code provided more detailed definitions of direct and indirect discrimination and sexual harassment while also outlining the terms for exemptions and specifying the procedures for addressing sexual discrimination (Wiedermann 2008). The new Employment Act outlined the procedures for equal access to employment and strengthened the overall application of the EU Directive on Employment Equality. In addition, several other acts were changed to include gender equality principles: the Act of Service in State Administration (2002), the Act on Service in Security Forces (2003), and the School Act (2004). While many of the important legal acts were changed to transpose EU requirements on gender equality, the Commission and independent analysts considered these changes insufficient (Pavlik 2004). The Czech laws on gender equality appeared to have no single, binding anti-discrimination act. Thus, in 2007 the Czech Republic was in violation of nine out of ten EU Directives on gender equality (Röder 2007). Among major concerns are the inconsistencies of Czech equal treatment laws, insufficient provisions for finding redress in cases of discrimination, and prohibition of certain jobs for women, including mining and underground work. These laws violate the Equal Treatment Directive, provide insufficient definitions of sexual orientation and sexual identity, maintain inequality in social security calculations, and do not challenge the weakness of Czech gender equality institutions.[5]

The process of EU accession and the monitoring of Czech compliance with EU requirements coincided with a ruling left-wing government coalition (1998–2006). The left-wing government proved to be responsive to international pressures on gender equality, with the Czech government pursuing adoption of key legislative changes such as amendments to the Czech Labor Code (2001). The Czech reforms, however, exemplify a clear top-down initiative with no impact from non-governmental organizations. Although NGOs continued to lobby the government with their recommendations, their input was rather symbolic: all proposals by NGOs to elevate the status and functions of the equality institutions in the Czech Republic remained ignored (Pavlik 2004). Under pressures from the European Union, the government opened a body for state-NGO consultations in 2002, the Government Council for Equal Opportunities. It is an inter-ministerial consultative and advisory body with a mandate to promote EU policies on gender equality and equal treatment. But the Council was established after major changes to Czech legislation took place and NGO representatives did not have a chance to submit their comments and recommendations on the 2002 amendments.[6]

Marginalization of independent advisors in the process of negotiations and legislative reforms allowed the Czech government to pursue minor policy and institutional changes. Their main argument was that the principles of gender equality in labor relations and in the Czech social protection system are already satisfied (Drapal 2005). Many politicians believed that the Czech social protection laws inherited from the communist state already included strong protective measures for working women and only minor adjustment was required to satisfy the EU Directives. These attitudes not only stalled major amendments to existing laws, but also precluded the adoption of Anti-Discrimination Laws. The commentators on Czech reforms note that the transposition of EU laws in some areas of policy was an uncontroversial process (amendments to Labor Code and other acts) while in others it sparked political debates and opposition (Anti-Discrimination Law) (Havelková 2010; Hašková and Křižková 2008; Wiedermann 2008). The proponents of reforms reaffirmed to the supremacy of EU law and argued that the Czech Republic's chances for successful accession were being jeopardized by noncompliance. As a result, Vladimir Špidla, then a Minister of Labor and Social Affairs, often argued that EU provisions on gender equality had to be transposed exactly as they appeared in EU Directives ("copy and paste" method) (Wiedermann 2008), which could have resulted in the "mechanistic" transposition of these requirements into Czech laws (Hašková and Křižková 2008).

Anti-Discrimination Act 2008

General anti-discrimination clauses are articulated in the Charter of Fundamental Rights and Freedoms of the Czech Republic, adopted in 1993. In particular, Article 3 of the Charter guarantees equality in access to fundamental rights and freedoms, explicitly prohibiting discrimination on the grounds of sex, race, color, ethnicity, language, religion, political views, national origin, property, and other status. It does not include provisions or definitions for sexual identity and sexual orientation, referring to all other forms of discrimination as "other status" (Röder 2007). Moreover, only the Constitutional Court can interpret and apply the Charter to specific cases of discrimination, which makes the process of redress very cumbersome and unattainable in most cases. Ingrid Röder states that in 2005, for the first time, the Constitutional Court delivered a judicial decision in a case of discrimination (2007). To respond to this shortcoming and address international requirements on umbrella, anti-discrimination law, the Czech government initiated the preparation of an Anti-Discrimination legislation in 2000. With some input from human rights NGOs, the Czech government's Commission on Human Rights prepared the first draft of the law. The bill refers explicitly to the EU requirement: "Pursuant to the law of the European Communities, this Act regulates the right to equal treatment in the following matters. . . ." The footnote enumerates all relevant EU Directives (Wiedermann 2008, 43). Section 1 of the Act provided the scope of the application. Section 2 and 3 provided definitions to all terms in accordance with European Directives and the case law of the European Court of Justice. Section 5 identified some of the most typical exemptions from the principle of equal treatment. Part II of the draft provided measure of protection in cases of discrimination, focusing primarily on legal action in civil courts. Overall, the Act would have provided more comprehensive protection against discrimination than the multiple amendments to existing laws and acts passed in the early 2000s (Wiedermann 2008).

However, the Anti-Discrimination Act did not find strong support among parliamentarians. The Parliament reviewed the first draft of the Act in 2004 and was approved by the Lower Chamber. Social democrats, holding a majority of seats, generally supported the draft in its existing form. But their coalition partners, the Christian Democrats, the KDU-CSL, rejected the draft, arguing that no adjustments to existing laws are necessary because the new amendments to standing laws aptly satisfied all EU requirements. The neoliberal ODS party also largely opposed the bill on the grounds that the Act could distort the employer-employee relations. In addition, they argued that the major anti-discrimination clauses were already addressed by the recent amendments. The draft was sent for further review. In 2005 the government prepared a second version of the Act and it was finally heard in parliament in 2006. The amended

Act passed three readings in the Chamber of Deputies, was approved and forwarded to the Senate. The Senate rejected the Act, sending it back to the Chamber of Deputies for further work. At this point, the Act failed to gain the majority vote in the Chamber of Deputies and ultimately was rejected.

The new right-wing government that came to power in 2006 showed little support for the Anti-Discrimination Act; moreover, Prime Minister Mirek Topolánek, a well-known skeptic of gender equality and other forms of affirmative action, openly criticized the European Union for imposing such legislation on member states.[7] But political opportunity opened up for proponents of the Anti-Discrimination Act. In June 2007 the Czech Republic hosted an opening ceremony for the European Year of Equal Opportunities. EU pressure, as well as the pressure from multiple human rights and women's rights NGOs, increased. To avoid confrontation, the government of Mirek Topolánek made unprecedented concessions. First, it approved "The National Strategy of the Czech Republic for the European Year of Equal Opportunities for All (2007)— Towards a Just Society and Priorities of the European Year." Second, the government approved the Anti-Discrimination Act in June 2007—a draft that was defeated just a year earlier. The Parliament approved the Act in 2008. Finally, it created the new position of the Minister of Human Rights and Ethnic Minorities (although without a portfolio) within the structure of the Cabinet. While this position did not focus specifically on gender equality, its mandate contained gender-based discrimination as one of its responsibilities (Králiková 2007). While most experts recognize these changes as mere window dressing for the EU event (e.g., the position of the Minister of Human Rights was to be dismantled shortly after the new government took over[8]), the adoption of the Anti-Discrimination Act was a clear achievement.[9] Another favorable factor that aided in the re-introduction of the Anti-Discrimination Act to the parliament in 2007 was the fact that the Green Party supported the bill. The Green Party was part of the ODS coalition from 2006 to 2010. It is a small party that has existed since 1990 but was able to gain seats in Parliament only in the 2006 elections. It campaigned on the platform of human rights and saw the reintroduction of the Anti-Discrimination Act as one of its policy priorities.

The saga of the Anti-Discrimination Act did not end when the government and parliament approved the bill in 2008. President Václav Klaus vetoed the Act in May 2008. He stated that the Czech Republic had already addressed all issues discussed in the bill in individual amendments to various acts and the Labor Code and also derided that Act as being poor in quality. The next parliamentary meeting that addressed the rejected bill was held in October 2008. MPs largely agreed that they must pass the bill in order to address the EU requirement and to meet the deadline (2008) set by the European Commission. Financial repercussions and unnecessary embarrassment were the main arguments in support of the bill. The Act was supported by a majority of the ODS MPs, traditionally opposing any forms of affirmative action. This caused a split between President Václav Klaus and the ODS leadership, resulting in Klaus's resignation from the party he helped found in the early 1990s. A convinced Euroskeptic, Václav Klaus established another party with a strong, anti-EU integration focus. However, his party failed to gain enough support to take any seats in the 2010 parliamentary elections.

Czech Institutions on Gender Equality

Czech institutions for gender equality were created shortly after the Beijing conference. The Czech government had to submit its response to the *Questionnaire to Governments on Implementation of the Beijing Platform for Action* to the UN Division for the Advancement of Women. In April 1997, an MP from the Czech Social Democratic Party, Hana Orgoniková, sent a request to Prime Minister Václav Klaus to report on government activities with regard to the National Report on the implementation of the Beijing Platform of Action, which was due in 1998. In response to her request, the Ministry of Labor and Social Affairs was given the responsibility of coordinating the policy area concerning women in society. The UN requirement to create a women's policy machinery mirrored the EU's accession requirement of establishing a government office on gender equality policies. To respond to these international requirements, the government adopted Resolution #8/98 and charged the Ministry of Labor and Social Affairs with the task of establishing such an office. In the end, the Unit for Equality between Men and Women was created at the lowest organizational level; it is part of the Department for Integration to the European Union within the Ministry of Labor and Social Affairs (Maksová-Tominová 2003; Linková 2005; Watson and Vörös 2005). The very status of the unit suggests that it has been established in order to satisfy the EU conditional requirement for accession, not to promote gender equality principles. Even today, the state provides only limited personnel and financial resources to the office, thus impeding the task of implementation of gender policies. The unit has five employees; two of these employees are IT managers whose task is to provide the IT support to the whole department. The three other employees are charged with the task of coordinating issues related to equal opportunities between women and men across the ministries. Originally, the unit was designed to align Czech legislation with EU requirements on gender equality. But being so poorly staffed, the unit had a small impact on policy development. Today the unit's agenda includes legislative functions, development and dissemination of information related to gender equality and equal opportunity, organization of training seminars for civil servants, and subcontracting public opinion surveys regarding gender equality. Its largest responsibility, however, is preparing the Government Priorities and writing Reports on Government Priorities. In pursuing this task, the unit cooperates with other ministries, developing tasks and measures in order to improve their compliance with those Government Priorities. The unit does not have the power to enforce any laws and must rely on the good will of the ministries and other government administration offices to comply with its recommendations (Zhiriková 2005). In Zhiriková's words, "the unit functions as a secretariat for coordinating government work on gender equality" (2005).

In 2002 the Commission of the European Communities reprimanded the Czech government for disregarding the EC's requirements to develop "effective implementation and enforcement measures" (2002, 19). In response to this criticism, the government created the Government Council for Equal Opportunities (2002) to coordinate and shape Czech gender equality policies. This is a consultative advisory body with a mandate to promote EU gender equality policies. The Council includes about forty members, many of whom are ministers, top governmental officials, representatives from women's NGOs, and academics. The Council can develop policy recommendations, but cannot make binding decisions; it does not have an independent budget, or the capacity to legislate or enforce those decisions. It is the only government institution that allows cooperation and input from women's NGOs. But the NGO recommendations do not have a binding force on further government decisions. Overall, experts note the limited capacity of the Government Council to influence policy. They also remark that government officials show low interest in participating in the Council. The Council convenes two or three times a year. It is common for top government officials to send their low-ranking substitutes to the council meetings. Many regional representatives ignore the meetings altogether. All of this results in a highly inefficient and poor institution with a marginal impact on policy development. By 2005, the government has accepted only one recommendation made by the Council—to publish a methodology on gender budgeting, which was prepared by the Ministry of Finance (Niklová 2005). Other issues discussed by the Council, such as amendments to the existing Penal Code in support of the victims of domestic violence, were not signed into the Law.

To assist in greater coordination in the area of gender mainstreaming in state institutions, Vladimir Špidla, then Minister of Labor and Social Affairs, and now the EU Commissioner for Employment, Social Affairs, and Equal Opportunities, proposed to create Gender Focal Points and enforce twinning projects (exchanges with Western counterparts) at the ministry level. Pursuant to Government Resolution #456 from May 9, 2001, the Gender Focal Points were established in all ministries in 2002. These positions are part time with responsibilities shared between gender equality coordination and advancement within the ministry, as well as other duties. The ministries had to make a decision about the status of this position. In most ministries, the position was created in the Department of Human Resources at the secretariat level. The most important task of this position is to develop a program for gender mainstreaming within each ministry. The quality and the prominence of the Gender Focal Points varies dramatically across the ministries. Since their establishment, this position at the ministry-level was one of the most notable ones, as it was charged with a task of developing a program on Gender Budgeting (Niklová 2005). Overall, Gender Focal Points are believed to have marginal effect on policy development (Pavlik 2004).

The Position of the Public Defender of Human Rights, the Ombudsman, was established in 1999. Originally, the main responsibilities of this position included analysis and review of cases of administrative mismanagement by authorities. The Ombudsman did not hold specific responsibilities to address issues on gender discrimination. Since the approval of Anti-Discrimination Act in 2007, the responsibilities of the Ombudsman offices have expanded to include all cases of discrimination, including gender-based violations. The position of the Minister on Human Rights, Minorities and Equal Opportunities, established in 2007, received a mandate to monitor and address cases of violations of the Anti-Discrimination Act, and propose programs to combat discrimination. The mandate, however, was largely restricted to cases of ethnic minorities. The position was abolished in 2010.

To sum up, the Czech institutions created to oversee the implementation of gender equality principles have critically limited functions; none of them have the power to assign tasks, issue binding recommendations, or effectively inspect other government bodies (Haškova 2005). None of them have the competence to independently assist victims of discrimination as it is required by Article 8a of Council Directive 2002/73/EC.

International Pressures and Czech Compliance

Czech reforms in the area of gender equality took place in response to coercive and noncoercive international pressures. The UN Conference on Women in Beijing (1995) and the responsibility of the Czech government to submit periodic reports to the UN Division for the Advancement of Women were the main reasons why the Czech government established the first office on women's affairs, the Unit for Equality between Men and Women. The main responsibility of this office was to prepare and draft responses to international organizations as regards to gender equality in the country. The status, agenda, and responsibilities of this office have not changed since then. Political conditionality during the EU accession did not create an opportunity for elevating the status of this office.

In the Czech case, EU conditionality on gender equality brought about some policy and institutional reforms. As part of accession obligations, the Czech government adjusted the state Labor Code and several other relevant acts, like the Wages Act and Salary and Bonus Act. However, accession conditionality could not trump the resistance to the adoption of a separate anti-discrimination law. In response to EC criticism of weak equality institutions, the Czech government established an intergovernmental council on equal opportunity, but it was an insignificant institution which was disregarded by its own members. Overall, I find that accession conditionality secured minimal policy reforms and created weak institutions on gender equality in the Czech Republic.

In the post-accession period, pressures to assimilate to other EU members prevented the dismantling of EU required policies and institutions. The status of policies and institutions on gender equality remained the same. But EU pressures to assimilate to group rules created an opportunity for the adoption of a generic anti-discrimination act despite some stern criticism and opposition from many government officials. Overall, the Czech case demonstrated how social and conditional pressures from international organizations generated symbolic formalistic compliance with international requirements and resulted in minimal reforms on gender equality.

Conclusion

As in other EU Enlargement countries, Czech reforms on gender equality and equal treatment of women and men were driven by the desire to accommodate international pressures. The early reform efforts were a response to UN requirements to act on the Beijing Platform of Action, and since 1998 the EU accession requirements dominated state discourse on the issue of gender equality. In contrast to the Polish case, we did not observe public confrontation surrounding the role of men and women in society. Both public and state officials believed that gender equality was not a critical issue for Czech society because equality between men and women was achieved during the communist era. The Czech Republic inherited the communist legacy of gender equality in the labor market with women enjoying access to education, employment, and promotion, and most believed that no further guarantees to improve the status of women in society were necessary. While these beliefs are based on false assumptions and poor awareness about gender discrimination, the NGOs failed to mobilize a significant portion of the public in support of gender equality policies and also failed to appeal to government officials with demands to advance policies and institutions on gender equality. All proponents of gender equality, both in the government and in the non-governmental sector, appealed to their opponents with arguments about gender equality being part of the EU conditional requirements for accession. Such arguments implied that the adoption of these laws should mimic the language of EU directives ("copy and paste"), rather than engage in debate about the value of gender equality principles for Czech society. Lack of constituency and public support for these policies contributed to formal transposition of gender equality policies into Czech laws and allowed the government to co-opt the reforms without much input from women's NGOs.

The largest policy and institutional changes took place during accession conditionality and coincided with left-wing parties being in power. Left-wing parties are hypothesized to be more supportive of gender equality laws than right-wing parties, and we find support for this general finding in the case of Czech Republic. But despite the fact that top officials, e.g., Vladimir Špidla, Prime Minister 2002–2004, endorsed gender equality policies, they failed to pursue comprehensive legislative and institutional reforms. Leftist governments also failed to establish meaningful cooperation with Czech women's NGOs, marginalizing them in the process of accession negotiations and disregarding their input on policy recommendations.

Key political figures, who were supportive of gender equality, endorsed policy and institutional reforms, but they could not overcome general resistance to these policies from the Czech political establishment. Among the key politicians whose role in policy reforms was so indispensable are Vladimir Špidla, Prime Minister 2002–2004, Michaela Maksová-Tominová, an NGO activist, who joined the Ministry of Labor and Social Affairs, and Anna Čurdová, who served as a Chairperson of the Council for Equal Opportunities for Men and Women. While the role of individual politicians was important, the pure number of women in parliament did not have an impact on policy enforcement. First of all, women took a very small number of seats in the Czech parliament during the studied period. Second, women voted along the party lines on the changes concerning gender equality (Drapal 2005). Female MPs from liberal and conservative parties tended to criticize gender equality guarantees, albeit for different reasons; parliamentarians representing social-democratic parties tended to support these changes.

In the post-conditionality period, we do not observe a dramatic dismantling of the policies and institutions that were created during the accession period. Moreover, the rightist governments that came to power after the EU accession continued, albeit with delay, the reforms on gender equality and their efforts resulted in the adoption of the Anti-Discrimination Act in 2008. We also observe that the right-wing government expanded institutional capacities by creating a position for Minister on Minority and Equal Opportunity, but failed to give her a portfolio. Even if this position was sustained for two years, its creation by a Prime Minister who notoriously opposed any type of affirmative action is indicative of a state response to international pressures, on one hand, and the influence of concerns regarding international reputation, on the other hand. Overall, we observe that in the case of the Czech Republic, EU conditionality encouraged a government-led reform on gender equality policies and institutions. Such cooptation of reforms resulted in delayed and marginal policy transposition of gender legislation, weak institutional reform, and formalistic conformity to EU requirements in the post-accession period.

7

Lithuania

Policy Emulation and Strong Compliance

Lithuania was the first of the former Soviet Union republics to officially apply for EU membership in December 1995. Negotiations on the terms of membership started in early 2000, after the Commission's decision to begin the accession process for several Eastern and Central European candidate states was announced at the EU Helsinki Summit (December 1999). Since the late 1990s, the accession process has had an important impact on shaping the state building efforts and policies of Lithuania.

Lithuania experienced a harsh economic downturn following its independence in 1991. Severe fiscal austerity, skyrocketing unemployment, and hyper-inflation ensued as the government introduced measures to transform the state-controlled economy to a market economy. Despite the punitive economic situation, the first discussion about the law on gender equality and equal treatment of women in the labor market took place in 1992, when several women's NGOs addressed the government with a proposal to protect equal access to work for men and women (Taljunaite 2002). As a former Soviet Union republic, Lithuania inherited Soviet-style gender equality provisions in its Constitution and labor code. Linked to a command planned economy of full employment, these provisions proved to be unenforceable after the collapse of the state-controlled economic system. The state had to respond to international demands to reform its policies on gender equality in preparation for the UN World Conference on Women in Beijing. In 1994 the government established a position of the Government Advisor on Women's Issues to initiate the work on the National Action Plan for the Advancement of Women. In 1996 the government established the Women's Advisory Board to coordinate the work on the draft of the Law on Equal Opportunities for Men and Women, which was prepared in 1995 with support from the United Nations Development Programme (UNDP). The Law was signed and ratified on December 1, 1998 and came into force on March 1, 1999. Lithuania became the first CEE state to adopt a law establishing the equal status of men and women. To oversee the enforcement of the law, the government established a ministry-level office, the Ombudsman on Equal Opportunities, modeled after similar Ombudsman institutions in the Nordic states. The office received broad powers, including the responsibility to represent the rights of victims of discrimination in court and the ability to initiate investigations of alleged discrimination. The office reached an agreement with statewide labor inspectorates to monitor compliance with the Law and report cases of gender discrimination. This feature is largely absent from the agendas of other gender equality offices in CEE Enlargement states, where offices mainly perform advisory functions. Overall, the Lithuanian office of the Ombudsman on Equal Opportunities received broader powers than comparable offices in other Enlargement states.

What explains Lithuania's early adoption of the law on gender equality and its commitment to law enforcement? The right-left modality of parties in power does not explain early state compliance with international requirements. In fact, in Lithuania the right-wing government initiated the policy and institutional reforms in the mid-1990s. The voting record for the draft law on gender equality and its subsequent amendments and the relevant amendments to the labor and civil codes reveals a broad-based multi-partisan support for these amendments. Thus, in Lithuania we do not find party battles over gender equality laws like the ones observed in many other parliaments in CEE states. The case of state compliance with gender equality requirements is also very different from another gendered policy which I discussed above, violence against women. The Lithuanian government was able to block any legislative changes in the area of violence against women for over a decade. What helped to overcome such barriers in the area of gender equality in the labor market?

In this chapter I will examine the case of Lithuanian compliance with international gender equality requirements. I recognize that this is an outlier case, which does not easily fit into a theoretical model developed in this study: the main factors such as political parties and strong women's NGOs focused on gender equality do not explain early comprehensive reforms in Lithuania. First, the reforms were initiated by the right-wing government. Second, Lithuania has multiple women's NGOs but only a few of them focus on gender equality. Moreover, state compliance on gender equality began before these NGOS became strong organizations.

Therefore, the case of Lithuania is a theory-building exercise in which I examine and demonstrate that another set of factors had a dramatic impact on policy development and enforcement in this post-communist state. In particular, I reveal that three factors played an important role in shaping the reforms on gender equality. They reflect the interplay between domestic and international actors and between state and non-state institutions. First, the human rights-oriented approach of Lithuania's UNDP had an important impetus for reforms. The UNDP Resident Representative initiated and facilitated early reforms on gender equality opportunities and on human rights in Lithuania. UNDP proposed and assisted the establishment of two Ombudsman institutions, Lithuania's Parliamentary Ombudsman Office and the Office of the Equal Opportunities Ombudsman. Both of these institutions were created in partnership between UNDP and governments of Lithuania, Denmark, Finland, Sweden, and Norway. In addition, UNDP proposed legislative reforms preparing a draft Law on Gender Equality and Equal Opportunities between Women and Men, and several key Action Plans in the area of gender equality and human rights.

Second, the reforms on gender equality were endorsed by an activist NGO, the Women's Issues Information Center (WIIC). Established by UNDP, the WIIC developed its independent voice and authority to work with the government on the equality legislation. Initially this activist women's lobby group served as a channel for facilitating dialogue between the government and civil society. In recent years it received government authorization to evaluate government programs on gender equality and inclusion, e.g., the project "Women and Men in All Areas of Changes in the Extensive Survey and Evaluation by the National Equal Opportunities 2005–2009 Program Year." Experts from Women's Issues Information Center took an active part in preparing the drafts of the Law on Equal Opportunities for Men and Women and National Action Plans.

Finally, an activist women's parliamentary group, the women's caucus, endorsed the draft law in the Seimas and ensured the MP's support for the law. Female parliamentarians formed a multi-partisan caucus in 1997. The caucus united very prominent politicians, active promoters of laws that supported the position of women in politics and in the labor market. The high status and recognition of some of these women in parliament, like Kazimira Prunskienė, the former Prime Minister of Lithuania, and Giedrė Purvaneckienė, a feminist scholar and advocate of women's rights, allowed the women's caucus to influence the policy agenda and facilitated the adoption of the Law on Equal Opportunities for Women and Men as well as subsequent amendments to the law. Together, the efforts of these actors created substantial pressures on the Lithuanian government and improved state compliance.

The impact of international pressures on compliance with gender equality requirements in Lithuania differs from the effect of international factors in many other Enlargement states. Most of the reforms in Lithuania began in the pre-accession period, or before coercive conditional pressures of the European Union were applied. International socialization and social pressures to assimilate other Western democracies, therefore, had an important impact on Lithuania's early adoption of policies and institutions on gender equality. Many observers, including the Lithuanian politicians and experts, note that the Lithuanian government was very responsive to international pressures. The desire of the state to become part of the European and world community steered many policy decisions toward aligning the Lithuanian law with international norms (Krupavičius and Matonytė 2003; Taljunaite 2004; Women's Information Issues Center 2009). In addition to reforms on gender equality, Lithuania was a pioneer in pursuing progressive reforms on human rights. Lithuania is the only state among new EU member states that has fully established institutional structures that deal with human rights issues. In this regard, Lithuania's Parliamentary Ombudsman Office, founded in 1995, is the first office of its type in Central and Eastern Europe (Reynolds 2005). Lithuania's National Human Rights Action Plan, 2003–2005, is the first such plan in the CEE region. It is regarded as exemplary and is being emulated in other countries, e.g., Moldova, Nepal, and Mongolia (Reynolds 2005). Thus, progressive human rights-oriented reforms in Lithuania are not restricted solely to gender equality issues, but encompass a broad spectrum of human rights protection. International conditionality had a minimal impact on Lithuania's level of compliance, which confirms that Lithuania is an outlier among other Enlargement states.

In the following, I will review the political transformation in Lithuania since independence and examine its reforms on gender equality policies and institutions.

Gaining Independence:
Transition and Lithuanian Governments, 1995–2010

Lithuania's path to independence was long and tenuous. In 1795 the Russian empire absorbed the Grand Duchy of Lithuania, and for more than a century Lithuania remained a Russian province. In 1918 the Soviet Union recognized its independence, but Lithuanian statehood was short-lived. The Molotov–Ribbentrop Pact signed by Germany and the Soviet Union in August 1939 divided the Baltic countries into German and Soviet spheres of influence. According to the pact, Latvia and Estonia came under the Soviet control, and Lithuania was given to the Germans. In 1940 the Lithuanian government was forced to accept the terms of a mutual assistance treaty with the USSR, and Soviet troops entered the country (Eglitis 2011). After World War II the Soviet leaders made concerted efforts to integrate the Baltic states into the Soviet Union, most importantly by relocating a large number of ethnic Russians to these states. By the late 1980s the Russian population of Lithuania was considerably smaller than in other Baltic states (8 percent as compared to 30 percent in Latvia and 25 percent in Estonia). The collapse of the Soviet Union paved the path to Lithuanian independence in 1991.

A popular independence movement emerged in the Baltic states in 1988. Lithuania was the first of the Soviet republics to push for secession. The Lithuanian movement, Sajudis, placed its candidates on the 1989 ballot for the All Union Congress of People's Deputies and won 36 out of 42 seats. In the first semi-free parliamentary elections in March 1990, Sajudis won 91 out of 141 seats in the Lithuanian Supreme Soviet (Krickus 1997). Following the elections the Sajudis-dominated Parliament declared Lithuania an independent state. In response, the Soviet leadership imposed an economic embargo on Lithuania. Trying to suppress the secession, Soviet tanks entered Vilnius in January 1991 after which popular protests ensued. The death of fifteen protesters received global coverage and, consequently, the Soviet efforts to prevent the secession of Baltic states were deemed illegitimate. In the following months, the opposition grew ever stronger and more radicalized. Lithuania became independent in September 1991, following the failed coup against Gorbachev, which signaled the collapse of the Soviet Communist Party and the Soviet Union itself (Eglitis 2011).

In the first days of independence Lithuanian politicians debated the constitutional foundations of the new state. Politicians who sided with Sajudis proposed a strong presidential system; politicians from the ex-communist camp proposed a parliamentary system. As a compromise the camps agreed on a semi-parliamentary system in which a popularly elected president shares powers with the government and the prime minister. *De facto*, however, the Lithuanian state functions as a parliamentary system (Fritz 2007). In the 1992 parliamentary elections, Sajudis lost heavily to the reformed ex-communist party, the Lithuanian Democratic Labor Party (LDDP). Due to this victory, ex-communists received a large advantage when negotiating the terms of the Constitution and, as a result, multiple limitations on the president's power were introduced. The government is appointed by the president but only upon the approval by the Seimas, the Lithuanian Parliament. The president cannot express a vote of no confidence in the government; only the Parliament has this right. Presidential powers of issuing decrees are also limited. Presidential decrees must be approved by the prime minister or a minister responsible for the implementation of the order (Fritz 2007).

The 1992 parliamentary elections were unfortunate for Sajudis. The party which led the Lithuanian independence movement just a few years ago lost heavily to the ex-communist party. Facing severe criticism and low public support, Vitautas Landsbergis, the leader of Sajudis, removed himself from the presidential campaign. Dire economic crises and hasty privatization, which was perceived by the public as unfair and corrupt, explain this unexpected election result. The LDDP won the 1992 parliamentary elections in a landslide and the LDDP leader, Algirdas Brazauskas, won the first presidential election. While ex-communist parties joined the political competition in most post-communist states, the LDDP was the first to win the parliamentary and presidential elections in the region.

In the times of harsh economic downturn, the LDDP government came to power with support of the working class and farmers on the promise to protect their interests. At the same time the party sought support from the European Union and declared its intention to join the Union. These goals, however, often proved to be contradictory as the state's support of EU liberalization and austerity policies inevitably hurt the Lithuanian working class. As a result of political maneuvering and trying to cater to both sides, the LDDP lost the support of its voters and subsequently was defeated in the 1996 elections. The Homeland Union-Conservatives of Lithuania (HU-CL), a successor party of Sajudis, won the majority of seats in parliament and formed a conservative government. By 1996 Lithuania developed one of the most stable party systems among the former post-Soviet states with clear boundaries drawn between the reformed communists, the LDDP, and the conservatives, which included several parties that emerged from the independence movement Sajudis (Krupavičius and Matonytė 2003).

Table 7.1. Governments in Lithuania, 1995–2010

Government	Parties	Seats in the Chamber of Deputies	Total Seats in the Chamber of Deputies, Government Ideology
President:			
Algirdas Brazauskas, 1992–1998	LDDP*	73	73/141
	Sajudis	30	Left-Wing
	LCDP	18	
	LSDP	8	
	YL	1	
	LCM	2	
Prime Ministers:	MLP	4	
Adolfas Slezevicius, 1993–1996			
Lurynas Stankevicius, 1996	LNM	4	
President:	HU-LC	70	86/141
Valdas Adamkus, 1998–2003	LCDP	16	Right-Wing
	LDDP	12	
	LCM	13	
	LSDP	12	
	YL	1	
	LWP	1	
Prime Ministers:	LCDU	1	
Geiminas Vagnorius, 1996–1999	EAPL	1	
Ronaldas Paksas, 1999	LMN	4	
Andrius Kubilius, 1999–2000	LDP	2	
	LUL	1	
	LPP	1	
	LUPPD	1	

continued on next page

Table 7.1. Continued.

Government	Parties	Seats in the Chamber of Deputies	Total Seats in the Chamber of Deputies, Government Ideology
	LDDP	**26**	**51/141**
	SDPL	**19**	**Left-Wing**
	URL	**3**	
Presidents:	**NDP**	**3**	
Ronaldas Paksas, 2003–2004	NU	28	
	LUL	33	
Prime Ministers:	HU-LC	9	
Ronaldas Paksas, 2000–2001	CDU	1	
Algirdas Brazauskas, 2001–2004	LPP	4	
	LCD	2	
	LCU	2	
	NKS	1	
	EAPL	2	
	LLU	1	
	YL	1	
	Independents	3	

Union, LUL: Liberal Union of Lithuania, LPP: Lithuanian Peasant Party, LUPPD: Lithuanian Union of Political Prisoners and Deportees, EAPL: Electoral Union of Poles of Lithuania, NKS: Union of Moderate Conservatives, OJ: Order and Justice, NRP: National Resurrection Party, LM: Liberal Movement, LCU: Liberal and Center Union, LPPU: Lithuanian Peasant Popular Union

President:
Valdas Adamkus, 2004–2009

Prime Ministers:
Algirdas Brazauskas, 2004–2006
Gediminas Kirkilas, 2006–2008

Party	Seats
LP	**39**
SDPL	**20**
NU-SL	**11**
HU-LC	25
OJ	10
LCU	18
LPP-NKS	10
EAPL	2
Independents	6
39	

101/200
Left-Wing

President:
Dalia Grybauskaitė, 2009–present

Prime Ministers:
Andrius Kubilius, 2008–2012

Party	Seats
HU-LC	**45**
NRP	16
OJ	15
SDPL	25
LP-YL	10
LM	11
LCU	8
EAPL	3
LPPU	3
NU	1
Independents	4

100/200
Right-Wing

*Governing Party or Party of a Government Coalition in Bold

Acronyms: LDDP: Lithuanian Democratic Labor Party, LCDP: Lithuanian Christian Democratic Party, LSDP: Social Democratic Party of Lithuania, YL: Young Lithuania, LCM: Lithuanian Center Movement, MLP: Movement of Lithuania's Poles, LNU: Lithuanian Nationalist Party, HU-LC: Homeland Union–Lithuanian Conservatives, LWP: Lithuanian Women's Party, LCDU: Lithuanian Christian Democratic

As in many other post-communist states, in the 1990s, the Lithuanian governments were often short-lived. Since its victory in 1993 elections the LDDP, under the leadership of Lubys, Slezevicius, and Stankevicuis, formed three governments in the period of three years. The average survival of conservative governments from 1996 to 2001 was also one year. During this period the prime ministers, Vagnorius, Paksas, Kubilius, and Paksas again, formed their governments. Fritz reports that in the eleven years from 1990 to 2001 Lithuania has had seen eleven governments (2007, 248).

Government instability, however, did not imply the instability of parties. From one election to another, the same major parties competed for seats in parliament. Moreover, the party ideological programs were clear-cut and reflected a traditional left-right division (Krupavičius, 1999). The Homeland Union represents the conservative wing of the political spectrum. This party developed as a main opposition party in 1992–1996, when the LDDP controlled the parliament, and became part of the ruling coalition in 1996–2000. In the 2000 elections the Homeland Union lost and was replaced by a centrist coalition with two middle-size parties, the Liberal Union and the New Union/Social Liberals, which formed a center-right minority government. In 2001 the LDDP successfully merged with the Lithuanian Social Democratic Party and created a new government under the leadership of Algirdas Brazauskas (RFE/RL Features, July 12, 2001). The LDDP managed to form its second consecutive government after the 2004 elections. It was the first time in Lithuanian modern history that one party won two consecutive elections. This time the LDDP formed a coalition with four parliamentary parties. But the coalition proved to be unstable and was torn by internal conflicts and scandals. It survived only until 2006, when the president, Valdas Adamkus, citing violations of ethical principles, expressed no confidence in two of the ministers of the government from the Lithuanian Labor Party. The scandals tarnished the reputation of the Brazauskas government, and the government was forced to resign because the Labor Party, one of the left-wing coalition parties, left the government.

The Lithuanian Labor Party was founded by one of the wealthiest men of Lithuania, a Russian-born businessman, Victor Uspaskich. The party quickly gained popular support and received the highest vote in the 2004 elections to the European Parliament. In the 2004 elections to the Lithuanian Seimas, the Lithuanian Labor Party received 37 out of 141 total seats. The party won on a populist platform with a promise to expand social programs, raise pensions and salaries, and cut down

Table 7.2. Ideology of Major Lithuanian Parties

Party	Ideology
Homeland Union–Lithuanian Christian Democrats	Anti-communist, Christian democracy, neoliberalism, conservativism, right-wing.
Lithuanian Christian Democratic Party	Christian democracy, social conservativism, right-wing.
Lithuanian Democratic Labor Party	Social democracy, Keynesianism, center-left.
Social Democratic Party of Lithuania	Social Democracy, center-left.
Labor Party	Centrism, populism, center.
New Union (Social Liberals)	Social liberalism, neoliberalism, center-right.
Electoral Action of Poles of Lithuania	Nationalism, populism, regionalism.
Order and Justice	National conservatism, mild Euroskepticism, social conservatism, right-wing
National Resurrection Party	National conservatism, social conservatism, right-wing.
Liberal movement	Neoliberalism, social liberalism, center-right

the costs of utilities and housing. The party leader, Victor Uspaskich, became the Minister of Economic Affairs, but he had to step down due to accusations of partiality and conflicts of interest. In 2006 his party was accused of income violations and fraud by the financial police. The party was investigated for taking kickbacks from the European Union grants, breaching campaign-finance limits in the 2004 election and receiving money from Russia (Economist, June 8, 2006). Viktor Uspaskich resigned as a party leader and left Lithuania for Russia, where he was believed to be hiding from police and Interpol (BBC, August 30, 2006).

The conflict over the Lithuanian Labor Party and its leader was not the only political scandal that shattered Lithuanian politics in recent decades. As in many other post-communist states, Lithuanian politicians were often accused of corruption. The hastened privatization launched by the Landbergis government in 1991 was largely perceived as a fraudulent process. The privatization scandals cost the Sajudis government a loss in the following elections. Rolandas Paksas is another politician notorious for his involvement in corruption. During his term as Prime Minister, heading the Homeland Union, he had to resign due to a shady sale of one of Lithuania's major oil refineries to an American company (Fritz 2007). After that scandal, Paksas did not disappear from the Lithuanian political scene, however. In 2003 he was elected as president of Lithuania on a populist platform of fighting corruption and foreign conspiracy. Ironically, in 2004 he was impeached on the allegation of smuggling and large-scale fraud during the privatization of the alcohol industry (Economist 2004). To some commentators, the impeachment of Paksas signaled that Lithuanian elites were committed to democratic reforms and broadly agreed on the goal to join the European Union (Fritz 2007). Others suggested that Lithuanian politics during this time was divided not along the ideological lines, but into groups made up of the old "nomenklatura" politicians and the newcomers. Neither Paksas nor Uspaskich belonged to the old elites and some believe that this is the reason they were ousted (Economist, June 8, 2006).

During the early 2000s Lithuania's economy was booming. The GDP growth reached an incredible 8 percent in 2007, but the economic growth came to an abrupt end and the economy contracted by 17 percent in 2009. The global financial crises revealed the dependency of the Lithuanian economy on foreign investment and credit, which slumped as financial markets collapsed. The country's economy experienced the deepest crisis since the collapse of the planned economic system in the early 1990s. The labor market shrank, wages declined, and unemployment rose to a record high of 18.3 percent by mid-2010, as compared to the beginning of 2008, when it was as low as 4.2 percent. Youth unemployment reached 37 percent in 2010, forcing a large wave of emigration. To preserve its macroeconomic stability, the country devalued its currency internally. The total amount of fiscal consolidation, which included cuts in public expenditure and tax reforms, constituted nearly 12 percent of GDP for 2009 and 2010 (Transformation Index Report 2012).

Frustration over the crises, cuts in government spending, and tax hikes escalated into the riots in January 2009. Protests turned violent. The work of the government was paralyzed as it was facing low public support. Lithuanian political elite needed a new figure to lead the country out of the crises. In May 2009, Lithuanian people elected Dalia Grybauskaitė, former European Commissioner and Minister of Finance, to be their next president. Dalia Grybauskaitė was the first female to be elected to the country's highest political post. She won the elections in a landslide. President Grybauskaitė represents a new cohort of politicians whose careers did not originate in the movement for independence in the late 1980s and early 1990s. Although backed by the dominant conservative party, HU-LC, she ran as an independent candidate (BBC, May 19, 2009). Known as an Iron Lady, President Grybauskaitė changed the relations between the branches of government in favor of a more assertive presidential policy style. She expanded the presidential authority to include the field of domestic politics, earlier reserved for the prime minister and the government. The President's Office is the only political institution that continues to enjoy significant popular support, whereas the political parties, the Seimas, and the government remain the least-trusted institutions (Transformation Index Report 2012).

The UNDP Presence and Activities in Lithuania: Setting the Agenda for Protection of Human Rights

The UNDP was one of the first international organizations to open its office in Vilnius in October 1992. At this initial stage the task for the first UNDP Resident Representative was to establish broad contacts with the government and set preliminary goals for cooperation. Using the Ministry of Foreign Affairs of Lithuania as a core partner in the government, UNDP reached out to all central and regional authorities and negotiated the content of the first Country Program (CP) for Lithuania. The key priorities for the UNDP First Country Programme (1993–1996) focused on democratization and civil society, public administration reform, adaptation to market economy, and poverty reduction. During this period, the UNDP supported over twenty projects at the national and regional level with the largest portion of financial aid spent on projects on governance and institution building. In the language of UNDP, the "democratic institution building" meant the development of civil society organizations and support of government initiatives that aimed at strengthening the transparency of state institutions, developing their public outreach and cooperation with non-state actors, and personnel training and education. The initial investment in these programs in Lithuania constituted three million U.S. dollars. The UNDP supported the establishment of the following organizations: the Public Servants Language Center, the Public Administration Training Center, the Lithuanian Innovation center, the International Business School, the Human Rights Center, the NGO Information and Support Center, the Judicial Training Center, and the Women's Issues Information Center, one of the most outspoken women's rights lobby organizations (Reynolds 2005). The support included the provision of seed funds for opening the organization, expert and personnel training, program and project development, support of networks between regional, national, and international NGOs and partnership programs. In addition, the UNDP served as a mediator between the state and non-state institutions, creating a platform for their cooperation and dialogue. The introduction of the cost-sharing mechanism was one of the strategies to induce government cooperation in joint initiatives with NGOs. This was a successful strategy even if the initial contribution by the government was very modest (it constituted about 2.5 percent of the total cost) (Reynolds 2005).

From the beginning of its mission in Lithuania, the UNDP pursued a strong human rights agenda. The UNDP assisted the establishment of two Ombudsman institutions, both regarded as comprehensive institutional structures for addressing human rights violations by international experts. The Parliamentary Ombudsman Office was established in 1995 in partnership with several government ministries and policy experts from Denmark, Sweden, Finland, and Norway. This was the first office of its type in the CEE region. In a similar cooperative project, the UNDP assisted the establishment of the Office of the Equal Opportunities Ombudsman in 1999. It provided initial financial, administrative, and technical assistance for the office, including personnel training, capacity building, developing administrative procedures, and public awareness raising. The EOO became one of the main partners of the UNDP in addressing the issues of equality. The agenda of the office was extended in the early 2000s to incorporate age, ethnicity, and disability as grounds of discrimination. In addition, the government created the position of a Children's Ombudsman in 2000.

The Second Country Programme period (1997–2000) built on the initial UNDP program by providing over eight million U.S. dollars in support to programs in four key areas: poverty reduction, democratic governance, human security, and environmental protection with cross-cutting themes of the advancement of women, the promotion of NGOs, and the HIV/AIDS prevention programs. The UNDP introduced a new financial mechanism, the Country Cooperation Framework (CCF) for Lithuania, reflecting the creation of the country-specific channel of funding. The first Country Program in Lithuania was supported from the Global Cooperation and Regional Cooperation financial mechanisms. During 1997 through 2000, the environment had become the most important theme in terms of allocation of resources, accounting for more than half of total recourses spent in this period. But the institution-building effort has continued and the funding for these programs did not change much in comparison with the first CP in absolute terms. The UNDP supported the establishment of the following organizations: the Crime Prevention Center, Information Center for Sustainable Development, and a network of Citizen Advice Bureaus across the country (Reynolds 2005). In addition, the UNDP initiated a course on Human Development at three universities and supported the edition of a country-specific textbook for the course. The second program was the most generous period in terms of UNDP financial support of projects in Lithuania. As democratic institutions became more and more mature and once Lithuania became an official candidate to the European Union, the UNDP dramatically decreased its financial support, moving the funds to the east, on one hand, and allowing the European Union and other European donors to take the leading position in preparing Lithuania for accession. While the UNDP Representative in Lithuania disagreed with the UN position on limiting resources of UNDP programs, the UNDP Third Programme was cut in half with 4.5 million U. S. dollars invested in Lithuania from 2001 through 2003.

The Third Country Programme (2001–2003) pursued an explicit programmatic approach to human rights enforcement. It set the goal to develop a comprehensive action plan on human rights to identify and address social imbalances in the country. The UNDP closely cooperated with different governmental and non-governmental institutions, including the Ministry of Justice, the Ministry of Social Affairs and Labor, the Ministry of the Interior, the Chancellery of Parliament, the Ministry of

Education and Science, the Human Rights Center, the Association for Human Rights, and the UN High Commissioner on Human Rights. The work on the Action Plan proceeded in two stages. During the first stage, a national working group was organized, which carried out an initial assessment including a public survey. The second stage involved the development of a baseline study, which included a multilevel analysis of the situation culminating in five regional studies and a national conference on human rights. These measures provided the data for developing concrete policy recommendations in the first draft of the National Action Plan on Human Rights. The draft identified several social groups as particularly vulnerable, including the elderly, disabled, children, and women. The National Action Plan strengthened the institutional structures for consistent human rights monitoring and supported several national campaigns on public awareness about human rights discrimination.

The UNDP supported the work on National Action Plans for Advancement of Women. The first such plan was developed in cooperation with the Women's Information Center and Women's Advisory Board in 1996 as a follow-up to the Beijing Conference on Women. In 2002, the UNDP assisted the drafting of the second National Action Plan for the Advancement of Women. While the first plan concentrated on developing legal human rights framework for women's advancement and creating institutional mechanisms for law implementation and control the second Action Plan focused efforts on improving women's competitiveness through access to information and communication technology, assistance in starting up small businesses, and combating gender based violence.

The UNDP final Country Programme for Lithuania (2004–2005) focused on supporting the government in closing the gaps for successful integration to the European Union and prepared Lithuania to serve as a donor for development assistance. The UNDP closed its mission to Lithuania in 2005 when the country became an official member of the European Union.

Women's Organizations in Lithuania: The Interplay of NGOs and Women's Groups in Formal Organizations

Lithuania has a relatively long history of women's organizing. The first women's organization in Lithuania, the Lithuanian Women's Catholic Association (LCWA), was established in 1907 (Trinkūniene and Trinkūnas 1999). At the turn of the twentieth century, Lithuania was a backwater of Europe. A Western province of the Russian Empire, it was an agrarian state with a large rural population. In a deeply Catholic society, the women's organization served to unite women through informal interactions and provided opportunities for women to help those in need. The functions of social assistance, charity, and dissemination of Catholic values were important for the LCWA. When Lithuania gained its independence in 1918, the LCWA entered into the political realm (Trinkūniene and Trinkūnas 1999). It was an active supporter of granting suffrage to women, which was granted following independence. The LCWA also promoted women into politics. Women elected to the Lithuanian parliament in 1920 were members of the LCWA who competed on a joint list of Catholic organizations (Trinkūniene and Trinkūnas 1999).

During the Soviet era, all independent organizing ceased to exist. Women's organizations were part of the Communist political system. The revival of independent activity after the collapse of Communist rule brought about a plethora of non-governmental organizations, including women's organizations. About nine thousand organizations operated in the Lithuanian non-governmental sector in the mid-2000s (Ilgius 2004). It is an impressive number, taking into account that the total population of Lithuania is about ten million people. The range of their activities encompassed education, environmental protection, and legal help to service-providing functions. Like many post-communist states, newly founded NGOs filled the multiple spaces opened after the collapse of the communist welfare state (Lemke 2001). This is especially true of women's NGOs, which tended to focus on self-help, education and social services. The number of NGOs was growing following the adoption of new regulations that harmonized the Law on Foundations, Associations and Public Institutions with the new Civil Code. These amendments came into force in July 2002. Their goal was to approximate the Lithuanian laws on non-governmental organizations with EU requirements. New regulations allowed for more flexibility in terms of the structure of organizations. They improved the prevention of fraud, set standards for defining conflicts of interest, and introduced the requirement of an annual report for all types of organizations in hopes of improving organizational transparency, especially in the use of public funds. New registration requirements eased the process of founding a new organization. In addition, the amendments clarified and extended the concept of a mission-related economic activity and specified that these activities would be tax exempt. Leaders of NGOs and legal experts positively evaluated the new amendments (Ilgius 2004). The amendment of the Law on Charity was crucial for the survival of many NGOs because previously it did not allow nonprofit organizations to generate any income (Mecajeva and Tereseviciene 2000).

The first women's organizations appeared in 1989 as part of the independence movement, and their number has been growing ever since. The Women's Information Center website reported 63 women's organizations in 1999 (Taljunaite 2004). Currently, this list includes 165 women's organizations; it is estimated, however, that only half of them are fully functional (Glade 2010). The activities of these organizations focus on a diverse range of social services, such as social care, health, unemployment, domestic violence and trafficking, training, and education; but some of these organizations are advocacy groups seeking to promote public awareness about gender violence, gender equality, and non-discrimination, and support women's political and business activity. NGO categorization presented by the Women's Issues Information Center includes the following spheres of activity: education, employment, policy and decision making, human rights, health, environment, institutional management, statistics, and public information and stereotypes. The largest number of organizations indicate education, employment, human rights, and public information and stereotypes as their primary activity.

Most women's advocacy NGOs grew out of professional associations, branches of international organizations, and formal organizations, such as political parties and academia (Taljunaite 2004). Glade estimates that about twenty women's NGOs focus on gender equality and non-discrimination (Glade 2010). The Women's Issues Information Center (WIIC), founded by the UNDP in 1993, is the largest advocacy women's NGO. It serves as an umbrella organization that unites and connects multiple women's organizations in Lithuania. The activities of the WIIC include public awareness campaigns, educational seminars, conferences, workshops and training on gender equality and nondiscrimination, violence against women, and employment for diverse groups of people. The Center's website is an important information resource for communication between NGOs, activists, and the public. The WIIC has a strong outreach program. It publishes a monthly magazine, *Woman's World*, along with other educational and awareness-raising materials. Lobbying the government is another important function of the Center. The WIIC works collaboratively with the Women's Caucus in Parliament, the Lithuanian National Women's Board, and the advisor of the Prime Minister on gender related issues and NGOs. The work of the WIIC is supported by the UNDP, other foreign donors, and the Ministry of Social Security and Labor. The Women's Issues Information Center is the most visible women's advocacy organization in Lithuania, but it is not the only one.

The Lithuanian Coalition of Non-Governmental Organizations for Protection of Women's Human Rights is another umbrella organization for NGOs concerned with gender equality. It calls itself "a non-formal union of NGOs" that aims to enforce gender equality laws through raising public awareness and creating a public movement. It is supported by the European Commission Delegation in Lithuania, the Baltic-American Partnership Program, the U.S. Embassy in Lithuania, and the Ministry of Social Security and Labor, while being coordinated by the Social Innovation Fund, a research and policy think tank. The Coalition works with the Office of the Ombudsman of Equal Opportunities, the government Commission on Equal Opportunities for Women and Men, Women's Parliamentary Caucus, and the Prime Minister's advisor on gender equality and NGOs. It unites sixty NGOs from all ten counties of Lithuania. Since its establishment in 2001, the Coalition has carried several important projects together with other NGOs. Using its multi-regional structure, it regularly partners with the Social Innovation Fund and the European Innovation Fund to enable research on the status of women across Lithuania. Overall, however, the Coalition did not receive a lot of public visibility as an organization (Pilinkaitė-Sotirović 2008).

The Lithuanian women's NGOs suffer from the same problems as their partners all across the Eastern and Central European countries: lack of funds, fragmentation, low sense of solidarity, and low public support. Foreign donors are the main source of financial assistance for women's organization projects. National and local funding remains insignificant, although it grew in the 2000s. The experts observe that the Lithuanian law lacks serious incentives for developing a culture of civic engagement and charity (Mecajeva and Tereseviciene 2000). The general weakness of civil society and lack of grassroots connections explain a narrow membership base of women's NGOs. As is typical for post-communist states, the Lithuanian public tends to distrust the non-governmental sector. In general, the public is suspicious of these organizations and reluctant to support them. The narrow membership base and weak connections with the public prevent NGOs from engaging in active political action. In addition, financial constraints, lack of staff, and poor organizational resources inhibit the development of coordinated political action by these organizations. Such circumstances push NGOs to concentrate on socio-economic and cultural-ethnic problems, rather than on women's issues, and to provide services, rather than to engage in lobbying and campaigning. Non-governmental actors championing women's rights remain largely unknown to the Lithuanian public (Laja 2000, Paluckienė 2000). As a result, the influence of non-governmental organizations on policy depends on the government, which either establishes avenues for collaboration between the governmental and non-governmental sectors or shuts down such collaboration. In the Lithuanian case, women's groups within formal organizations, such as political parties and the parliament, served an important role of connecting governmental and non-governmental sector.

Women's groups inside formal organizations appeared for different reasons, but often they were a result of emulation of practices of similar institutions in other countries. The creation of women's groups within political parties best demonstrates this type of institutional copying. The five largest parties of Lithuania have internal women's groups. The first women's party organization dates back to the communist time. The successor of the CPSU in Lithuania, the Lithuanian Democratic Labor Party (LDDP) inherited this organizational unit and encouraged its activity over time. The second largest leftist party, the Lithuanian Social Democratic Party, established the party women's group in 1991. This organizational unit was emulated from its international partner, the Socialist International, the united organization of social democratic parties (Krupavičius and Matonytė 2003). The major right-wing parties also founded their women's groups. The Christian Democratic Party of Lithuania established a party women's organization following the example of Christian Democratic parties in Scandinavian states (Krupavičius and Matonytė 2003). The Center Union and the Homeland Union-Conservatives of Lithuania founded their women's groups in 1996, at least partially in response to the founding of the Women's Party of Lithuania. By then it became evident that women's issues were of importance to a large proportion of the electorate and parties wanted to signal their readiness to articulate these issues with the help of internal women's organizations (Krupavičius and Matonytė 2003).

The Women's Party was a genuine effort to demonstrate that the major political institutions in Lithuania were dominated by men and were unresponsive to women's interests. The first Prime Minister of Lithuania since its independence, Kazimira Prunskienė, founded this party to expand women's representation in politics and to better articulate women's interests (Krupavičius and Matonytė 2003). The decision was dictated by harsh competition in the 1992 parliamentary elections, when she lost to her opponents from the Sajudis movement. The Women's Party secured only one seat in the 1996 parliamentary elections. The leader of the party, Kazimira Prunskienė, won the race in a single-member district. In 2000, the renamed New Democracy/Women's Party joined the coalition of leftist parties and won three seats in parliament. Eventually, the Women's Party was absorbed by Social Democratic Party of Lithuania, but it had a lasting influence on all political parties in Lithuanian because they all started to include women on party lists and support the establishment of internal women's party organizations (Krupavičius and Matonytė 2003).

Among the women's groups within formal organizations, the women's caucus in the Lithuanian Seimas is by far one of the most influential platforms for voicing women's issues. It was pivotal for advancing the Lithuanian law and institutions on gender equality. The women's caucus was established in 1997 under the initiative of Kazimira Prunskiene and other female deputies from left-wing parties. The caucus was open to women from all parties, but in the beginning was ignored by women from conservative parties (Krupavičius and Matonytė 2003). Later, however, most female deputies joined the caucus. The women's caucus declared that its policy agenda was all-encompassing, but gender-related policies were the main focus of the group. Members of the caucus were active supporters of the Law on Equal Opportunities for Men and Women. Upon their insistence, in 1997 the Council of Seimas appointed a working group to prepare a draft law. The draft was signed into a Bill in 1998 and came into force in March 1999. In addition, the women's caucus was instrumental for introducing changes to Lithuanian legislation, including amendments to the Labor Code, the Law on Maternity and Sickness that introduced paternity leave (although due to a strong conservative lobby, leave was restricted to married men only) and flex-security, or flexible return to work during the period of maternity leave.

At the initiative of the women's caucus, the Seimas re-established one of its consultative boards, the Lithuanian National Women's Advisory Board, in April 2003. Originally, this consultative board was established in 1996 after the Beijing conference. The main responsibilities included the development of the National Action Plan on the Advancement of Women, which was adopted in 1996, and the preparation of the Law on Equal Opportunities for Women and Men. The consultative board was closed down in 1999, shortly after the adoption of the Law. The new office was open to coordinate the work on policy harmonization with EU requirements between different branches of the government, parliament, and women's NGOs. The Board took an active part in developing and supporting the National Action Plan, "The Vision of Development of the

Egalitarian Society in Lithuania, 2004–2014." The role of several activist female MPs, Giedrė Purvaneckienė, Ina Dagytė, Esmeralda Kuliešytė, Ramunė Trakymienė, and Vilija Vasiliauskienė, was especially crucial for the adoption of "The Vision." The same group of activist MPs prepared another important document, a strategy for NGO-government cooperation, which later was incorporated in the Lithuanian Social Inclusion Programme.

The role of individual activist deputies was crucial for interpreting the meaning of EU directives, introducing them and popularizing them among politicians, and adapting them to the Lithuanian policy context. In this regard, the role of Giedrė Purvaneckienė cannot be underestimated. A native of Kaunas, Lithuania's second largest city, Giedrė Purvaneckienė graduated with a degree in physics and worked at Vilnius State University. During her tenure her professional interest changed and expanded and she defended her doctoral dissertation in sociology in 1982. In 1994 she was appointed the Government Advisor on Women's Issues and led the work on Lithuania's National Action Plan on the Advancement of Women. The collaboration with international organizations allowed her to become the UNDP Advisor in 1997. Giedrė Purvaneckienė authored multiple reports on the status of women in Lithuania, and she advised the government on policy harmonization with international requirement in the area of gender equality and women's rights. As a politician, she joined the Social Democratic Party of Lithuania in 1998 and became the Vice President of the Lithuanian Social Democratic Women's Union. Her election in the Seimas in 2000 was pivotal for empowering the activity of the Women's Parliamentary Group, which she joint as a Deputy Chair. In addition, Giedrė Purvaneckienė was a member of the Committee on Social Affairs and Labor and the Chairman of the Commission on Family and Child Affairs. Through these appointments she was involved in drafting amendments to the Lithuanian Labor Code, the Law on Equal Opportunity, and the Law on Equal Treatment to incorporate provisions required by international organizations.

Activist parliamentarians are known for their non-legislative activity in support of gender equality as well. MPs from the women's caucus regularly organize public awareness events to encourage women to become more active in politics and to raise public awareness about gender discrimination in society. For instance, members of parliament, Giedre Purvaneckiene and Birutė Vėsaitė, worked in the Maxima and Iki supermarkets during busy national holidays to bring to the attention of other government officials that female workers are exploited in the labor market (Jurėnienė 2010). The women's caucus held several campaigns in support of women's participation in politics and the introduction of quotas. The social democrats supported the legislative initiative on quotas for women in the Seimas, but liberals and conservatives rejected these propositions and defeated the draft law on quotas.

Policies and Institutions on Equal Opportunity for Women and Men

The Soviet Constitution and the Soviet Labor Code recognized gender equality as a fundamental right of Soviet citizens. The Soviet equality principles were mimicked in Lithuanian sovereign laws after the independence. The Lithuanian Constitution of 1992 guaranteed formal recognition of equality between men and women. While Lithuania formally embraced the principles of gender equality, however, it lacked administrative and legal mechanisms for their enforcement, as well as state commitment and political will to pursue policy implementation. This situation started to change in 1995, the year of the Fourth World Conference on Women in Beijing and Lithuania's ratification of CEDAW. Lithuania's ratification of the Beijing Declaration and Action Plan and CEDAW opened avenues for international actors, most importantly organizations acting on behalf of the UN, such as the UNDP, to influence the agenda of Lithuanian government. As part of international requirements, Lithuania adopted the first National Action Plans for Advancement of Women on November 8, 1996 (State Order No. 1299). The Action Plan was a collaborative project between the Government Advisor on Women's Issues, the National Women's Advisory Board, the UNDP, and women's organizations. In the opinions of many experts, the adoption of the Action Plan was a necessary and formal follow-up to international obligations. The reactions of several Lithuanian ministries reflected their pragmatic position on the issue of gender equality with some members of the government arguing that gender equality can be enforced only in economically developed societies. In the opinion of some politicians, Lithuania's painful transition to market economy and general impoverishments of society inhibited state capacities to enforce such policies. These politicians suggested that if international organizations were to require Lithuania's compliance with gender equality requirements they should be sponsoring gender equality programs in the country (Pilinkaite-Sotirović 2008, 11). The initial compliance with international gender equality norms, therefore, reflected instrumental adoption of policies and programs.

Similar arguments were raised during the debate on the Law on Equal Opportunities for Men and Women. The first draft of the law was prepared in 1995 by Women's Information Center experts and the UNDP. On June 17, 1997, the Board of Seimas appointed a working group to review the draft upon the introduction and lobby by the Women's Caucus. Nijole Oželytė-Vaitiekūnienė from Homeland Union (Lithuanian Conservatives) and a member of the Conservative Women's Union was appointed a chairperson of the group to lead the work on the Law on Equal Opportunities. The working group included members of parliament from different political parties, and representatives from the Ministry of Justice, the Seimas Ombudsman Office, and several NGOs. The working group released the draft of the bill for open public debate soliciting comments and feedback from trade unions, academia, research institutions, and non-governmental organizations. But the commentators noted that the Law did not get much attention in the media, most of the political parties remained uninterested in it, the bill did not become an issue for public debate, and the largest bulk of work in the preparation of the Law was done by the members of the Women's Caucus and, in particular, members of the Women's Party and the Center Union (Krupavičius and Matonytė 2003). Despite some criticism and skepticism about the need for such a bill in Lithuania, the parliamentary debates revealed the general perception that it was a positive bill with negligent consequences. Many parliamentarians agreed, however, that the bill was an important path for modernizing the Lithuanian legal system. The bill was overwhelmingly supported by all parties: 34 members of parliament voted for the bill, seven voted against the bill, and five people abstained. Interestingly, Nijole Oželytė-Vaitiekūnienė, the chair of the working group responsible for the Law, was not present on the day of the vote. The Law was passed on December 1, 1998 and came into force on January 3, 1999. It banned gender-based discrimination in the public sphere and prohibited sexual harassment in the workplace.

While many saw this Law as inconsequential, one important immediate result of its adoption was the establishment of the Office of the Ombudsperson for Equal Opportunities to oversee the enforcement of the Law. This office is accountable to the Seimas and is granted the status of a ministry without portfolio with a small but independent budget. It takes overall responsibility for the supervision and the enforcement of the Law on Equal Opportunities for Women and Men. The Office of the Ombudsperson investigates individual complaints about gender-based discrimination and sexual harassment and has the right to initiate the investigations on its own initiative. The office has the right to supervise the mass media regarding the content of the publication and releases and can prevent the publication of discriminatory advertisement or other content in which one gender is treated superior to the other. In addition, the Ombudsperson can participate in job interviews and monitor the admission tests to educational institutions.

The Ombudsperson has broad powers of representing victims of discrimination in court. In cases of discrimination on the grounds of sex, the office can send the material to pre-trial investigation institutions. It can investigate cases of administrative violations and impose administrative sanctions for violating the Law on Equal Opportunities for Women and Men, an effective tool for enforcing the principles of equality into practice. The Ombudsperson's office provides victims with relatively fast assistance: the Law asserts that the Office must review the case and respond to the complainant within a month of receipt of the complaint. Such efficiency in resolving individual complaints ensured the effectiveness of the Office in considering cases of discrimination, reflected in the growing popularity of the office as a resort for seeking remedy in cases of discrimination. This is reflected in the number of investigations per year: in 1999 the office investigated 31 complaints and carried out 4 investigations at the initiative of the Ombudsperson. In 2005 these numbers grew to 128 received complaints and 5 carried out at the initiative of the office. In 2008 the office investigated 219 complaints and initiated the review of 3 cases (The Office of the Equal Opportunities Ombudsperson, 2009).

In addition to monitoring discrimination, the Office of the Ombudsman for Equal Opportunities has broad powers of policy recommendation and review. The office has the right to review existing laws and propose amendments to satisfy the requirements of gender equality and equal opportunities. The proposals for amendments can be submitted directly to Parliament for review.

In 2002–2004 the Ombudsperson's office promulgated amendments to the Law on Equal Opportunities for Women and Men, Labor Code, and several other acts to fully harmonize Lithuanian Law with EU directives on equality. New amendments introduced the missing concepts of indirect discrimination, introduced the concept of affirmative action (although some experts believe these concepts must be expanded even further), expanded the areas of gender equality opportunities to include the consumer services, and included the provisions for the reversal of the burden of proof in cases of discrimination. In 2003 the mandate of the Ombudsperson on Equal Opportunities was expanded to include discrimination on grounds of age, disability, ethnic origin, sexual orientation, religion, and belief. The new Law on Equal Treatment was passed to incorporate and reflect these changes in the mandate of the Office. In 2004, the Law on Equal Opportunities for Women and Men was amended to grant victims of sex discrimination the right to claim compensation for moral and material damage. These procedures were strengthened with amendments to the Civil and Penal Codes that defined administrative procedures for claiming the compensation. While the parliamentary debates reflected tensions and disagreements on the proposals, the voting record reveals multi-partisan support for these laws and amendments. This observation suggests that EU requirements trumpeted the individual opinions of MPs, who overwhelmingly voted in favor of the laws.

Giving a general assessment of Lithuania's compliance with EU requirements on gender equality, experts agree that the Lithuanian government pursued comprehensive policy change and supported the establishment of strong rights-oriented institutions. Overall, Lithuania is an example of a best complying state among the EU Enlargement states, although some problems remain here as well. Among the problematic areas, the experts note inadequate equal treatment procedures and guarantees in relations to self-employed individuals, limited attention to affirmative action or cases of positive discrimination, and absence of suitable administrative pressures on private employers (Mackeviciute 2005).

International Factors of Compliance

In Lithuania, like in all other post-communist EU Enlargement states, international organizations were the driving force behind the reforms on gender equality. At the same time the case of Lithuania is different from many other EU accession states because here noncoercive pressures from international organizations brought about strong compliance with international requirements on gender equality, whereas in most other accession states EU conditionality ensured compliance with international gender equality requirements. In Lithuania, EU conditionality strengthened policy and institutional reforms, but the direction for state programmatic consistent action in protecting the rights of women workers was taken before the European Commission started monitoring the progress of Lithuania towards accession.

Under conditional pressures, the Lithuanian government expanded powers of its equality institution and strengthened legal guarantees of gender equality in 2002 amendments to the Law on Equal Opportunities. In the post-accession period, Lithuania continued its strong compliance in this area of international law supplementing legal guarantees with programmatic national action plans. Lithuania represents the case of post-accession compliance as opposed to post-accession conformity observed in most other EU Enlargement states. These reforms are supported by domestic political actors and general government multipartisan commitment to guarantee equal access to work and promotion and nondiscrimination on the labor market. Despite initial opposition to these policies, politicians from the right-wing parties supported the introduction of gender equality reforms and generally regarded them as modernizing and progressive initiatives. In Lithuania, we observe that a broad range of politicians from the left and from the right embraced the ideas of gender equality on the labor market and promoted these policies and institutions. Thus, Lithuania is a state where the role of successful international socialization brought about normative change among the elites and ensured strong levels of compliance with EU requirements on gender equality. Arguably, Lithuania is the only state in my sample where international socialization was able to achieve high levels of normative congruence between the international norms on gender equality and normative positions of elites on this issue.

Conclusion

Several factors explain Lithuania's successful adoption of policies and institutions on gender equality. First, it was a positive role model for international socialization and model emulation that provided Lithuanian government with good examples of best practices and motivated compliance. International conditionality strengthened these positive international influences. Second, Lithuania had an accommodating domestic political environment characterized by several factors, such as multi-partisan support for policies and institutions; activist women's caucus and a large number of female MPs who could get organized in support of this issue regardless of their party affiliation; and an activist women's NGO that gained prominence among other women's organizations and created strong working relationship with the government regardless of which party was in power.

The case of Lithuania's adoption of policies and institutions to promote gender equality and to combat gender discrimination is in many
ways a unique example of success in policy compliance among the EU
Enlargement states. Lithuania was the first to pass the Law on Equal
Opportunities for Women and Men and to pass a number of amendments to satisfy EU requirements on gender equality. It was also the
first state to establish the Office of Ombudsperson for Equal Opportunities as an institutional mechanism for law enforcement. The structure
of this office, in particular, the self-enforcing mechanism built into the
Ombudsperson institution, had unintentional positive consequences for
the anti-discrimination policy enforcement. The number of complaints
received by the office was steadily growing, until it stabilized at a relatively high number of 180 cases per year (with 2008, marked by a severe
economic crisis, bringing the number of applicants to the record high of
218). The relative efficiency of the office, easy access, and autonomy from
the state and businesses, allowed it to develop a reputation as a reliable
defender of women's rights and a last resort for those who are seeking
redress. As the number of disputes resolved in favor of the complainants
increased, the public support and awareness about the Ombudsperson's
Office grew as well. The analysis shows that several factors contributed
to Lithuania's success story.

The role of international pressures is critical for understanding the
path of Lithuanian reforms. The legislative activity on gender equality
started around the time of the World Conference on Women in 1995
and continued as Lithuania ratified international treaties on women's
rights. The initiation of the European Union monitoring for accession
strengthened the reforms even further. But in the case of Lithuania, international advising with a strong human rights orientation complemented
international coercion and incentives and reshaped the routes of reforms.
The major player, the UNDP, was pivotal for introducing the model of
human rights— and women's rights—oriented legislation and institutions
to Lithuanian government, mediating the negotiation on policy among
state actors, NGOs, and international advisors.

The domestic context was conducive for these reforms as well.
Although in principle opposed to the reforms, the conservative branch
of Lithuanian parliament voted in support of all bills and amendments in
relation to gender equality. Regardless of party affiliation, Lithuanian MPs
displayed overwhelming support for these policies and institutions in
the name of "progress and future modernization" (parliamentary debates).
The introduction and support for the laws was facilitated by an activ-

ist women's caucus, who undertook multiple initiatives in drafting and popularizing the bills among parliamentarians and government officials.

Overall, I note that Lithuanian political establishment embraced the norms of gender equality, regarding them as an important guarantee of a modern democratic state. Thus, successful international socialization was able to achieve necessary normative congruence between international legal requirements and personal beliefs and policy positions of the Lithuanian political establishment, which guaranteed strong compliance with EU gender equality directives.

8

Conclusion

Main Findings

Recent scholarship has increasingly confirmed the importance of international institutional influence for promotion of women's rights around the globe (Boyle and Preves 2000; Htun and Weldon 2012; Keck and Sikkink 1998; Krook 2009; True and Mintrom 2001; Zippel 2006). This study took the question, do international influences matter, one step further by analyzing what kind of international pressures matter and how they matter. The study investigated how ten EU Enlargement states complied with EU accession requirements to reform their policies and institutions on gender equality. The time span of the study begins before the accession negotiations started and ends after these states became members of EU, allowing for analysis of how the levels of compliance changed during three periods of accession: pre-accession, accession conditionality, and post-accession. Three distinct mechanisms of international influence characterize each of these periods. During the pre-accession period international organizations relied on socialization (referred to in this book as normative pressures or pressures to embrace EU normative values and policy positions) and social pressures (pressures to assimilate other members of the group). Accession conditionality relied heavily on coercive mechanisms of changing states' behavior by linking compliance with EU requirements to membership guarantees. In the post-accession period coercive powers of EU have shrunk significantly as the EC lost powers to punish noncomplying states by withdrawing their membership in the organization. While maintaining the powers to shame and even fine states violators, the EC's ability to punish noncomplying states has decreased dramatically with candidate states gaining EU membership. Accession could have changed the incentive structure of compliance for national governments, especially in cases of domestic opposition or prohibitive cost of compliance. In this concluding chapter I will present a summary of major findings of this study and discuss their implications for future theoretical and empirical work on mechanisms of protecting women's rights worldwide.

International Influences

The study finds that international institutional mechanisms of influence were pivotal forces behind state reforms on gender equality policies and institutions in EU Enlargement states. While all states had constitutional guarantees of gender equality and nondiscrimination replicated from the 1936 Soviet Constitution, the notion of these guarantees was declarative, because none of these states provided legal avenues for redress in cases of discrimination. In communist states gender equality in the labor market was embedded in the structure of a state-planned economy and mandatory full employment for women and men. With the collapse of communist-planned economies, these state guarantees vanished as the state retreated from the total control of the economic systems and could not guarantee full employment and benefits. Protecting the rights of women workers on the labor market was not a priority for newly democratizing transition states with crumbling economies. At the same time, in the mid-1990s we observe state activity in drafting national programs, such as National Action Plans, to address the issues of gender equality and gender discrimination. While many of these programs remained declarative rather than implemented, it was remarkable to see how international governmental organizations like the UN and the European Union could change the agenda of transition states. It is even more remarkable to note that these early international efforts at promoting women's rights relied purely on noncoercive mechanisms of influence, such as socialization (strategies to change policy positions and beliefs of elites through teaching and persuasion) and social pressures (pressures to assimilate others in a community of states by replicating their policies and institutions).

What kind of policy did these early international socialization efforts produce? Did they influence state policies on protecting women workers? My statistical study reveals modest attempts to change state policies and create institutions on gender equality; my case studies, however, present a picture of mixed results. I find that the UN World Conferencess on Women (particularly those held in 1985 and in 1995) provided an impetus for states' activity in the area of gender equality. All states took part in the 1995 conference and signed and ratified the CEDAW, which opened their governments for monitoring by the UN Division for the Advancement of Women. While the UN could not enforce policy compliance, it employed a variety of socialization and social pressure mechanisms, including the publication of best and worst practices, or a strategy of shaming and praising, and an obligation to submit state reports on their compliance progress which encouraged state action in this area. At a bare minimum, states had to open offices on women, or women machineries bureaus, which became responsible for drafting responses to the DAW *Questionnaire on the Status of Women* in coordination with several state institutions, most notably a ministry of social affairs and labor, a ministry of education, and a ministry of health. In general, noncoercive international mechanisms of influence generated declarative "window dressing" action on behalf of state governments. While most of the examined states created offices or working groups to draft state responses to the *Questionnaire* and develop National Action Plans on Women, by and large these programs did not specify enforcement instruments and tools and, thus, remained unenforced and marginalized. Since the UN conventions do not entail a significant incentive to comply or do not involve a sizable punishment for noncompliance, states tend to engage in declarative formal compliance with UN treaties with intent to demonstrate that they, in principle, agree and support the norms embedded in the treaties, but states rarely follow up with enforcement of these principles in domestic policy practice. This is the lesson learned from the country case studies, with the exception of Lithuania, where noncoercive international pressures generated high-level compliance and resulted in the adoption of a separate law on equal treatment of women and men and the establishment of a ministry-type institution on gender equality. Thus, in some exceptional cases international socialization can generate high-level compliance.

The calculation for EU Enlargement states changes dramatically when they achieve a candidate status. The EU conditionality links compliance with the award of EU membership, and noncompliance with a withdrawal of this award. This incentive structure generated unprecedented reforms of gender equality policies and institutions in accession states: all states amended their labor codes, administrative codes, acts on social security and wages, and other relevant laws; most of the states adopted separate laws on gender equality or generic anti-discrimination acts. All states opened offices for women, or women's policy machineries, at different levels in their administrative hierarchies with a varying range of responsibilities and functions, but the overall scope of state action in response to international conditionality was remarkable.

When we turn from the question of policy and institutional adoption to policy enforcement, the overall picture is much less impressive. The EU accession conditionality was based on the premise of "rapid rewards" for "rapid reforms" to provide a clear incentive for states to engage in costly transformation of their legal and institutional structures in exchange for a credible promise of membership. Short time horizons of the costly and complicated conditional agreement between the EU and candidate states are generally recognized as one of the explanations for the success of the fifth wave of EU Enlargement (Schimmelfennig and Sedelmeier 2004). The notion of rapid reforms, however, created a set of unintended consequences. First, they allowed for state cooptation of reforms, when all social partners were excluded from policy formulation and decision making. Second, they encouraged the use of "copy and paste" practice, when EU Directives were formally transmitted into national laws but were not publicly debated. Thus, new laws were not adapted to national circumstances and, therefore, lacked enforcement and application mechanisms. Conditional compliance, thus, generated formalistic reforms of policies and institutions in many accession states.

Did states improve their compliance with EU gender equality requirements after gaining membership or did they dismantle these policies and institutions? By and large, states maintained their policies and institutions established under conditional pressures; except for Romania where the gender equality office was closed down in 2010. Some states improved their policy compliance in the post-accession period with the adoption of anti-discrimination acts (Poland and the Czech Republic); many other states adopted administrative orders, or national action plans, on promoting women's rights, including gender equality in the labor market. The overall picture demonstrates that states maintained their institutions on women and gender equality created under conditional pressures, confirming the stability of accession conditionality reforms. In-depth investigation of policy practice and institutional capacity to enforce these policies, however, reveals that formalistic compliance of the accession period grew into conformity with EU requirements in the post-accession period, described as policy marginalization and stagnation. While the states kept these policies and institutions on the books, they did not expand their powers, they did not improve their enforcement and monitoring capacities, and they maintained minimal protection guarantees. Overall, I observe that EU Enlargement states preserved gender equality policies and institutions that conformed with EU requirements.

In doing so, the states signaled to the European Commission that they formally respected EU-imposed norms. Since EC's monitoring capacities of policy enforcement have shrunk significantly following the accession, the states do not have an incentive to develop gender equality policies and institutions further and can get away with minimal measures. Post-accession conformity with EU pressures to maintain gender equality policies and institutions lead to marginalization and stagnation of these policies in EU Enlargement states.

Domestic Factors of Compliance

While the general trends of state "rapid reforms" under conditionality and policy marginalization and stagnation in the post-accession period are observed across the studied region overall, I note a significant variation of when and to which degree governments engaged in reforms of policies and institutions across states and across time. To explore this variation in state compliance, I analyze the domestic factors of compliance. Relying on the extensive literature, I identify several key actors of gendered policy reforms: political parties in power, social non-governmental actors both in support and in opposition to gender equality laws, the sex composition of national parliaments, and the sex composition of prime ministers' cabinets. Below I will review my findings in regard to each of these actors of political process.

First, my analysis finds that political parties are important mediators of reforms on gender equality policies and institutions. Left-wing parties, on average, are found to be supportive of these reforms, and the right-wing parties are found to oppose these reforms and delay compliance. Case studies support these findings from statistical analysis. The case of Polish compliance demonstrates that right-wing parties were able to reverse the course of reforms and change the agenda of gender equality institution to embrace a conservative family-oriented agenda, while the left-wing parties sided with liberal women's NGOs and supported the reforms of policies and institutions. But the party positions on gender equality and their influence on reforms are not always so clear-cut, as the Czech case demonstrates. In the Czech Republic neither right-wing, nor left-wing parties engaged in comprehensive reforms of policies and institutions. In fact, it was the right-wing government that adopted the anti-discrimination act under pressures from the European Union. The left-wing government did not pass such a bill. Thus, left-wing governments alone are not going to pursue comprehensive reforms on gender equality. The statistical analysis of state compliance demonstrates that left-wing parties are more likely to pursue reforms of policies and institutions when they are confronted by strong autonomous women's NGOs. In this study, I focused specifically on the activity of women's NGOs with agendas on gender equality policies and institutions. The outlier case of Lithuania, however, reveals that right-wing parties in some rare cases can also engage in comprehensive reforms on gender equality. Thus, while a general trend of party effects holds statistical significance, our case studies reveal a much more nuanced role of political parties in power. It becomes obvious that international conditional or social pressures (such as shaming and naming) can create a substantial incentive or threat for right-wing parties to change their policy positions and support domestic reforms.

The second important factor in predicting the scope of reforms on gender equality is supportive social actors. In particular, I focused my analysis on the role of autonomous women's non-governmental advocacy organizations with an agenda on gender equality. I looked at the organizational capacities of these NGOs, their cohesiveness and cooperation with other women's NGOs and with the government. I analyzed and recorded actions of these NGOs in support of EU reforms and their capacity to mobilize other sympathetic women's organizations to back up this cause. I find that the role of autonomous women's advocacy groups was indispensable for ensuring the comprehensiveness of policy reforms and for expanding the powers of government institutions on gender equality. In states where women's NGOs were able to create working coalitions with the government, we observe higher levels of reforms than in states where NGOs could not establish such relations with parties in power. This finding is confirmed by case study analysis. In Poland, where liberal women's NGOs emerged and developed quite high organizational capacity and cohesiveness, they were able to create working relationship with the left-wing government and had an influence on the course of the reforms. In the Czech Republic, liberal women's NGOs could not establish strong ties with a communist-time large NGO, which hampered the cohesiveness of women's social organizing and marginalized these groups in the process of policymaking, even under the leftist government. On average, I find that women's NGOs were more likely to work with left-wing parties, but in some states, like Lithuania, they were able to create working relations with right-wing parties as well. The reference to EU conditionality by these groups was one of the most effective strategies used to persuade the government to support the reforms. Thus, the success of women's NGOs' mediation of reforms relied heavily on EU conditionality.

The third actor considered in this study is women in national parliaments. The argument about women having a unique perspective on policies is quite prominent in critical feminist research, which would predict that a larger number of women in national parliaments leads to more women-friendly policies. In the case of gender equality policies and institutions in EU Enlargement states, I find that increasing the number of female parliamentarians does not guarantee the support for gender equality policies and institutions. Women in post-communist parliaments tend to vote along party lines and, thus, women who affiliated with conservative and liberal parties are more likely to oppose gender equality reforms if this is a general position of their parties. Country case study evidence greatly supports this point: women elected on the ballot of center-conservative movement of King Simeon II in Bulgaria and the ultra-conservative League of Polish Families in Poland, which both had a record high number of women in their parliaments, were notoriously outspoken against any type of emancipation policies. At the same time female MPs from multiple parties in Poland, Hungary, Slovenia, and Lithuania were pivotal supporters of gender equality policies and institutions. Women's caucuses articulated and promoted amendments to national labor codes and supported bills on gender equality in these states (although the adoption of these bills could have failed overall). Thus, women's organizing in parliament in support of gender equality reforms (sometimes these were multiparty efforts, like in Lithuania and Hungary) mattered more than the mere number of women in national parliaments.

Finally, a number of women in national cabinets had a positive impact on institutional reforms. This finding is important and remarkable as well: female cabinet members often were Ministers of Social Affairs and Labor, the key institution directly responsible for the promulgation of policies on gender equality. No wonder that if female heads of this Ministry were part of the cabinet of ministers, the states' highest governing office, they had more power to enforce policies and negotiate greater powers for gender equality institutions. In addition to this finding, the case studies illuminate that individual high-level government officials were instrumental for policy and institutional promotion. All three cases demonstrate how important was the support of key governmental officials, both men and women, for promoting the amendments and overseeing the creation of gender equality institutions.

Lessons Learned and Future Research

The process of admitting new members to international organizations presents a unique opportunity for promoting and implementing global policy priorities on the domestic policy level by linking admission to change in policy and practice. Membership conditionality is an effective and powerful tool for introducing and promoting international human rights norms by creating incentives for states to participate and respect their international obligations not only toward their international partners, but most importantly, in their domestic policy practice. It is well established in the literature, that governments are often reluctant to recognize and combat women's rights violations, because they regard them as an issue of minor public concern. The public too, may remain unaware of habitual discrimination and may disregard their right to protect themselves, thus, even democratic societies may fail to protect and enforce women's rights (Weldon 2002, 2011). In this situation, international organizations become important sources of issue articulation and public education, on the one hand, and shaming and naming of noncomplying governments, on the other. While these mechanisms of influence are credited with global promotion of women's rights norms, the link between "soft influences" and policy enforcement on the domestic level remains weak (Avdeyeva 2007; Hafner-Burton and Tsutsui 2005). Membership conditionality, however, can be an effective tool for policy enforcement. This research demonstrated that EU conditionality created an opportunity to introduce policies protecting women workers amidst a stern political opposition and low public awareness. Thus, the accession process presents a rare occasion for international organizations to change state calculation about the costs and benefits and pursue significant policy changes regardless of domestic issue support (or the lack of support) and political opposition. The first lesson learned from the study is that international organizations can exploit the power of membership conditionality more often to encourage state enforcement of their human right obligations.

At the same time, the structure of membership conditionality embedded in the formula of "rapid rewards for rapid reforms" may encourage superficial enforcement of new policies, leading to their marginalization in the post-accession period. This finding constitutes the second lesson learned from this study: encouraging international organizations to develop and implement programs for policy sustainability and enforcement in the post-accession period. These strategies may rely on international and domestic tools of enforcement. The remarkable effectiveness of conditional measures suggests that coercive incentives for compliance should not be abandoned after states gain membership in an organization. They may include a variety of conditional mechanisms linking compliance to specific group benefits and noncompliance to their withdrawal. Structuring states' incentives around their compliance with women's rights and other human rights obligations is an important imperative for scholars and practitioners alike. Noncoercive measures should definitely accompany conditional measures: socialization and shaming and naming are effective strategies of communicating group values and norms to all participants and, thus, should not be disregarded. Socialization is also the only strategy to achieve "normative congruence" or change in normative positions both in public and among the elites. As the case study evidence demonstrates, the highest levels of compliance occur in instances when elites' policy positions match or fit with international norms. Therefore, international organizations should pursue various strategies of communicating these norms to elites and the public, encouraging debate and discussion.

Third, international organizations should coordinate their agendas for sending a consistent and clear message to state governments. Coordination and cooperation between different international organizations is crucial as our case studies show, and their message should align. While the UN and the European Union embrace similar principles, the EU is by far more detailed in specifying what constitutes gender equality and nondiscrimination on the labor market. If these requirements were aligned between these two organizations, they could have been more efficient in pursuing similar goals. Fourth, the more the merrier: as many international organizations as possible should criticize and shame governments violating their obligations to protect women on the labor market. In Europe, the list of these organizations can include, besides the European Union: the UN, the International Labor Organizations, and the Council of Europe.

The fifth important lesson is that domestic actors and domestic policy environment cannot be disregarded in the study of state compliance with international norms. To ensure future compliance, international organizations should foster alliances with the critical domestic actors; in my specific case these are not limited to women's NGOs, but include the whole spectrum of these organizations: political parties and women's organizations inside political parties, legislators, and women's parliamentary caucuses.

Policy process is a complex phenomenon. The analysis in this book demonstrated that successful reforms took place because of strategic alliances formed between various political actors. This is the sixth lesson we can draw from this study: international actors should encourage partnerships between various governmental and non-governmental organizations in support of policy initiatives and activities. Since political parties, women's parliamentary groups, and women's NGOs are important mediators of policy and institutional reforms on gender equality, different forms of activities that could encourage the collaboration of these actors in the post-accession period could have an impact on policy enforcement. International organizations can also encourage the use of government co-pays for international and national activities in support of women's rights. It is generally observed that state co-pays are an effective way of improving state involvement into policy enforcement.

Finally, since implementation of policies lags behind the policy adoption, international institutions should continue rigorous compliance monitoring after accession. Continuous monitoring could be enforced until satisfactory levels of compliance are reached. Positive practices, like twinning and expert exchange, can be encouraged after accession as well. Policy enforcement will remain a challenge even in well-complying states, because the support and stability of these policies depend on favorable domestic political environment, but international organizations should pursue divergent strategies to create incentives for domestic governments to participate in positive policy practices.

This study took international incentives and mechanisms of influence seriously, but no study is perfect. Future research could tease out independent effects of each particular mechanism of international involvement, conditional measures, socialization and persuasion measures, and shaming and naming (social group pressures), and evaluate their outcomes for policy sustainability and the depth of compliance and policy enforcement. The question of policy sustainability is an important one for the post-accession period. Which strategies of policy promotion and what kind of institutional incentives are most effective in inducing compliance with human rights norms among member states? Careful case study investigation into this question could complement and expand the findings in this book and provide invaluable insight to students of international norms, scholars, and policy practitioners.

Appendix I

Table 1. Laws and Legislation Acts Reviewed in EU Enlargement States.

Country	Laws Enacted
Bulgaria	Decree no. 68 of 1996 of Council of Ministers; Anti-Discrimination Bill (2003); Law of Ombudsman (2004); 2001 amendments to Labor Code; Employment Promotion Act of 2001; Pensions Act of 1958, amended in 1996; Decree no. 116 of 1996 on Procedures and Means of Pension Payments; Act of 1999 on Complementary Voluntary Pension Insurance, amended in 2000; Compulsory Social Security Code 2000; Act of 2002 to Amend and Supplement the Act on Social Assistance.
Czech Republic	Anti-Discrimination Act 2008; Charter of Fundamental Rights and Freedoms (2/1993); Employment Act (435/2004); Act on Wages (1/1992); Act on Salary (143/1992); Collective Bargaining Act (99/1963, 150/2002, 309/1999); Labor Code (65/1965, 221/1999, 218/2002, 1/1991, 154/1994, 2/1991, 9/1991, 236/1995, 201/1997, 186/1992—repealed by 361/2003, amended 2001, 2004); The State Service Act, amended 2004; the Military Act (amended 2004); ILO no. 100 (1996);
	Government Resolution of April 8, 1998 no. 236 on the Priorities and Procedures of the Government to Enforce Equality between Men and Women;
	Pension Insurance Act (155/1995, 100/1988, 54/1956, 32/1957, 117/1995, 482/1991, 582/1991, 150/2002).
	Business Code (513/1991); Family Act (94/1963); Civil Code (40/1964); Social Security Act (1000/1988); Civil procedures Act (99/1963), 309/1999 regarding Law Collection and Collection of International Contracts;

the Decree of Ministry of Health no. 261/1997 on work prohibited to all women, pregnant women, and new mothers and to juveniles; Notice 208/2003 regarding the prohibition of pregnant women, breastfeeding women and from particular types of work; Regulation 178/2001 determining protection of employees during work; Law no. 361/2003; Law no. 218/2002; Law no. 221/1999 on special types of occupations;

Law regarding Minimum Wage (303/1995).

Estonia	Constitution (1992, amended in 2002, article 12); Gender Equality Act (2004); Wages Act (1994); ILO no. 100 (1996); Amended Wages Act (2002); Employment Contract Act (1992, amended 2004); Gender Equality Act (2004);
	Health Insurance Act (1998), Unemployment Insurance Act (2002), Funded Pension Act (2001), Aliens Act (1993/1997), Social Welfare Act (1995, amended in 2001); Occupational Health and Safety Act (1999); Social Protection of Unemployed Act (1994); Old-Age Pensions at Favorable Conditions Act (1992);
	Holidays Act (1992, amended 2001); Occupational Health and Safety Requirements for Work of Pregnant and Breastfeeding Women (Regulation no. 50 of the Government, 2001); Parental Benefit Act (2004, amended 2007); State Family Benefits Act (1997, 2001 repealed and replaced; 2003 repealed and replaced by Parental Benefit Act); Child Benefit Act (1994).
Hungary	Constitution (1949 amended 1989, 70/B (2), bb (1) and 70/A (1); Labor Code (Section 5 (1) of 1967 and 142/A (1) of 2001; Act LVII/2000 on the Announcement of the Agreement No.100 Accepted at the 34th Meeting of the ILO; Bill No. T/4244 on the Equal Treatment and the Ban of Discrimination; Act CXXV/2003 on Equal Treatment and Promotion of Equal Opportunities.
	Act XIV/2007 on the Amendment of the ACT CXXIII/2004 on the Promotion of Employing Entrant Youth, People above the Age of 50, and Job-Seekers Following Care-giving for Children or Other Family Member, and Scholarship Holders; Act LXX/2005 on the Amendment of the Act IV/1991 on the Advancement of Employment and Social Assistance to the Unemployed.

Eligibility for Social Security Provisions and Private
Pensions and the Coverage of These Services (1997, Act
LXXX, amended in 2001); Social Insurance Pension
Provision (1997, Act LXXXI); Private Pension and Private
Pension Funds (1997, Act LXXXII); Mandatory Health
Insurance Provisions (1997, Act LXXXIII); Furthering
Employment and Provisions for the Unemployed 1991,
Act III/1993 on Social Administration and
Social Provisions (amended in 2002); Act XCI/2003
on the Amendment of the Laws Concerning Taxes,
Contributions and other Public Incomes. Establishment
and Management of Voluntary Mutual Insurance Funds
(1993), Act CLXX/2005 on the Amendment of the Act
III/1993 on Social Administration and Social Provisions.

Labor Code (1992, Sections 54, 58, 85 (1), 90 (1), 102
(2), 107, 121, 138 (1), (6)); Decree no. 33 of 1998; Act
LXXXIV on Family Provisions (1998); Act LXXXIII on
Mandatory Health Insurance (1997); Act XCII on Labor
Safety (1993) and Decree no. 5 (1993) issued by the
Ministry of Labor on the Executive Provisions of the Act;
Decree no. 33 (1998) issued by the Ministry of Welfare;
Government Degree no. 2401 (1995); Government Decree
no. 218 (1999); Act XI/2004 on the Amendment of the
Act XCIII/1993 on Labor Safety.

Government Decree no. 1031 (1994) on the Principles
of Long-Term Demographic Policy; Act LXXI/2005 on
the Amendment of Act LXXIV/1997 on Short-Term
Employment Contracts and the Simplified Payment of
Common Charges.

Labor Code (1992, Sections 5 91), 42, 90 (1), 125, 138
(5);

Decree no. 33 of 1998; Act LXXXIV on Family Provisions
(1998, amended in 2001, 2002); Government Decree No.
305/2002 on Fathers with Babies Measures; Act IV/2003
on the Amendment of Certain Laws on Social Affairs;

Act CXXVI/2005 on the Restructuring of the Family
Support System.

Latvia	Labor Code (2002, amended in 2004, 2006); Law on Labor Protection (2002, amended 2005); Law on Consumer Protection amended in 2008; Social Insurance Law (1995, amended 2005). Pension Act 1995, Law

on Private Pension Funds 1997. Law on Insurance and Maternity Illness 1995.

Law on Consumer Protection, amended 2008; The Criminal Law amended in 2007 (directly refers to other forms of discrimination, not gender-based discrimination); Law on Prohibition of Discrimination of Natural Persons Engaged in Economic Activity (2012).

Lithuania	Constitution (1992); Employment Contracts Act (1991); Wages Act (1991); Collective Agreements Act (1991); Equal Opportunities Act (1999, amended 2002); Labor Code (2003); 2004 Law no. IX-2086 on ratification of ILO no. 156 Convention Regarding Equal Opportunities and Equal Treatment of Women and Men with Family Responsibilities. Act on Labor Protection (1993, amended 2000); Employment Contracts Act (1991). Act on Labor Disputes (2000); Act on Administrative Proceedings (1999). Social Insurance Law (1995, amended 2005); Act on the Principles of the Social Security System (1990, article 5); Act on State Social Security (1991); Act on State Social Security Pensions (1994); Pension Funds Act (2000); Act on Farmers (1999); Act on Collective Agreements and Contracts (1991); Act on Holidays (1991); Act on State Benefits for Families Raising Children (1995); Law on Sickness and Maternity Leave (amended 2004, 2006, 2007).
Poland	Constitution (1997, articles 32, 33); Labor Code (1974 amended in 2001, 2004); Act on the Implementation of Certain Provisions of the European Union in the Field of Equal Treatment (2011); Employment and Unemployment Act (1994). Act on Social Security Systems (1998); Decision of Constitutional Tribunal on retirement age of women and men, ref. K. 15/99; Judgment of March 28, 2000, ref. K. 27/99 on the Decision of Constitutional Tribunal on Retirement Age of Women and Men; Judgment of December 5, 2000, ref. K. 35/99 on the Decision of Constitutional Tribunal on Retirement Age of Women and Men; Government Regulation on the Coordination of Social Security Schemes with EU Requirements (2010); Act on Social Security of Farmers (1990); Act on Commercial Activity (1999). Government Ordinance on Safe Working Conditions (2002); Ministerial Directive on

30.07.2002 on the List of Work Prohibited to Women (127/1092); Justification of the Proposal to Terminate Convention no. 45 of ILO (2006); Law on Family Allowances (2006).

Romania	Constitution (2003, article 38 (4), Labor Code (2003); Code of Civil Proceedings; Law 202/2002 on Equal Opportunities for Women and Men (amended 2006); Governmental Ordinance 137/2000 on Preventing and Punishing all Forms of Discrimination (2002); Government Decisions no. 970/2006 approving the National Action Plan for Employment; Chapter VIII, Horizontal Initiatives—Equal Opportunities for Women and Men.
	Law no. 19/2000 on Public System of Pensions and Other Social Security Schemes; Law no. 577/2003 approving Government Ordinance no. 9/2003 for Amending Provisions in Law 19/2000 on Public System of Pensions and Other Social Security Rights; Law no. 145/1997 on Health Social Insurance; Law no. 76/2002 on the Unemployment Insurance System and Labor Occupancy; Law no. 418/2001 Regarding the Minimum Guaranteed Income; Emergency Governmental Ordinance no. 105/2003 Regarding Complementary Family Allowances and Support for Single Parent Families; Government Ordinance no. 148/2005 on Supporting Families with Children; Law on Privately Administered Mandatory Pension Funds (2005); Law no. 577/2003 Approving Government Ordinance no. 9/2003 for Amending Provisions in Law 19/2000 on Public System of Pensions and Other Social Security Rights; Law no. 204/2006 on Optional Private Pensions; Emergency Government Ordinance no. 96/2003 on Maternity Protection in a Work Place Approved and Modified by Law no 25/2004.
Slovakia	Labor Code (311/2001, amended 2003 and 2007); Civil Service Act (312/2001); Public Service Act (552/2003 and 553/2003); Collective Bargaining Act (2/1991), Anti-Discrimination Act/Act on Equal Treatment in Some Areas and Protection against Discrimination (365/2004); Health Safety and Protection Act (330/1996); Act on Further Education (386/1997); Act no. 125/2006 on Labor Inspection; Act no.564/2001 on the Public Defender of Rights; Social Insurance Act (461/2003, amended 2006).

Slovenia   Constitution (1946, amended 1991); ILO no. 100 (1952);
                         Employment Relationship Act (1990, amended 2002);
                         Equal Opportunities for Women and Men Act (2002);
                         The Employment and Insurance against Unemployment
                         Act (2002, amended 2006); Pension and Disability
                         Insurance Act (1999); Health Care and Health Insurance
                         Act (1992); Labor and Social Courts Act (1994);
                         Employment and Insurance Against Unemployment Act
                         (1991); Parental Protection and Family Benefit Act (2001,
                         amended 2003, 2006); Health Care and Health insurance
                         Act (1992); Employment Relationship Act (1990, amended
                         2002), Employment Regulation Act (1977, amended
                         2002); Occupational Health and Safety Act (1999); Rules
                         on Protection of Health at Work of Pregnant Workers
                         and Workers who Have Recently Given Birth and are
                         Breastfeeding (2003); Rules on the Preparation of Safety
                         Statement with Risk Assessment (1999); Health Services
                         Act (1992); General Practitioner's Service Act (1999);
                         Rules Concerning Preventive Medical Examinations of
                         Workers (1971, 1996).

Table 2. Maternity Leave Provisions in CEE States, 2010.

Country	Length of Leave	Benefit
Bulgaria	135 days (45 days before birth); job protection until child is 3.	Normal Salary for first 135 days; after that 50% of minimum monthly salary until child is 2; unpaid until child is 3.
Czech Republic	28 weeks (37 weeks for multiple birth and single mothers) is woman participated in sickness insurance for at least 270 days during last 2 years.	90% of net earnings for 28 (37 for multiple births) weeks; then maternity or paternity allowance, a monthly lump sum of 1.54 times the living wage until child is 4.
Estonia	70 days before and 56 days after birth (70 days in case of multiple or complicated birth).	Childbirth allowance, a lump sum (120 days before and 6 months after birth), followed by one-month parental benefit based on average income (or minimum wage for unemployed or students).
Hungary	24 weeks (4 weeks before birth).	70% of average monthly income if mother participated in social security insurance; in addition, a lump sum for mothers who attended medical consults.
Latvia	8 weeks before and 8 weeks after birth; parental leave with job protection until child is 3.	Paid at 100% of previous income.
Lithuania	8 weeks before and 8 weeks after birth; parental leave with job protection until child is 3.	100% of previous income for 70 days before birth and 56 days after birth; then parental benefit 70% of average daily wage for the 1st year, lower fixed rate during 2nd and 3rd year; a lump sum after birth.

Poland	16 weeks (first child), 18 weeks (subsequent children), 26 weeks (twins); 2 weeks before delivery.	Before birth leave is paid at 100% of income, followed by maternity allowance equal to average pay during 6 months of work preceding birth.
Romania	Total 126 days (52 days before delivery).	85% of average monthly wage.
Slovakia	28 weeks (or 37 weeks for multiple births or single mothers).	55% of gross earnings, after 28 (37 for multiple births) weeks lump sum until child is 3.
Slovenia	365 days of parental leave, including 105 days of maternity leave and at least 28 days before expecting delivery; 260 days can be used by mother or father; possibility of part-time work until child is 17 months old.	Benefit is 100% of the previous year average income for 260 days; social security payment for remaining 75 days.

Appendix II

Table 1. Institutions on Gender Equality in Central and Eastern States, 1995–2010.

Country	Institutions
Bulgaria	*Executive branch:* The Department of Human Rights within the Ministry of Foreign Affairs, 1999; Unit on equal Opportunities for Women and Men within the Policy of Labor Market Directorate at the Ministry of Labor and Social Policy, 2004–2005; Equal Opportunities Department at the Demographic Policy, Social Investments and Equal Opportunities Market Directorate at the Ministry of Labor and Social Affairs, 2005–present.
	Legislative branch: Human Rights and Religious Affairs Committee, Sub-committee on Women's Rights and Gender Equality.
	Consultative: the National Women's Forum, 1995–1997; the Consultative Commission on Equal Opportunities for Women and Men, 2003–present; the National Council on Gender Equality, 2004–present.
Czech Republic	*Executive branch:* Unit for Equal Opportunities within the Department for Integration into the European Union, Ministry of Labor and Social Affairs, 1998–present; Gender Focal Points, 2002–present.
	Legislative branch: Permanent Commission on Family and Equal Opportunities in the Parliamentary Committee for Social Affairs and Healthcare, 2002–present.
	Consultative: the Government Council for Human Rights, 1999–present; the Government Council for Equal Opportunities, 2002–present.
	Ombudsman: 1999–present.

Estonia	*Executive branch:* Gender Equality Bureau in the Ministry of Social Affairs, 1996–2004; reorganized into the Gender Equality Department, 2004–present.
	Consultative: Working Group for Promoting Gender Equality, 2002–present; Gender Equality Council, 2004–present.
	Ombudsperson: Gender Equality Commissioner, 2005.
Hungary	*Executive branch:* the Secretariat For Women's Policy, the Ministry of Labor, 1995–1996; the Secretariat for Equal Opportunities, the Ministry of Labor, 1996–1998; the Secretariat for the Representation of Women, the Ministry of Social and Family Affair, 1998–2002; The Directorate for equal Opportunities, in the ministry of Employment Policy and Labor, 2002–2003; the Governmental Office for Equal Opportunities (a ministry-level institution), 2003–2004; The Women's Directorate within the Ministry of Social and Labor Affairs, 2004–2006; Equal Opportunity Department, 2006–present.
	Consultative: the Council for the Social Equality of Women and Men, 1999.
	Ombudsperson: Parliamentary Commissioner for Civil Rights, 1995–present.
Latvia	*Executive branch:* Unit on Gender Equality, the Department of European and Legal Affairs, Ministry of Welfare, 2003–present.
	Consultative: Inter-ministerial Working Group and Council for Gender Equality, 2001–present.
	Ombudsperson: National Human Rights Office, 1996–present.
Lithuania	*Executive branch:* Department of Labor and Equal Opportunities, Ministry of Social Security and Labor, 2001–2006; Department of Equal Opportunities, Ministry of Social Security and Labor, 2006–present; Gender Equality at the Municipal level—Vilnius.
	Legislative branch: Parliamentary Commission for Family and Child Affairs, 1996–present; Parliamentary Human Rights Committee, 1998.
	Consultative: Governmental Adviser on Women and Family Issues, 1995–2002; reorganized into Advisor

to the Prime Minister, 2002–present; Inter-Ministerial Commission on Equal Opportunities for Women and Men, 2000–present.

Ombudsperson: the Office of the Equal Opportunities, 1999-present, ministry-level institution.

Poland	*Executive branch:* Government Plenipotentiary for Equal Status of Women and Men, 1986–present (existed under various names, institutional status, and policy agenda); Gender equality offices at the municipal and regional level. *Legislative branch*: the Parliamentary Group of Women, 1992–present. *Ombudsperson:* The Commissioner for Civil Rights Protection, 1989; The Constitutional Tribunal, 1985.
Romania	*Executive branch:* Department for Strategies for Promoting Women's Rights and Family Policy, 1995–1998; Division for Equal Opportunities, 1998–2000; reorganized in 2000 into two low-level divisions in the Ministry of Labor and Social Affairs and in the Ministry of Health and Family, 2000–2003; The Directorate for Equal Opportunities (within the Ministry of Labor, Family and Social Protection), 2003–July 2010; The National Agency for Family Protection, 2003–present (focused on violence against women). *Legislative branch*: The Parliamentary Sub-Commission for Equal Opportunities between Women and Men, 1997–2000; the Deputy Chamber Commission on Equal Opportunities for Women and Men and the Senate Commission on Equal Opportunities for Women and Men, 2000–present. *Consultative:* Inter-ministerial Commission for Equal Opportunities between Women and men, 1999–present; The National Council for Combating Discrimination, 2002–present. *Ombudsperson:* the People's Advocate, 1997–present.
Slovakia	*Executive branch:* the Department for Equal Opportunities of Women and Men, the Ministry of Labor, Social Affairs, and Family, 1999–2003; The Department of Equality and Anti-Discrimination, the Ministry of Labor, Social Affairs,

and Family, 2003–2005; The Department of Family and Gender Policies, 2005–2007; the Ministry of Labor, Social Affairs, and Family; The Department of Gender Policies and Equal Opportunities, the Ministry of Labor, Social Affairs, and Family, 2007–present.

Legislative branch: the Committee for Human Rights, Minorities, and Status of Women, 2002–present.

Consultative: The Coordination Committee for Women's Issues, 1996–2001; the Commission for Equal Opportunities and Status of Women in Society, 2003;

Ombudsperson: the Slovak National center for Human Rights, 1994–present.

Slovenia	*Executive branch:* the Office for Women's Politics, a self-standing professional government body, 1992–2001; The Office for Equal Opportunities, 2001-present; The Advocate for Equal Opportunities, 2002–present.

Legislative branch: Commission for Women's Policy, 1990–1996; reorganized into the Commission of the National Assembly for Equal Opportunities Policy, 1996–2000; Committee for Petitions, Human Rights, and equal opportunities, 2004–present.

Consultative: the Commission for the Promotion of Women in Science, 2001; Expert Council on dealing with violence against women, 2001; Council of Government for the Implementation of the Principle of Equal Treatment, 2004;

Ombudsperson: Human Rights Ombudsperson, 1995–present.

Appendix III

Outcome Categorization Tables
Policy Harmonization Conceptualization and Coding

Table 1. Adoption of a Blueprint Policy.

Adoption of a specific law on gender equality	Adoption of a generic nondiscrimination act	No policy
1	0.5	0

Table 2. Adoption of a National Plan/Administrative Strategy on Gender Equality.

Adoption of an administrative strategy with specific orders/ goals/tasks/responsibilities on GE	Adoption of a generic plan of action/ administrative orders are poorly developed	No policy
1	0.5	0

Table 3. Policy Harmonization Assessment in Five Policy Areas.

Outcome	Leave Polocies, A1	Care and Informal Work, A2	Equal Pay, A3	Tax/ Benefits, A4	Non-Discrimination, A5
Comprehensiveness	0–1	0–1	0–1	0–1	0–1

Coding Rules for Table 3:

"0"—"non-compatible" (appropriate documents do not reflect compatibility; no fit between provisions and EU requirements).

"0.33"—"minimally compatible" (only few policy documents reflect compatibility, but not all appropriate documents are harmonized; only a few policy provisions are specified in domestic laws, not all EU policy provisions are addressed reflecting minimal fit in policy provisions).

"0.66"—"partly compatible" (only some appropriate policy documents reflect compatibility, but not all necessary documents are harmonized; only some of the policy provisions are specified in domestic laws, not all EU policy provisions are addressed reflecting partial fit in policy provisions).

"1"—"compatible" (all appropriate documents contain provisions on gender equality as required by the EU; policy provisions comprehensively cover all aspects of EU gender equality policies).

To analyze the overall level of state compliance in the area of policy harmonization, I develop the *Policy Harmonization Index*. This index adds scores for five policy areas to scores for the Blueprint Policy and to scores for the adoption of the National Plan/ Administrative Strategy.

The Policy Harmonization Index = (A1 + A2 + A3 + A4 +A5) + Blueprint Policy Adoption (0–1) + National Plan/Administrative Strategy (0–1).

The range of the *Policy Harmonization Index* is 0–7.

Table 4. Policy Harmonization Index.

Non-Compatible	Minimally Compatible	Partly Compatible	Compatible
0–1.75	1.76–3.5	3.6–5.25	5.26–7

Note on Calculation:

Non-compatible represents 0–25% of fully compatible; minimally compatible represents 26–50% of fully compatible; partly compatible represents 51–75% of fully compatible; compatible represents 76–100% of fully compatible.

Notes on Conceptualization:

A Blueprint policy refers to an overarching policy document that affirms the states commitment to secure the equality of men and women in all spheres of life, including labor relations. Such a policy-document includes a national Gender Equality Law or a general Anti-Discrimination Act, as recommended by the European Union as part of their compliance procedure. The general law on nondiscrimination does not focus on gender nondiscrimination, but addresses all grounds of discrimination, including ethnicity, religion, age, disability, origin, and class. Some experts view the adoption of Anti-Discrimination acts as a less potent solution for addressing the issues of gender discrimination (Röder 2009; Krizsán 2009). National plans (National Action Plans, National Priorities, etc.) are evaluated in terms of their effectiveness to provide administrative enforcement of gender equality laws. The study asks questions such as: Are these plans purely symbolic policy documents designed to fulfill international requirements, or are they effective avenues for administrative enforcement of new gender equality laws?

Governments must introduce changes to existing laws in order to make them compatible with EU accession requirements. These changes are evaluated along two sets of criteria: the *status of legal changes* (a type of document where policy adjustment is taking place) and the *comprehensiveness of policy provisions*. The status of legal changes measures whether changes are occurring in appropriate legal documents, such as a Constitution, Labor Code, Labor Acts, Acts on Social Security, etc. For each policy area, I determine the necessary legal documents in the hierarchy of national laws and evaluate if the government introduced the required changes in these laws (see Appendix I). In a similar manner, I evaluate how comprehensively the existing policy and policy amendments fit the provisions of the EU equality directives.

Institutional Adjustment Conceptualization and Coding

Table 5. Institutional Adjustment: Coding Rules.

Institutional Status	0–0.5–1	"0"—no institution; "0.5"—office within the structures of relevant ministries; "1"—ministry or cabinet ministry level office.
Legislative and Policy Influence Functions	Advisory: 0–0.1; Coordination: 0–0.1; Cooperation with NGOs: 0–0.1; Regional Network: 0–0.1; Representing victims in courts: 0–0.1; Legislative: 0–0.3; Monitoring: 0–0.2.	"0"—no such function "0.1"—there is such function for those functions in range from 0–0.1; "0.2"—here is such function for those functions in range from 0–0.2; "0.3"—there is such function for those functions in range from 0–0.3.
Enforcement Capacity	Power of administrative orders and enforcement: 0–0.5; Independent budget: 0–0.5.	"0"—no such function; "0.5"—there is such function for those functions in range from 0–0.5.
The Score Range and Total Possible Score for Institutional Adjustment:	0–3	

Table 6. Institutional Adjustment Index.

Non-Compatible	Minimally Compatible	Partly Compatible	Compatible
0–0.75	0.76–1.5	1.6–2.25	2.26–3

Note on Calculation:

Non-compatible represents 0–25% of fully compatible; minimally compatible represents 26–50% of fully compatible; partly compatible represents 51–75% of fully compatible; compatible represents 76–100% of fully compatible.

Notes on Conceptualization:

The *institutional status* of gender equality offices considers where the offices on gender equality are placed in the hierarchy of governmental institutions. The UN Division for the Advancement of Women (DAW) establishes a classification of women's policy machineries, which divides them into high-profile and low-profile government institutions. Gender equality offices placed within the structures of the Ministries on Labor and Social Affairs or other relevant ministries are defined as low-profile institutions. These institutions have very limited policymaking capacities and have no access to other branches of power. Such institutions are found in Bulgaria, the Czech Republic, Estonia, Latvia, Romania, and Slovakia. High-profile institutions on gender equality are those that have the status of an independent ministry or are placed within the Cabinet of the President or the Prime Minister. High-profile institutions on gender equality are found in Lithuania, Slovenia, Hungary from 2003–2004, and Poland from 2001–2005.

The analysis takes into consideration the declared and actual agenda of the government offices on gender equality. Sometimes the declared agenda of the office did not coincide with the practices or policies that it put into place/instituted/followed. For instance, the office on women's affairs in Poland from 1997 to 2001 promoted a very conservative agenda, which, in turn, undermined the purpose of a gender equality institution. In my analysis, I consider this dissonance between stated purpose and practical application to nullify the effectiveness of the gender equality office in Poland during this period.

The *legislative and policy influence* functions of gender equality offices include: advising, coordinating (between various government ministries), legislating, monitoring of compliance, cooperating with NGOs, establishing regional network, and providing legal assistance to victims of discrimination. The *enforcement capacity* of gender equality institutions measures the powers of the administrative orders that the gender equality office has or does not have as well as measures the independent budget allocated for the office to ensure enforcement, monitoring, and conducting of various activities, including public campaigns and public outreach programs. This measure does not take into account the moneys channeled to these institutions from the EU funds. It evaluates only the state allocation of funds for such programs.

In the coding rules of institutional capacities, I note that different values were assigned to different functions. Some scholars use the same value for different aspects of the policy with the assumption being that each specific component has as much weight, or functional importance, as all other independent components of the policy (e.g., Weldon 2002; Weldon 2011). While this approach can be used in the evaluation of specific policy functions, using the same treatment for institutional functions can be problematic. Since I am measuring the institutional capacity to enforce policies, then the powers of administrative order and enforcement are valued higher than policy coordination or policy advising. Similarly, the legislative function, or the ability to draft and propose bills for parliamentary debates and government consideration, has more weight than the coordination and advising function.

Appendix IV

Coding Rules for Independent and Control Variables

Table 1. Description and Coding of Independent Variables.

Variable Description	Coding
Conditionality	"Present"—1/"Absent"—0
Normative Pressure	"Present"—1/"Absent"—0
Women's NGO	"Absent"—0/"Weak"—0.33/ "Moderate"—0.66/"Strong"—1
Social Opposition	"Absent"—0/"Weak"—0.33/ "Moderate"—0.66/"Strong" 1
Party Ideology	"Right"—0/"Center-right"—1/ "Center"—2/"Center-left"—3/"Left"—4
Proportion of Female MPs	Percent of all members
Proportion of Female Cabinet Ministers	Percent of all members
Level of Unemployment	Percent of workforce
Gender Pay Gap	Percent of men's pay
GDP per capita	In real US dollars

Notes

Chapter 1

1. Newly accepted members of EU Eastward Enlargement were the Czech Republic, Estonia, Hungary, Latvia, Lithuania, Poland, Slovakia, and Slovenia. Governments of these states applied for EU membership between 1994 and 1996 following the collapse of the Soviet bloc.

2. "Opening Statement of the Polish Government Delegation" at the beginning of negotiations on EU membership, Brussels, March 31, 1998.

3. The European Commission monitored candidate state compliance with Equality Directives evaluating state progress towards compliance in the EC Opinion reports. Non-complying states faced the EC criticism and threats to close the accession negotiation process, e.g., Poland received a warning from the EC to close Social Chapter negotiations due to noncompliance with EU gender equality requirements in 2001.

4. For instance, see Barbara Einhorn 2000, Barbara Einhorn and Charlie Sever 2005, Fabian et al. 2010, Susan Gal and Gail Kligman 2000*a,b*, Janet Johnson and Jean Robinson 2007, Valerie Sperling 1999, Anna Titkow 1999, Jacqui True 2003, Peggy Watson 2000, and Georgina Waylen 2007.

5. The study is concerned with state actions to adopt policies on gender equality and establish institutions to enforce these policies into practice; the study does not take into account the outcomes of these efforts, e.g., changes in gender pay ratios, number of cases of discrimination taken to courts, or changes in public awareness about gender equality laws. Thus, the study is concerned with *government input*, rather than policy outcomes.

6. Cichowski documents that at the time of the writing of the Treaty of Rome. France was the only country with a legal provision of the equal pay among the founding states of the European Community (2002, 222). French authorities demanded to include the same provision in the Treaty of Rome to avoid disadvantages of "equal pay" provisions in a broader European economic union.

7. Judgment of the European Court of Justice of February 10, 2000, in Case *C-270/97 Deutsche post AG v Elisabeth Sievers* and *Case C-271/97 Deutsche post AG v Brunhilde Schrage*. ECR 2000, p. I-00929.

8. For the extensive review of EU gender equality policies and the history of their development, see Ellina 2003, Hantrais 2000, and Hoskyns 1996.

9. The principal directives are as follows: Council Directive 75/117/EEC of 10 February 1975 on the approximation of the laws of the Member States relating to the application of the principle of equal pay for men and women, O.J.E.C., 19 February 1975; Directive 76/207/EEC of 9 February 1976, amended by Directive 2002/73 of 23 September 2002 (O.J.E.C., 5 October 2002) on the implementation of the principle of equal treatment for men and women as regards access to employment, vocational training and promotion, and working conditions, O.J.E.C., 14 February 1976; Council Directive 79/7/ EEC of 19 December 1978 on the progressive implementation of the principle of equal treatment for men and women in matters of social security, O.J.E.C., 10 January 1979; Directive 86/378 on the implementation of the principle of equal treatment for men and women in occupational social security schemes, amended by Directive 96/97, O.J.E.C., 12 August 1986; Directive 86/613 on the application of the principle of equal treatment between men and women engaged in an activity, including agriculture, in a self-employed capacity, and on the protection of self-employed women during pregnancy and motherhood, O.J.E.C., 19 December 1986; Directive 97/80 on the burden of proof in cases of discrimination based on sex, O.J.E.C., 20 January 1998; Directive 2004/113 implementing the principle of equal treatment between men and women in the access to and supply of goods and services, O.J.E.C., 21 December 2004; Directive 2006/54 on the implementation of the principle of equal opportunities and equal treatment of men and women in matters of employment and occupation (recast), O.J.E.C., 26 July 2006.

10. Explanatory Memorandum, Proposal for a Directive of the European Parliament and of the Council on the implementation of the principle of equal opportunities and equal treatment of men and women in matters of employment and occupation (recast version) of 21/04/2004, COM(2004) 279 final.

11. The list of Equality Directives since 2006 includes the following: Recast Directive 2006/54/EC, which repeals and replaces the directives on equal pay, equal treatment in employment, training, promotion and working conditions, social security schemes and burden of proof (formerly Council Directive 75/117/ EEC of 10 February 1975 on the principle of equal pay for work of equal value (as amended by Directive 2006/54/EC), Council Directive 97/80/EC on the burden of proof in cases of discrimination based on sex; Directive 79/7/EEC on the progressive implementation of the principle of equal treatment for men and women in matters of social security; and Council Directive 86/613/EEC on equal treatment of men and women in the field of social security—occupational social security schemes).

Directive 86/613/EEC on the application of the principle of equal treatment between men and women engaged in an activity, including agriculture, in a self-employed capacity, and on the protection of self-employed women during pregnancy and motherhood. There is currently a proposal to amend this directive.

Directive 92/85/EC on the introduction of measures to encourage improvements in safety and health at work of pregnant workers and workers who have recently given birth or who are breastfeeding. There is currently a proposal to amend this directive.

Directive 96/34/EC on the Framework Agreement on Parental Leave concluded by the social partners in 1996. The social partners concluded a new framework agreement on 18 June 2009.

Directive 96/97/EC on equal treatment of men and women in the field of social security—statutory social security schemes.

Directive 97/81/EC concerning the framework agreement on part-time work concluded by UNICE, CEEP and the ETUC.

Directive 2004/113/EC implementing the principle of equal treatment between men and women in the access to and the supply of goods and services.

12. Recast Directive 2006/54/EC, Article 33.

13. From my analysis, I excluded one equality directive 2004/113/EC implementing the principle of equal treatment between men and women in the access to and the supply of goods and services, as it does not directly apply to gender equality on the labor market. I analyze state compliance with ten directives on gender equality in the labor market and in social security calculations (see note vii).

14. Ivan Kostov, Interview to Reuters *Sofia, Tuesday, March 9, 1999.* Accessed on July 7, 2011 at <http://sun450.government.bg/old/eng/prime_minister/interviews/reuters-01-03-99_eng.htm>.

15. Open Society Institute and Network Women's Program. 2002. "Monitoring the EU Accession Process: Equal Opportunities for Women and Men 2002," accessed July 24 2005 at <www.eonet.ro>. Open Society Institute and Network Women's Program. 2005. "Equal Opportunities for Women and Men: Monitoring Law and practice in New Member States and Accession Countries of the European Union," accessed October 15 2007 at <www.soros.org/women>.

16. For a detailed overview of socialist provisions on gender equality, see Amanda Sloat (2004). "Legislating for equality: The Implementation of the EU equality *Acquis* in Central and Eastern Europe." Jean Monnet Working Paper 08/04.

17. Iglehart and Norris developed a Gender Equality Scale by combining five questions from the pooled 1995–2001 World Values Surveys and European Values Surveys. Three items use statements with Lickert five-point agree–disagree responses, while two others use dichotomies. The items were coded that higher values represent support for gender equality. MENPOL Q118: "On the whole, men make better political leaders than women do." (Agree coded low). MENJOBS Q78: "When jobs are scarce, men should have more right to job than women." (Agree coded low). BOYEDUC Q119: "A university education is more important for a boy than a girl." (Agree coded low). NEEDKID Q110: "Do you think that a woman has to have children in order to be fulfilled or is this not necessary?" (Agree coded low). SGLMUM Q112: "If a woman wants to have a

child as a single parent but she does not want to have a stable relationship with a man, do you approve or disapprove?"

Chapter 2

1. For instance, see several edited volumes that bring all theoretical perspectives together and assess their utility for explaining the results of Europeanization processes in "old" and "new" EU states: Cowles, Caporaso, Risse (2001); Schneider and Aspinwall (2001); Schimmelfennig and Sedelmeier (2005); and individual studies: Andonova (2004); Checkel (2001); Kelley (2004); Schimmelfennig et al. 2003; and Schimmelfennig and Sedelmeier (2004) to name just a few.

2. For instance, Judith Kelley demonstrated low support for socialization efforts on citizenship and ethnicity policies in Latvia (2004), while Jeffrey Checkel demonstrates high support for international socialization on citizenship laws in Ukraine (2001).

3. We observe a parallel to the opening move in economic trust games, in which an investor and trustee each receive an equal amount of money (M). The investor can share any proportion of his/her money with the trustee (0 to M). Whatever amount the investor hands over to a trustee is tripled by the experimenter. The trustee is then free to return any amount to the investor. There is a large literature on the outcomes and strategies for trust games (Camerer 2003; Heinrich et al. 2004). The lab and field experiments demonstrate that the more the investor shares with the trustee; the more the trustee is likely to repay. Camerer and Fehr describe this as "feeling of obligation to repay more to an investor who has exhibited trust" (2004, 74). This feeling is also known in the game theoretic literature as "positive reciprocity" (Heinrich et al. 2004; Ostrom 1999).

4. For full review of mechanisms of international influence—coercion, persuasion (socialization), and social pressures (acculturation)—please see Avdeyeva's article on state compliance with international treaties (2007).

5. Berkovitch offered a detailed account of the critical role played by international organizations in the promotion of women's rights in individual nation-states (1999). Boyle and Preves considered the importance of local constituencies versus international normative influence in creating and enforcing laws against female genital cutting (2000). Katzenstein and Mueller looked at the role of women's movements in the diffusion of feminist ideas in the United States and Europe (1987). Krook examined the rapid diffusion of quotas for women in national and local parliaments and parties in a global study of gender and candidate selection (2010). True and Mintrom demonstrated the importance of the World Conferences on Women for global diffusion of state women's policy machineries in national bureaucracies (2001). Zippel investigated the emergence of sexual harassment policy in the United States and its travel across the Atlantic, where this concept was taken up first by the European Union, the United Kingdom, and Ireland and later, more gradually, in other European countries (2006).

6. For more details, see Banaszak, Beckwith, and Rucht 2003; Cohen and Arato 1992; Della Porta 2005; Epstein 2001; Mazur 2002; Klandermans and Staggenborg 2002; Rochon 1998; Rochon and Mazmanian 1993; Tilly 1997; Weldon 2002, 2011.

7. Among such systematic studies are Women's Movement and Reconfigured States (WMRS), Research Network on Gender Politics and the State (RNGS), Enlargement, Gender and Governance: The Civic and Political Participation and Representation of Women in Central and Eastern Europe (EGG), and Gendered Citizenship in Multi-Cultural Europe: The Impact of Contemporary Women's Movements (FEMCIT). For more details on these and other systematic comparative projects, see the review by Mazur 2007. Of these projects, only one focuses on EU Enlargement countries (the EGG project); however, it largely relies on descriptive analyses in examining the contribution of women's movements to women's policies in these countries. Another important source of data on gender policies in EU Enlargement states is the QUING Project coming from the Queens University in Belfast. It was indispensable in collecting and evaluating data for this book.

Chapter 3

1. My dependent variable, state compliance, is measured through state actual behavior, rather than beliefs and identity. Some scholars argue that the effect of normative pressures "cannot be revealed by studying behavior" (Payne, 2001, 42), because normative change requires active acceptance of a new norm. Following Kelley (2004), I do not think it is inappropriate to examine the ability of normative pressures to change the behavioral outcome.

2. At the Luxembourg summit in 1997 (December 12–13) the European Union accepted the opinion of the European Commission to invite Poland, Czech Republic, Hungary, Slovenia, Estonia, and Cyprus to start talks on their accession to the European Union. The preliminary condition for the inauguration of negotiations was maintenance of the criteria by the countries operating within the Copenhagen framework. These are the countries of the first accession wave. The second accession wave began in 1999 (December 10–11) at the Helsinki summit, when the European Union invited Slovakia, Latvia, Lithuania, Romania, and Bulgaria to begin accession talks.

3. None of the candidate states had a paternity leave prior to accession.

4. This study evaluates policies "on the book" and institutions created to enforce these policies. A study of policies "on the books" is critical for political scientists, activists, and students concerned with human rights and democratic policymaking for several reasons. First, the absence of policies indicates a state violation to provide legal protection against discrimination; "no policy" disadvantages and silences gender inequality in the labor market and allows treating women as secondary workers. Second, we can think of a government policy as

a signal about national priorities, which define the meaning of social justice and equality and furnish incentives for the mobilization of social forces in support of these policies. Third, policy implementation is not possible, if policies are not adopted. While translating law into action often takes time and effort, the law can be a powerful force for social change (Htun and Weldon 2012).

5. In the text, I use interchangeably several terms to describe state actions on policy harmonization: policy reform, policy adjustment, and policy change. All of these terms describe the process of policy harmonization at the national level with EU directives on gender equality.

6. In the text, I use interchangeably several terms to describe the process of institutional adjustment: creation of institutions, expansion of institutional powers, institutional reform, reversal of institutional reform, and institutional change to refer to processes of institutional adjustment to comply with EU requirement on establishing and maintaining government offices on gender equality.

7. The coding for institutional conditionality and normative pressures are conceptualized through three distinct periods in EU: EU Enlargement states relations: pre-accession negotiations (1995–1997/1999), or period prior to EU decision to initiate accession talks with these states; accession conditionality (1999/2000–2004/2006), or period of EU monitoring of candidate state compliance for accession; and post-accession period (2005/2007) or period when these states gained membership in European Union. To account for these periods in statistical analysis, I create several variables: year, period 1, period 2, and period 3. Then I create interaction terms for three periods: year* period 1, year* period 2, and year* period 3. The constitutive terms of these interactions are periods and year. Following the rules for dummy variable inclusion in model, I omit the following dummies: period1 and year. The final model is as follows: $\hat{y} = \alpha + X_1\beta_1 + X_2\beta_2 + X_3\beta_3 + X_4\beta_4 + X_5\beta_5$, where $X_1\beta_1$ – period 2(constitutive term), $X_2\beta_2$ – period 3 (constitutive term), $X_3\beta_3$ – interaction for period 1, $X_4\beta_4$ – interaction for period 2, and $X_5\beta_5$ – interaction for period 3. In this model the coefficients for period interactions will tell us the rate of slope change for this period from 0.

8. Random effects models require that much more strenuous assumptions be met. The model diagnostics results in the Breusch-Pagan and Sargan Hagen Tests suggest that the model meet these assumptions. The random effects model is not suggested for lagged dependent variables; I do not lag the dependent variables, so it is practical to use random effects.

9. The lagged dependent variables are not suited for the type of response I am exploring. The study explores state responses to international pressures, and the effects of these pressures are observed within a year of its receipt. The states either respond or do not respond to these international efforts. One year is a sufficient period to explore the effectiveness of international engagement. Moreover, a one-year period is best suited to observe the effect of domestic political forces; change in governments, for instance, leads to changes in levels of compliance with gender equality requirements, and this is exactly the point of my analysis. Qualitative case studies support and explore these statistical findings. In addition,

requiring the change to occur in the same period of observation presents a more stringent test for the effectiveness of the tools. Other scholars did not use lagged dependent variables in studies similar to my own (Kelley 2004).

10. For simplicity, I combine two waves of accession into one, by considering a conditional requirement starting from 2000 to 2004, and although we can see that compliance slightly improves already in 1999 (the first year of monitoring for four countries) and continues to 2007 (the last year for Romania and Bulgaria).

Chapter 4

1. See for instance: Klasen and Schuler, 2011. "Reforming the Gender-Related Development Index and the Gender Empowerment Measure: Implementing Some Specific Proposals." *Feminist Economics* 17(1), 1–30. World Economic Forum, 2012. *The Global Gender Gap Index*. Available at <http://www.weforum.org/issues/global-gender-gap>.

2. In particular, the authors note "the credibility of the EU's threat of withholding rewards in the case of non-compliance, and conversely, the credibility of the EU's promise to deliver the reward in the case of rule adoption" (Schimmelfennig and Sedelmeier 2005, p.13).

3. Among other factors, the authors note that "the longer the temporal distance to the payment of rewards, the lower the incentive to comply . . . A gradual process with several levels of progress at which compliance is checked and intermediate rewards are paid reduces this problem even if the ultimate reward— EU membership—is distant" (Schimmelfennig and Sedelmeier 2005, p.13).

4. It is important to note the conceptual difference of compliance between the proponents and the opponents of rapid reforms: Schimmelfennig and Sedelmeier in their 2005 analysis concentrate on rule adoption (policy adoption), whereas the opponents of rapid reforms analyze policy enforcement and implementation (for instance Falkner, Treib, and Holizleithner (2008) argue that a great majority of adopted rules and policies remain "dead letters" both in EU Enragement states and in the 15 "old" EU members).

5. See for instance, Elena Stoykova. 2007. "Issue Histories Bulgaria: Series of Timelines of Policy Debates." Institute for Human Sciences: Vienna; Raluca Maria Popa. 2007. "Issue Histories Romania: Series of Timelines of Policy Debates." Institute for Human Sciences: Vienna; Falkner, Treib, and Holzleithner. 2008. Compliance in the Enlarged European Union: Living Rights or Dead Letters? Ashgate: Aldershot, Hampshire.

6. The weakness of EU binding law (directives) to guarantee enforcement of policies by national and regional governments in member states is a well-researched question in various policy areas regulated by the European Union: social policy (see De Burca, De Witte and Ogertschnig 2005; Falkner, Treib, Hartlapp, and Keiber 2005; Falkner, Treib, and Holzleithner 2008; Shaw 2000;

Zeilin and Pochet 2005 to name just a few); economic and monetary policy
(Hosli 2005; Verdun 2000, 2002); environmental policy (Jordan 2005; Jordan and
Liefferink 2004; Jordan 2010; Knill and Liefferink 2007; McCormick 2001); and
foreign, security and defense policy (Howarth 2007; Kagan 2004; Jones 2007;
Smith 2008). Lacking direct enforcement powers of policy enforcement in areas
such as environment, social policy, labor safety, and gender equality the European
Union relies on the network of interest groups and social partners to challenge
state incompliance. In recent years, when the European Union faced serious
legitimacy challenges, often concerning the traditional Community policymaking method. To address these concerns, the European Union introduced "new
governance" tools, including the Open Method of Coordination, to substitute the
traditional Community method. New Modes of Governance are not homogenous
and are used differently according to the specific conditions of the policy area.
Greater reliance on this method of policy decision making is embraced by the
Lisbon Treaty (Warlegh-Lack and Drachenberg 2010).

    7. Hafner-Burton and Pollack (2009) investigate the EU commitment
to the "mainstreaming" of gender issues across all policy areas embraced by the
Union during the 1990s. They find that a decade later after the Union's initial
engagement, there has not been consistent and effective implementation of gender mainstreaming in EU institutions. The problem, they argue, lies in the failure
to create effective incentives mobilizing sufficient interest among crucial actors.
The European Commission did not provide any "hard" incentives for bureaucrats
to implement reforms, relying on "soft" incentives such as persuasion and socialization. In contrast, the Commission has utilized hard incentives in the adoption
of another mandate, on equal opportunities for men and women officials within
the Commission, which resulted in rapid observable progress.

    8. The full question wording in the WVS questionnaire is as follows:

> V161.—Many Things may be desirable, but not all of them are
> essential characteristics of democracy. Please tell me for each of the
> following things how essential you think it is as a characteristic of
> democracy. Use this scale where 1 means "Not at all an essential
> characteristic of democracy," and 10 means "it definitely is an essen-
> tial characteristic of democracy." (Read out and code one answer for
> each): "Women have the same rights as men."

    9. The exact wording of the question from the WVS questionnaire is as
follows:

> V168.—In 2000, leaders representing almost all of the world's coun-
> tries agreed to carry out a number of programs to improve the lives
> of the people of low-income countries. These programs are known as
> the Millennium Development Goals. I am going to read out some
> of the problems that these programs involve. I would like you to

indicate which of these problems do you consider the most serious one in your own country? The list of problems: "1. People living in poverty and need; 2. Discrimination against girls and women; 3. Poor sanitation and infectious diseases; 4. Inadequate education; 5. Environmental pollution."

10. The full version of the Speech by Mirek Topolánek can be found on the Czech government website <www.vlada.cz>.

Chapter 5

1. Poland submitted an official request to initiate negotiations regarding association between Poland and the European Union in 1990. The 1991 European Pact included a statement about Poland's ultimate goal to join the European Union. In January 1993, the Polish government developed a plan of action for aligning Polish economy and legislation with those of the European Union. In 1994 Poland officially applied for the EU membership. Negotiations started in 1997 and were closed in 2002 (Lohmann and Seibert 2003).

2. Thomas Remington used this expression to describe painful consequences of economic transformation in Russia (*Politics in Russia*. Sixth Edition. Longman/Pearson. 2010, p. 199).

3. Extensive history of early women's mobilization in Poland is reviewed by Borkowska 1996, Czajkowska 1992, Mrozik 2007, and Walczewska 1993.

4. For instance, the Citizen's Committees of Lech Wałęsa organized in support of the first semi-free elections (Curry 2007).

5. For additional analysis of policy change in Poland in regard to EU gender equality directives, please see Zielińska 2002, Sloat 2004, and Dąbrowska 2007.

6. In 2005 it employed 22 full-time workers, a remarkable number of staff for the CEE gender equality offices at the executive branch.

Chapter 6

1. All experts agree that Prime Minister Vladimir Špidla (2002–2004), who became the EU Commissioner on Equal Opportunity in 2004, Anna Čurdová, a former Chairperson of the Council for Equal Opportunities for Men and Women, and Michaela Maksová-Tominová, an NGO activist, who joined the Ministry of Labor and Social Affairs, were active supporters of reforms on gender equality and equal opportunity in the Czech Republic.

2. Among EU Enlargement states, Latvia and Hungary exhibit similar levels of Euroskepticism; among old EU members, Czech levels of Euroskepticism is close to those in the UK.

3. In 1990 the first umbrella organization, the Women's Council, was established to provide greater cooperation and coordination between various NGOs in order to achieve full compliance with the CEDAW requirements. But this organization was short-lived. It disbanded in 1993 without achieving any of the stated goals (Hašková and Křižková 2008).

4. Maxime Forest analyzes strategies of Czech NGOs to influence the government focusing on lobbying and consulting in his 2007 article.

5. Detailed reviews of legislative changes are provided by Sloat (2004), Röder (2007), and Wiedermann (2008).

6. Petr Pavlik, ed., provides critical review of government action in "Shadow Report on equal treatment and equal Opportuntiies for Women and Men." Prague: Gender Studies, 2004.

7. For an excellent review of Mirek Topolanek's position on gender equality, please see Elaine Weiner (2010). "Morality, biology and the free market: (De) Naturalizing the EU's gender equality agenda in the Czech Republic." *Women's Studies International Forum* 33 (2010): 13–20.

8. The current Czech Prime Minister Petr Nečas (ODS) abolished the position of a Minister without a portfolio on Human Rights and Minorities. In his explanation of this decision, the Prime Minister was very clear and succinct: "The ministry is a luxury the country cannot afford" (cited in Albert, 2010).

9. Alena Králiková notes that no women's NGOs received grants provided within the framework of the European Year of Equal Opportunities (EYEO). Most grants were given to the cause of ethnic minorities, most importantly, the Roma minority. For detailed analysis of the effect of the EYEO on state action and women's NGO marginalization, see Králiková (2007).

Personal Interviews

Warsaw, Poland, February, 2005

Stana Buchowska, program coordinator. La Strada Foundation.
Lidia Goldberg, Head, International Cooperation and EU Integration Division. Council of Ministers of the Republic of Poland.
Agnieszka Grzybek, expert and program coordinator. OŠKA.
Anna Jancewicz, President. Fundacja Centrum Promocji Kobiet.
Anna Jawor, Plenipotentiary on the Equal Status of Women and Men. Mazowiecky Wojwodship.
Sylvia Korlak, EC Representative Office.
Monika Ksieniewicz, specialist on Education. Government Plenipotentiary on Equal Status of Women and Men. Council of Ministers of the Republic of Poland.
Joanna Rozynska, lawyer. Women's Rights Center.
Anita Seibert, expert and program coordinator. Karat Coalition.
Krzysztof Šmiszek, specialist Government Plenipotentiary for Women and Men. Council of Ministers of the Republic of Poland.
Maciej Stadejek, specialist. Government Plenipotentiary for Equal Status of Women and Men. Council of Ministers of the Republic of Poland.

Prague, the Czech Republics, March 2005

Maire Boháčová, Vice President of the Union of Catholic Women.
Stanislav Drapal, Chair. Cesky Statistycky Uřad.
Zdenka Hajna, President, the Czech Women's Union.
Alena Kraliková, program coordinator. Gender Studies, o.p.s.
Marcela Linková, researcher and program coordinator. Contact Center for Women and Science.
Dagmar Lorenz-Meyer, researcher and professor. Gender Studies, Charles University.
Katerina Niklová, specialist. Gender Focal Point in the Ministry of Finance of the Czech Republic.

Geraldina Polavčiková, specialist. Gender Focal Point in the Minister of the
    Interior of the Czech Republic.
Klara Zhiriková, coordinator. Unit on Gender Equality, the Ministry of Labor
    and Social Affairs of the Czech Republic.

References

Albert, Gwendolyn. 2010. "On the Chopping Block: Women and Minority Rights Have Joined the Long List of Cuts Planned by the New Nečas Government." www.Praguepost.com. Posted: July 21, 2010. Accessed October 17, 2011.

Alter, Karen. 2001. *Establishing the Supremacy of European Law.* Oxford: Oxford University Press.

Amenta, Edwin, Neal Caren, Elizabeth Chiarello, and Yang Su. 2010. "The Political Consequences of Social Movements." *Annual Review of Sociology* Vol. 36: 287–307.

Anderson, Leah S. 2006. "European Union Gender Regulations in the East: The Czech and Polish Accession Process." *East European Politics and Society* 20 (1): 101–125.

Aronson, Elliot, Timothy D. Wilson, and Robin M. Akert. 2002. *Social Psychology,* 4th ed. New York: Prentice Hall.

Ashwin, Sarah, and Valery Yakubovich. 2005. "Cherchez la Femme: Women as Supporting Actors in the Russian Labour Market." *European Sociological Review* 21 (2):149–164.

Atchison, Amy, and Ian Down. 2009. "Women Cabinet Ministers and Female-Friendly Social Policy." *Poverty & Public Policy* 1:1–23.

Avdeyeva, Olga A. 2007. "When Do States Comply with International Treaties? Policies on Violence against Women in Post-Communist Countries." *International Studies Quarterly* 51 (4): 877–900.

———. 2009. "Enlarging the Club: When Do States Enforce Gender Equality Laws?" *Comparative European Politics,* March 2009. 7 (1): 158–177.

———. 2010. "States' Compliance with International Requirements: Gender Equality in EU Enlargement Countries." *Political Research Quarterly,* March 2010. 63 (1): 203–217.

———. 2012. "Does Reputation Matter for States' Compliance with International Treaties? States Enforcement of Anti-Trafficking Norms," *International Journal of Human Rights* 16 (2): 298–320.

Banaszak, Lee Ann. 1996. *Why movements succeed or fail: Opportunity, culture, and the struggle for woman suffrage.* Princeton, NJ: Princeton University Press.

Banaszak, Lee Ann, Karen Beckwith, and Dieter Rucht. 2003. *Women's Movements Facing the Reconfigured State.* New York: Cambridge University Press.

Banaszak, Lee Ann, ed. 2006. *The U.S. Women's Movement in Global Perspective.* Boulder, CO: Rowman & Littlefield Publishers.

Balcerowicz, Leszek. 1995. *Socialism, Capitalism, Transformation.* Budapest: Central European University: 311–312.

Bashevkin, Sylvia. 1998. *Women on the Defensive: Living through Conservative Times.* Chicago: University of Chicago Press.

Baumgartner, Frank R., and Christine Mahoney. 2008. "Forum Section: The Two Faces of Framing Individual-Level Framing and Collective Issue Definition in the European Union." *European Union Politics* 9 (3): 435–449.

BBC. 2006. "Lithuania Seeks Minister's Arrest." August 30, 2006. Accessed January 2012 at http://news.bbc.co.uk/2/hi/europe/5299786.stm.

BBC. 2009. "Lithuania's new leader: Your views." May 18, 2009. Accessed January 2012 at http://news.bbc.co.uk/2/hi/europe/8056247.stm.

Bearce, David H., and Stacey Bondanella. 2007. "Intergovernmental Organizations, Socialization, and Member-State Interest Convergence." *International Organization* 61 (4): 703–733.

Beckwith, Karen. 2000. "Beyond Compare? Women's Movements in Comparative Perspective." *European Journal of Comparative Research* 37:431–468.

———. 2005. "The Comparative Politics of Women's Movements." Review Essay. *Perspectives on Politics* 3 (3): 583–596.

———. 2007a. "Numbers and Newness: The Descriptive and Substantive Representation of Women." *Canadian Journal of Political Science* 40 (01): 27–49.

———. 2007b. "Mapping Strategic Engagements: Women's Movements and the State." *International Feminist Journal of Politics* 9 (3): 312–338.

Berkovitch, Ninza. 1999. *From Motherhood to Citizenship: Women's Rights and International Organizations.* Baltimore: John Hopkins University Press.

Bird, Graham. 2001a. "IMF Programmes: Is There a Conditionality Laffer Curve?" *World Economics* 2 (2): 29–49.

———. 2001b. "IMF Programs: Do They Work? Can They Be Made to Work Better?" *World Development* 29 (11): 1849–1865.

Blauberger, Michael. 2009. "Compliance with Rules of Negative Integration: European State Aid Control in the New Member States." *Journal of European Public Policy* 16 (7): 1030–1046.

Bochel, Catherine, and Jacqui Briggs. 2000. "Do Women Make Difference?" *Politics* 20 (2): 63–68.

Borza, Iona. 2010. "A Lacking Legitimacy in the Transposition of the EU's Equal Opportunity Directives: The Case of Romania." *Women's Studies International Forum* 33:47–53.

Boyle, Elizabeth H., and Sharon E. Preves. 2000. "National Politics as International Process: The Case of Anti-Female-Genital-Cutting Laws." *Law and Society Review* 34:401–35.

Brambor, Thomas, William Clark, and Matt Golder. 2006. "Understanding Interaction Models: Improving Empirical Analysis." *Political Analysis* 14 (1): 61–82.

Bratton, Kathleen A., and Leonard Ray. 2002. "Descriptive Representation, Policy Outcomes, and Municipal Day-care Coverage in Norway." *American Journal of Political Science* 46 (2): 428–437.

Bretherton, Charlotte. 2001. "Gender Mainstreaming and EU Enlargement: Swimming against the Tide?" *Journal of European Public Policy* 8 (1): 60–81.

Buchowska, Stana. 2005. La Strada Foundation. Interview with the author. February 24, 2005. Warsaw: Poland.

Bugajski, Janusz. 2002. *Political Parties of Eastern Europe: A Guide to Politics in the Post-communist Era*. Armonk, NY: M. E. Sharpe.

Bull, Anna, Hanna Diamond, and Rosalind March, eds. 2000. *Feminism and Women's Movements in Contemporary Europe*. New York: St. Martin's Press.

Bystydzienski, Jill M. 1992. *Women Transforming Politics: Worldwide Strategies for Empowerment*. Bloomington: Indiana University Press.

Caiazza, Amy. 2007. *I Knew I Could Do This Work: Seven Strategies That Promote Women's Activism and Leadership in Unions*. Washington, DC: IWPR.

Camerer, C. F., and Fehr, E. 2004. "Measuring Social Norms and Preferences Using Experimental Games: A Guide for Social Scientists." In J. Heinrich, R. Boyd, S. Bowles, C. Camerer, E. Fehr, and H. Gintis, eds. *Foundations of Human Sociality*. New York, NY: Oxford University Press: 55–95.

Caporaso, James, and Joseph Jupille. 2001. "The Europeanization of Gender equality Policy and Domestic Structural Change." In Maria G. Cowles, James Caporaso, and Thomas Risse, eds. *Transforming Europe*. Ithaca, NY: Cornell University Press: 21–43.

Castles, Francis Geoffrey, ed. 1993. *Families of Nations: Patterns of Public Policy in Western Democracies*. Hanover, NH: Dartmouth Pub. Co.

Celis, Karen. 2008. "Gendering Representation." In Gary Goertz and Amy G. Mazur, ed. *Politics, Gender, and Concepts*. Cambridge: Cambridge University Press.

Čermáková, Marie, Hana Haŝková, Alena Křižková, Marcela Linková, Hana Mařiková, and Martina Musilová. 2000. *Relations and Changes of Gender Differences in the Czech Society in the 90's*. Prague: Institute of Sociology of Academy of Sciences of the Czech Republic.

Checkel, Jeffrey. 1998. "The Constructivist Turn in International Relations Theory: A Review Essay." *World Politics* 50:324–348.

———. 1999. "Norms, Institutions and National Identity in Contemporary Europe." *International Studies Quarterly* 43:83–114.

———. 2001. "Why Comply? Social Learning and European Identity Change." *International Organization* 55 (03): 553–588.

———. 2005. "International Institutions and Socialization in Europe: Introduction and Framework." *International Organization* 59 (4): 801–826.

Chołuj Bozena, and Claudia Neusüß. 2004. "EU Enlargement in 2004. East-West priorities and Perspectives from Women Inside and Outside the EU." Discussion Paper. New York: UNIFEM.

Ciocoiu, Paul. 2011. "Gender Equality Missing from Romania's Public Debate." *Southeast European Times* July 20, 2011.

Clarke, Simon. 1998. "Structural Adjustment without Mass Unemployment: Lessons from Russia." In Simon Clarke, ed. *Structural Adjustment Without Mass Unemployment: Lessons from Russia.* Cheltenham, UK: Edward Elgar: 9–86.

Cohen, Jean, and Andrew Arato. 1992. "Politics and the Reconstruction of the Concept of Civil Society." In Axel Honneth, Thomas McCarthy, Claus Offe, and Albrecht Wellmer, eds. *Cultural Political Interventions in the Unfinished Project of Enlightenment.* Cambridge: MIT University Press: 121–143.

Collier, Paul, Patrick Guillaumont, Sylviane Guillaumont, and Jan Willem Gunning. 1997. "Redesigning Conditionality." *World Development* 25 (9): 1399–1407.

Collier, Paul. 1997. "The Failure of Conditionality." In Catherine Gwin and Joan Nelson, eds. *Perspectives on Aid and Development.* Washington, DC: Overseas Development Council: 51–78.

Cook, Linda J., Mitchell Alexander Orenstein, and Marilyn Rueschemeyer, eds. *Left Parties and Social Policy in Post-Communist Europe.* Boulder, CO: Westview Press, 1999.

Coomaraswamy, Radhika. 2000. "Combating Domestic Violence: Obligations of the State." *Innocenti Digest* 6:10–11.

———. 2003. *Integration of the Human Rights of Women and the Gender Perspective: Violence against Women.* Report of the Special Rapporteur on Violence against Women, Its Causes and Consequences. New York: United Nations, Economic and Social Council.

Costain, Anne N. 1992. *Inviting Women's Rebellion: A Political Process interpretation of the Women's Movement.* Baltimore: Johns Hopkins University Press.

———. 2005. "Social Movements as Mechanisms for Political Inclusions." In Christina Wolbrecht and Rodney Hero, eds. *The Politics of Democratic Inclusion.* Philadelphia: Temple University Press.

Cowles, Maria G., James Caporaso, and Thomas Risse. 2001. *Transforming Europe.* Ithaca, NY: Cornell University Press.

Curry, Jane L. 2011. "Poland: The Politics of 'God's Playground.'" In Sharon L. Wolchik and Jane L. Curry, eds. *Central and East European Politics: From Communism to Democracy.* 2nd ed. New York: Rowman and Littlefield Publishers, Inc.: 161–186.

Dahlerup, Drude. 1986. *The New Women's Movement: Feminism and Political Power in Europe and the USA.* Bristol: Sage.

Daskalova, Klassimira. 2007. "How Should We Name the 'Women-Friedly' Actions of State Socialism?" *Aspasia* 1:214–219.

Davis, Rebecca Howard. 1997. *Women and Power in Parliamentary Democracies: Cabinet Appointments in Western Europe, 1968–1992.* Lincoln, NE: University of Nebraska Press, 1997.

Dąbrowska, Magdalena. 2007. "Issue Histories Poland: Series of Timelines of Policy Debates." Quality in Gender + Equality Policies (QUING). European Commission Sixth Framework Programme Integrated Project. Institute for Human Sciences. Vienna, 2007.

Deacon, Bob. 2000. "Eastern European Welfare States: The Impact of the Politics of Globalization." *Journal of European Social Policy* 10 (2): 146–161.

Dimitrova, Antoaneta. 2002. "Enlargement, Institution-Building and the EU's Administrative Capacity Requirement." *West European Politics* 25 (4): 171–190.

Downs, George W., David M. Rocke, and Peter N. Barsoom. 1996. "Is the Good News about Compliance Good News for Cooperation?" *International Organization* 50:379–406.

Drapal, Stanislav. 2005. Chairman of the Czech State Statistical Department. Interview with the author. March 14, 2005. Prague: Czech Republic.

Drezner, Daniel W. 2000. "Bottom Feeders." *Foreign Policy* 121 (November–December): 64–70.

Dryzek, John S. 1990. *Discursive Democracy: Politics, Policies, and Political Science.* New York: Cambridge University Press.

Economist. 2004. "Elites, Gherkins and Sugar-Beets." June 24th, 2004. Accessed January 2012 at http://www.economist.com/node/2792621.

Economist. 2006. "Lithuania's Government: Politics Exam." June 8, 2006. Accessed January 2012 at http://www.economist.com/node/7037599?zid= 309&ah=80dcf288b8561b012f603b9fd9577f0e.

European Commission. 2002. *Regular Report on the Czech Republic's Progress Towards Accession.* Brussels: European Commission. http//:ec.europa.eu/ enlargement/archives/pdf/key_documents/2002/cz_en.pdf./.

———. 2008. "Commission Acts Against Six Countries on Gender Equality Legislation." Press Release. IP/08/1821/ Brussels, 27 November 2008. http://ec.europa.eu/employment_social/gender_equality/legisltaion/index_ en.html. Accessed March 2012.

Eglitis, Diana Stukuls. 2011. "The Baltic States: Changes and Challenges in the New Europe." In Sharon L. Wolchik and Jane L. Curry, eds. *Central and East European Politics: From Communism to Democracy.* 2nd ed. New York: Rowman and Littlefield Publishers, Inc.: 231–249.

Einhorn, Barbara. 1993. *Cinderella Goes to Market: Citizenship, Gender, and Women's Movements in East Central Europe.* New York: Verso.

———. 2006. "Gender(ed) Politics in Central and Eastern Europe." *Journal of Global Ethics* 2 (2): 139–162.

Einhorn, Barbara, and Charlotte Sever. 2003. "Gender and Civil Society in Central and Eastern Europe." *International Feminist Journal of Politics* 5 (2): 163–190.

Ellina, Chrysttala. 2003. *Promoting Women's Rights: Politics of Gender in the European Union*. New York and London: Routledge.

Epstein, Rachel A. 2008a. *In Pursuit of Liberalism: International Institutions in Postcommunist Europe*. Baltimore, MD: Johns Hopkins University Press.

———. 2008b. The Social Context in Conditionality: Internationalizing Finance in Postcommunist Europe. *Journal of European Public Policy* 15 (6): 880–898.

Epstein, Rachel A., and Ulrich Sedelmeier. 2008. "Beyond Conditionality: International Institutions in Postcommunist Europe after Enlargement." *Journal of European Public Policy*. 15 (6): 795–805.

Esaiasson, Peter, and Sören Holmberg.1996. *Representation from Above: Members of Parliament and Representative Democracy in Sweden*. Hanover, NH: Dartmouth Pub. Co.

Escobar-Lemmon, Maria, and Michelle Taylor-Robinson. 2009. "Pathways to Power in Presidential Cabinets: What are the Norms for Different Cabinet Portfolios and Do Female Appointees Conform to the Norm? A Study of 5 Presidential Democracies." Unpublished manuscript. Paper presented at the APSA Annual Convention in Toronto, 2009.

Esping-Andersen, Gøsta. 1993. *Changing Classes: Stratification and Mobility in Post-Industrial Societies*. London: Sage Publications, Inc.

———. 1999. *Social Foundations of Postindustrial Economies*. New York: Oxford University Press.

Fábián, Katalin. 2010. "Introduction." In K. Fabian, ed. *Domestic Violence in Post-Communist States: Local Activism, National Policies, and Global Forces*. Bloomington: Indiana University Press.

———. 2013. "Mobilizing Against Domestic Violence in Postcommunist Europe: Successes and Continuing Challenges." Paper presented at the Third Conference of the European Consortium on Gender and Politics, Barcelona, March 2013.

Fagan, Colette, Jill Rubery, Damian Grimshaw, Mark Smith,Gail Hebson, and Hugo Figueiredo 2005. "Gender Mainstreaming in the Enlarged European Union: Recent Developments in the European Employment Strategy and Social Inclusion Process." *Industrial Relations Journal* 36 (6): 568–591.

Faulkner, Gerda, Oliver Traub, and Elizabeth Holzleithner. 2008. "Introduction: The Challenge of Implementation Research in the New Member States." In Gerda Faulkner, Oliver Traub, and Elizabeth Holzleithner, eds. *Compliance in the Enlarged European Union: Living Rights or Dead Letters?* Aldershot, Hampshire: Ashgate: 1–26.

———, eds. 2008. *Compliance in the Enlarged European Union: Living Rights or Dead Letters?* Ashgate: Aldershot, Hampshire.

Ferree, Myra Marx, and Patricia Yancey Martin. 1995. "Doing the Work of the Movement: Feminist Organizations." In Myra Marx Ferree and Patricia Yancey Martin, eds. *Feminist Organizations: Harvest of the New Women's* Philadelphia: Temple University Press: 3–23.

Fierke, Karin M., and Antje Wiener. "Constructing institutional interests: EU and NATO enlargement." *Journal of European Public Policy* 6, no. 5 (1999): 721–742.

Finnemore, Martha. 1996. *National Interests in International Society.* Ithaca, NY: Cornell University Press.

Finnemore, Martha, and Kathryn Sikkink. 1998. International Norm Dynamics and Political Change. *International Organization* 52 (4): 887–917.

Forest, Maxime. 2007. "The Changing Patterns of Gender Interest Representation in an Extended European Union: The Czech Republic and Slovakia in a Comparative Perspective." Paper presented at the ECPR General Conference, Pisa, September 6–8, 2007.

Fritz, Verena. 2007. *State-Building: A Comparative Study of Ukraine, Lithuania, Belarus, and Russia.* Budapest: Central European University.

Fukuyama, Francis. 1995. *Trust: The Social Virtues and The Creation of Prosperity.* New York: Free Press Paperbacks.

Furtlehner, Petra. 2008. "Slovenia." In Gerda Faulkner, Oliver Traub, and Elizabeth Holzleithner, eds. *Compliance in the Enlarged European Union: Living Rights or Dead Letters?* Ashgate: Aldershot, Hampshire: 125–156.

Fuszara, Małgorzata, and Eleonora Zielińska. 1995. "Obstacles and Barriers to an Equal Status Act in Poland." In Renata Siemienska, ed. *Women: The Past and the New Roles.* Warsaw: Information and Documentation. Unit on the Council of Europe. Warszaw University.

Fuszara, Małgorzata. 2001. "Organized Women's Movement in Poland" (Unpublished Manuscript).

———. 2003. "History of Women's Organizations" In Jasek Kurczewski, ed. *Civil Society in Poland.* Warsaw: Center for Social Research: 31–44.

———. 2004. "Mapping Women's Campaign for Change: Poland." Unpublished Manuscript.

———. 2005a. "Between Feminism and the Catholic Church: The Women's Movement in Poland." *Czech Sociological Review* (06/2005): 1057–1075.

———. 2005b. "Identifying Barriers to Women's Participation in Poland." Work Package 5. Enlargement, Gender and Governance (EGG) EU Framework 5, Project # HPSE-CT-2002-0015.

Gal, Susan, and Gail Kligman. 2000. *Reproducing Gender; Politics, Publics, and Everyday Life Aater Socialism.* Princeton, NJ: Princeton University Press.

Galligan, Yvonne, Sara Clavero, and Marina Calloni. 2007. *Gender Politics and Democracy in Post-Socialist Europe.* Opladen, Germany: Barbara Budrich Publishers.

Gelb, Joyce. 1989. *Feminism and Politics: A Comparative Perspective.* Berkeley: University of California Press.

———. 2003. *Gender Policies in Japan and the United States: Comparing Women's Movements, Rights, and Politics.* New York: Palgrave.

Geller-Schwartz, Linda. 1995. "An Array of Agencies: Feminism and State Institutions in Canada." in *Comparative State Feminism*, ed. Dorothy McBride Stetson and Amy G. Mazur. Newbury Park, CA: Sage.

Gender Equality Unit. 2000. *Priorities and Procedure of the Government in Promoting the Equality of Men and Women.* Prague: Ministry of Labor and Social Affairs.

George, Alexander, and Timothy McKeown. 1985. "Case Studies and Theories of Organizational D." *Advances in Information Processes in Organizations.* Greenwich: JAI Press.

Goerge, Alexander, and Andrew Bennett. 2005. *Case Studies and Theory Development in the Social Sciences.* Boston: MIT Press.

Ghebrea, Georgeta, Marina Tataram, and Ioana Cretoiu. 2005. "Implementing the EU Equality Acquis in Romania." Work Package 4. Executive Summary. Enlargement, Gender and Governance (EGG) EU Framework 5, Project # HPSE-CT-2002-0015.

Gheciu, Alexandra. 2005. "Security Institutions as Agents of Socialization? NATO and the 'New Europe.'" *International Organization* 59 (4): 973–1012.

Ghodsee, Kristen. 2004. "Emerging Capitalism, Cultural Feminism, and Women's Nongovernmental Organizations in Postsocialist Eastern Europe." *Signs* 29 (3): 727–753.

Glade, Nadine. 2010. "The Situation of Women's NGOs with Gender Equality Agendas in Modern Day Lithuania." Paper presented at the International Conference Civil Society and NGOs in Europe and Russia: Responding to New Challenges and Opportunities. St. Petersburg, November 12–14, 2010.

Goodman, Ryan, and Derek Jinks. 2004. "How to Influence States: Socialization and International Human Rights Law." *The Duke Law Journal* 54:621–703.

Government Plenipotentiary for Equal Status for Women and Men and Ministry of Foreign Affairs. 2004.

Grabbe, Heather. 1999. "A Partnership for Accession? The Implications of EU Conditionality for the Central and East European Applicants." Robert Schuman Center Working Paper 99/12, European University Institute.

———. 2001. "How Does Europeanization Affect CEE Governance? Conditionality, Diffusion and Diversity." *Journal of European Public Policy* 8 (6): 1013–1031.

———. 2005. "Regulating the Flow of People across Europe." In Frank Schimmelfennig, and Ulrich Sedelmeier, eds. *The Europeanization of Eastern Europe: Evaluating the Conditionality Model.* Ithaca, NY: Cornell University Press: 112–134.

———. 2006. *The EU's Transformative Power: Europeanization through Conditionality in Central and Eastern Europe.* Basingstoke: Palgrave.

Gray, Julia. 2009. "International Organization as a Seal of Approval: European Union Accession and Investor Risk." *American Journal of Political Science* 53 (4): 931–949.

Gray, Mark M., Miki Caul Kittilson, and Wayne Sandholtz. 2006. "Women and Globalization: A Study of 180 Countries, 1975–2000." *International Organization* Vol. 60 (2): 293–333.

Grzybek, Agnieszka. 2005. OSKA. National Women's Information Center. Interview with the author. February 18, 2005. Warsaw: Poland.

Hafner-Burton E., and K. Tsutsui. 2005. "Human rights in a globalizing world: The paradox of empty promises." *American Journal of Sociology* 110 (5): 1373–1411.

Hafner-Burton, Emilie, and Mark A. Pollack. 2009. "Mainstreaming Gender in the European Union: Getting the Incentives Right." *Comparative European Politics* 7 (April): 114–138.

Hantrais, Linda, ed. 2000. *Gendered Policies in Europe.* London: MacMillan.

Hašková, Hana. 2005. "Implementing the Equality Acquis: Czech Republic." Enlargement, Gender and Governance (EGG). EU Framework 5, Project No: HPSE-CT-2002-00115.

Hašková, Hana, and Alena Křižková, eds. 2003. *Sociological Papers.* Prague: Institute of Sociology, Academy of Sciences of the Czech Republic, 61–85.

Hašková, Hana, and Alena Křižková. 2008. "The Impact of EU Accession on the Promotion and Gender Equality in the Czech Republic." In S. Roth, ed. *Gender Politics in the* Expanding *European Union: Mobilization, Inclusion, Exclusion.* New York and Oxford: Berghahn Books: 155–173.

Hašková, Hana, and Marta Kolářová. 2003. "Women's Non-Governmental Organizations and Women's Groups in Left- and Right-Wing Social Movements." In Hana Hašková and Alena Křižková, eds. *Sociological Papers.* Prague: Institute of Sociology, Academy of Sciences of the Czech Republic: 45–60.

Havelková, Barbara. 2006. "The Effectiveness of Transposed EU Equality Law in the Czech Republic." *Croatian Yearbook of European Law and Policy* 2: 299–310.

———. 2010. "The Legal Notion of Gender Equality in the Czech Republic." *Women's Studies International Forum* 33 (2010): 21–29.

———. 2006. "The Effectiveness of Transposed EU Equality Law in the Czech Republic." *Croatian Yearbook of European Law and Policy* 2: 299–310.

Heinen, Jacqueline, and Stéphane Portet. 2002. "Political and Social Citizenship: An Examination of the Case of Poland." In Maxine Molyneux, and Shahra Razavi, eds. *Gender Justice, Development, and Rights.* Oxford: Oxford University Press: 141–169.

Heinrich, Joseph, Robert Boyd, Samuel Bowles, Colin Camerer, Ernst Fehr, and Herbert Gintis, eds. 2004. *Foundations of Human Sociality.* New York, NY: Oxford University Press.

Hellman, Judith Adler. 1987. *Journeys among Women: Feminism in Five Italian Cities.* New York: Oxford University Press.

Hollyer, James. 2010. "Conditionality, Compliance, and Domestic Interests: State Capture and EU Accession Policy." *The Review of International Organizations* 5: 387–431.

Hoskyns, Catherine. 1996. *Integrating Gender: Women, Law and Politics in the European Union.* London: Verso.

Htun, Mala. 2003. *Sex and the State: Abortion, Divorce, and the Family under Latin American Dictatorships and Democracies.* New York: Cambridge University Press.

Htun, Mala, and Laurel S. Weldon. 2012. "The Civic Origins of Progressive Policy Change: Combating Violence against Women in Global Perspective, 1975–2005." *American Political Science Review* 106 (3): 548–569.

Ilgius, V. 2004. Update on Lithuanian NGO Legislation. Accessed at http://www.nisc.lt.

Jacoby, Wade. 2001. "Tutors and Pupils: International Organizations, Central European Elites, and Western Models." *Governance* 14 (2): 169–200.

James, Simon. 1999. *British Cabinet Government.* 2nd ed. New York: Routledge.

Jaruga-Nowacka, Izabela. 2003. "Address of the Government Plenipotentiary for Equal Status of Women and Men." Presented at the Joint Conference on Gender Equality: Poland and Norway. Warsaw, 2003.

Jawor, Anna. 2005. Plenipotentiary for Mazowiecky Wojwodship on the Equal Status of Women and Men. Personal Interview. February 28, 2005. Warsaw.

Johnson, Juliet. 2008. "The Remains of Conditionality: The Faltering Enlargement of the Euro Zone." *Journal of European Public Policy* 15 (6): 826–841.

Johnson, Janet Elise. 2007. "Domestic Violence Politics in Post-Soviet States." *Social Politics* 14 (3): 380–405.

Johnson, Janet Elise, and Jean C. Robinson. 2006. *Living Gender after Communism.* Bloomington: Indiana University Press.

Johnstone, Alastaire I. 2001."Treating International Institutions as Social Environments." *International Studies Quarterly* 45 (4): 487–516.

———. 2005. "Conclusions and Extensions: Toward Mid-Range Theorizing and Beyond Europe." *International Organization* 59 (04): 1013–1044.

Jurėnienė, Virginija. 2010. "Stereotypical Character of Society in the 2nd Republic of Lithuania: Womne's Attempts to be Equal Partners in the State." In Liisa Husu, Jeff Hearn, Anna-Maija Lamsa, and Sinikka Vanhalam, eds. *Leadership Through Gender Lens: Women and Men in Organizations.* Helsinki: Hanken School of Economics: 198–206.

Kakusc, Naémi, and Andrea Pető. 2008. "The Impact of EU Accession on Gender Equality in Hungary." In S. Roth, ed. *Gender Politics in the Expanding European Union: Mobilization, Inclusion, Exclusion.* New York and Oxford: Berghahn Books: 174–192.

Kaplan, Gisela. 1992. *Contemporary Western European Feminism.* New York: New York University Press.

Katzenstein, Mary Fansoid. 1987. "Comparing the Feminist Movements of the United States and Western Europe: An Overview." In Mary Fansoid

Katzenstein and Carol Mueller, eds. *The Women's Movements of the United States and Western Europe.* Philadelphia: Temple University Press: 3–20.

Katzenstein, Mary Fansoid, and Carol Mueller, eds. 1987. The women's movements of the United States and Western Europe. Philadelphia: Temple University Press.

Keck, Margeret E., and Kathryn Sikkink. 1998. *Activist beyond Borders: Advocacy Networks in International Politics.* Ithaca, NY: Cornell University Press.

Kelley, Judith G., and Beth Simmons. 2012. "From Scrutiny to Shame: Social Pressure in US Anti-Trafficking Policy." Unpublished Paper Prepared for the Hauser Colloquium at NYU School of Law, October 25, 2012, New York.

Kelley, Judith G. 2004. *Ethnic Politics in Europe: The Power of Norms and Incentives.* Princeton and Oxford: Princeton University Press.

Keohane, Robert O. 1984. *After Hegemony.* Princeton, NJ: Princeton University Press.

Killick, Tony, with Ramani Gunatilaka and Ana Marr. 1998. *Aid and the Political Economy of Policy Change.* London: Routledge.

Kingdon, John W. 1984. *Agendas, Alternatives, and Public Policies.* Boston: Little, Brown.

Kittilson, Miki Caul. 2008. "Representing Women: The Adoption of Family Leave in Comparative Perspective." *Journal of Politics* 70 (2): 323–334.

———. 2011. "Women, Parties and Platforms in Post-Industrial Democracies." *Party Politics.*Vol. 17 (1): 66–92.

Kostelecky, Tomas. 2002. *Political Parties after Communism.* Baltimore, MD: John Hopkins University Press.

Korpi, Walter, and Joakim Palme. 2003. "New Politics and Class Politics in the Context of Austerity and Globalization: Welfare State Regress in 18 Countries, 1975–95." *American Political Science Review* 97 (3): 425–446.

Kotowska, I. E. 2002. "Zmiany Modelu Rodziny. Polska—Kraje Europejskie." *Polityka Społeczna* (4), 2002.

Králiková, Alena. 2005. Center for Gender Studies. Interview with the author. March 9, 2005. Prague: Czech Republic.

———. 2007. "Women in the Czech Republic in 2007." Friedrich Ebert Stiftung Papers: Analyses from the Czech Republic. December 8, 2007.

Krickus, Richard. 1997. "Democratization in Lithuania." In Karen Dawisha and Bruce Parrott, eds, *Democratization and Authoritarianism in Postcommunist Societies.* Cambridge: Cambridge University Press: 290–333.

Krizsán, Andrea. 2009. From Formal Adoption to Enforcement: Post-Accession Shifts in EU Impact on Hungary in the Equal Policy Field. European Integration Online Papers. Special Issue 2, Vol. 12 (2009), art. 22.

Krizsán, Andrea, and Violetta Zentai. 2006. "Gender Equality Policy or Gender Mainstreaming: The Case of Hungary." *Policy Studies* 27 (2): 135–151.

Krook, Mona Lena. 2009. *Quotas for Women in Politics: Gender and Candidate Selection Reform Worldwide.* Oxford: Oxford University Press.

Krook, Mona Lena, and Diana Z. O'Brien. 2010. "The Politics of Group Representation: Quotas for Women and Minorities Worldwide." *Comparative Politics* 42 (3): 253–272.

———. 2012. "All the President's Men? The Appointment of Female Cabinet Ministers Worldwide." *The Journal of Politics* Vol. 74 (03): 840–855.

Krupavičius, Algis. 1998. "The Post-Communist Transition and Institutionalization of Lithuanian Parties," In R. Hofferbert, ed. *Parties and Democracy: Party Structure and Party Performance in Old and New Democracies*. Oxford: Blackwell Publishers: 43–69.

Krupavičius, Algis, and Irmina Matonytė. 2003. "Women in Lithuanian Politics: From Nomenklatura Selection to Representation." In R. E. Matland and K. A. Montgomery, eds. *Women's Access to Political Power in Post-Communist Europe*. New York: Oxford University Press.

Laja, R. 2000. "Women's Organizations as Part of the Third Sector in Estonia." In UNDP Europe and CIS. *Toward a Balanced Society: Women and Men in Estonia*. Tallin: UNDP.

Laver, Michael, and Kenneth Shepsle. 1994. *Cabinet Ministers and Parliamentary Government*. New York: Cambridge University Press.

Leira, Arnaug. 2002. *Working Parents and the Welfare State: Family Change and Policy Reform in Scandinavia*. New York: Cambridge University Press.

Lemke, Christiane. 2001. "Social Citizenship and Institution Building: EU Enlargement and the Restructuring of Welfare States in East Central Europe." Working Paper Series 01.2. Center for European Studies Programme for the Study of Germany and Europe.

Levitz, Philip, and Grigore Pop-Eleches 2010. "Monitoring, Money and Migrants: Countering Post-Accession Backsliding in Bulgaria and Romania." *Europe-Asia Studies* 62 (3): 461–479.

Lewis, Jane, ed. 1997. *Lone Mothers in European Welfare Regimes: Shifting Policy Logics*. London: Jessica Kingsley.

Linden, R. H., and L. M. Pohlman. 2003. "Now You See It, Now You Don't? Anti-EU Politics in Central and Southeast Europe." *European Integration* 25 (4): 311–334.

Linková, Marcela. 2005. Institute of Sociology, Academy of Sciences of the Czech Republic. Personal Interview. March 18, 2005. Prague.

Lohmann, Kinga, and Anita Seibert (eds.). 2003. *Gender Assessment of the Impact of European Union Accession on the Status of Women in the Labour Market in Central and Eastern Europe. National Study: Poland*. Warsaw: Karat Coalition.

Lorenz-Meyer, Dagmar. 2003. "Policy Initiatives and Tools to Promote the Participation of Women and Gender Equality in the Process of the Czech Republic's Accession to the European Union." In Hana Hašková and Alena Křižková, eds. Sociological Papers. Prague: Institute of Sociology, Academy of Sciences of the Czech Republic: 61–85.

Lovenduski, Joni, and Pippa Norris, eds. 1993. *Gender and Party Politics.* Thousand Oaks, CA: Sage.

Mackeviciutė, Indre. 2005. "Equal Opportunities for Women and Men: Monitoring Law and practice in Lithuania." Budapest: Open Society Institute.

Maksová-Tominová, Michaela, ed. 2003. *Gender Assessment of the Impact of EU Accession on the Status of Women and the Labor Market in CEE.* Prague: Gender Studies.

Mansbridge, Jane. 1995. "What is the Feminist Movement?" In Myra Max Ferree and Patricia Yancey Martin, eds. *Feminist Organizations: Harvest of the New Women's Movement.* Philadelphia: Temple University Press: 27–34.

———. 2001. "The Making of Oppositional Consciousness." In Jane Mansbridge and Aldon Morris, eds. *Oppositional Consciousness: The Subjective Roots of Social Protest.* Chicago: University of Chicago Press.

Mansfeldova, Z. 2004. "The Czech Republic." In S. Berlung, J. Ekman, and F. Aarebrot, eds. *The Handbook of Political Change in Eastern Europe.* Cheltenham: Edward Elgar: 223–253.

March, James, and Johan Olsen. 1989. *Rediscovering Institutions: The Organizational Basis of Politics.* New York, NY: The Free Press.

Martinez, Manuela, and Monika Schrottle. 2006. "State of European Research on the Prevalence of Interpersonal Violence and Its Impact on health and Human Rights." Coordination Action on Human Rights Violations (CAHRV); funded by European Commission, 6th Framework, Project No. 506348.

Martinez-Vazquez, Jorge, Felix Rioja, Samuel Skogstad, and Neven Valev. 2001. "IMF Conditionality and Objections: The Russian Case." *American Journal of Economics and Sociology* 60 (2): 501–517, April 2001.

Matland, Richard. 1993. "Institutional Variables Affecting Female Representation in National Legislatures: The Case of Norway." *Journal of Politics* 55:737–755.

Matland, Richard, and Donley T. Studlar. 1996. "The Contagion of Women Candidates in Single Member District and Proportional Representation Electoral Systems: Canada and Norway." *Journal of Politics* 58:707–733.

Matland, Richard E. 2004. "The Representation of Women in Political Parties in Central and Eastern Europe." Presented at the European Consortium for Political Research, Joint Sessions of Workshops, Uppsala, Sweden, April 13–14.

Matland Richard E., and Kathleen E. Montgomery. 2003. *Women's Access to Political Power in Post-Communist Europe.* Oxford: Oxford University Press.

Matynia, Elzbieta. 2003. "Provincializing Global Feminism: the Polish Case." *Social Research* 70 (2): 499–530.

Mazur, Amy. 2002. *Theorizing Feminist Policy.* London: Oxford University Press.

———. 2007. "Gender and Public Policy in Europe: Current Research Trends." *European Politics and Society* 6 (1): 1–5.

McAllister, Ian, and Donley T. Studler. 1992. "Gender and Representation among Legislative Candidates in Australia. *Comparative Political Studies* 3:388–411.

McBride, Dorothy Stetson, and Amy G. Mazur. 2010. *The Politics of State Feminism: Innovation in Comparative Research.* Philadelphia: Temple University Press.

Mecajeva, Loudmila, and Margarita Tereseviciene. 2000. "Key Issues Affecting Women's Enjoyment of Human Rights in Lithuania." Shadow Report by Lithuanian NGOs Prepared for the 23d Session of CEDAW. Vilnius, 2000.

Mecajeva, Loudmila, and Audrone Kisieliene 2008. "Shadow Report on the Implementation of CEDAW and Women's Human Rights in Lithuania." Social Innovation Fund and European Innovation Center in cooperation with Lithuanian Coalition of Non-Governmental Organizations for Protection of Women's Human Rights. Submitted for the 41st CEDAW Session, July 2008. Kaunas, Lithuania.

Meehan, Elizabeth, and Selma Sevenhuijsen, eds. 1991. *Equality Politics and Gender.* London: Sage.

Meyer, John W., and Brian Rowan. 1977. "Institutionalized Organizations: Formal Structure as Myth and Ceremony." *American Journal of Sociology* 83:340–363.

Meyer, John W., John Boli, George M. Thomas, and Francisco O. Ramirez. 1997. "World Society and the Nation-State." *American Journal of Sociology* 103:144–181.

Minnesota Advocates for Human Rights 2008. Country Pages. http://www. stopvaw.org. Accessed January 5, 2012.

Miroiu, Michaela. 2006. "A Mayflower Turned Titanic: The Metamorphosis of Political Patriarchy in Romania." *Femina Politica* 15(1): 84–98.

Montoya, Celeste. 2009. "International Initiative and Domestic Reforms: European Union Efforts to Combat Violence against Women." *Politics and Gender* 5 (3): 325–348.

Morgan, Kimberly J., and Kathrin Zippel. 2003. "Paid to Care: The Origins and Effects of Care Leave Policies in Western Europe." *Social Politics* 10 (1): 49–85.

Morgan, Kimberly J. 2008. "Toward the Europeanization of Work-Family Policies? The Impact of the EU on Policies for Working Parents." In S. Roth, ed. *Gender Politics in the Expanding European Union: Mobilization, Inclusion, Exclusion.* New York and Oxford: Berghahn Books: 37–59.

Mueller, Carol McClurg. 1988. *The Politics of the Gender Gap: The Social Construction of Political Influence.* Vol. 12. London: Sage Publications, Inc.

Nagy, Beáta. 2003. Women in the Economic Elite in Hungary, In Michel Domsch, Désirée Ladwig, and Eliane Tenten, eds. *Gender Equality in Central and Eastern European Countries.* New York: Peter Lang: 151–168.

Nechemias, Carol. 2006. "Women Organizing Women in the Russian Federation." In Lee Ann Banaszak, ed. *The U.S. Women's Movement in Global Perspective.* Boulder, CO: Rowman & Littlefield Publishers: 151–170.

Niklová, Kateřina. 2005. Gender Focal Point Representative, Minister of Finance, Czech Republic. Personal Interview. March 2005. Prague.

Norris, Pippa, Elizabeth Vallance, and Joni Lovenduski. 1992. "Do Candidates Make a Difference? Gender, Race, Ideology and Incumbency." *Parliamentary Affairs* 45 (4): 496–517.

Nowakowska, Ursula. 1997. "The New Right and Fundamentalism." In Tanya Renne, ed. *Ana's Land: Sisterhood in Eastern Europe.* Boulder, CO: Westview Press: 27–33.

———. 2000. "Government Mechanisms for the Advancement of Women." In Polish Women in the 90s, ed. Nowakowska, Ursula. Warsaw: Women's Rights Center. http://free.ngo.pl/temida/family/htm (December 13, 2003).

O'Connor, Julia S., Ann Shola Orloff, and Sheila Shaver. 1999. *States, Markets, Families: Gender, Liberalism, and Social Policy in Australia, Canada, Great Britain, and the United States.* Cambridge: Cambridge University Press.

Office of the Equal Opportunities Ombudsperson. 2010. *2009 Annual Report.* Vilnius.

Orloff, Ann Shola. 2002. "Explaining US Welfare Reform: Power, Gender, Race and the US Policy Legacy." *Critical Social Policy* 22 (1): 96–118.

Ostrom, Elinor. 1990. *Governing the Commons: The Evolution of Institutions for Collective Action.* New York: Cambridge University Press.

———. 1998. "A Behavioral Approach to the Rational Choice Theory of Collective Action: Presidential Address." *American Political Science Review* Vol. 92 (1): 1–22.

———. 1999. "Coping with Tragedies of the Commons." *Annual Review of Political Science.* 1999. 2: 493–535.

Ostrom, Elinor, Roy Gardner and James Valkner. 1994. *Rules, Games, and Common Pool Resources.* Ann Arbor: University of Michigan Press.

Paluckienė, Jolanta. 2000. "Post-Socialist Welfare State and Gender: A Comparative Study in the Baltic States." In Raimo Blom, Meilute Taijunaite, and Harry Melin, eds. *Streaming Towards Social Stability.* Social Studies, Vol. 4. Vilnius-Tampere: LFSI.

Pascal, Gillian, and Jane Lewis. 2004. Emerging Gender Regimes and Policies for Gender equality in a Wider Europe. *Journal of Social Policy* 33 (3): 373–394.

Pascal, Gillian, and Nick Manning. 2000. "Gender and Social Policy: Comparing Welfare States in Central and Eastern Europe and the Former Soviet Union." *Journal of European Social Policy* 10 (3): 240–266.

Pateman, Carol. 1988. *The Sexual Contract.* Cambridge: Cambridge University Press.

Pavlik, Petr. 2004. "Shadow Report on Equal Treatment and Equal Opportunities for Women and Men." Prague: Gender Studies.

Petö, Andrea. 2003. "European Integration: Politics of Opportunity for Hungarian Women?" *European Integration Studies* 2 (2): 81–86.

Phillips, Anne. 1991. *Engendering Democracy.* University Park, PA: University of Pennsylvania Press.

———. 1995. *The Politics of Presence.* Oxford: Clarendon Press.

Pierson, Paul. 2000a. "Increasing Returns, Path Dependence, and the Study of Politics." *The American Political Science Review* 94 (2): 251–267.

―――. 2000b. "The Limits of Design: Explaining Institutional Origins and Change." *Governance* 13 (4): 475–499.

Pilinkaitė-Sotirović, Vilana. 2008. "Report Analyzing Intersectionality in Gender Equality Policies for Lithuania and EU." Quality in Gender + Equality Policies (QUING). Vienna: Institute for Human Sciences.

Pitkin, Hannah Fenichel. 1967. *The Concept of Representation*. Berkely: University of California Press.

Pollert, Anne. 2003. "Women, Work, and Equal Opportunities in Post-Communist Transition." *Work, Employment, and Society* 17 (2): 331–357.

Pollert, Anne. 2005. "Gender, Transformation and Employment in Central and Eastern Europe." *European Journal of Industrial Relations* 11 (2): 213–230.

Polish Government Delegation. 1998. "Opening Statement of the Polish Government Delegation." Brussels, March 31, 1998.

Pridham, Geoffrey. 1997. "The International Dimensions of Democratization: Theory, Practice, and Inter-regional Comparisons." In G. Prindham, E. Hering, and G. Sanford, eds. *Building Democracy? The International Dimensions of Democratization in Eastern Europe*. London: Leicester University Press: 7–29.

―――. 1999. "Complying with the European Union's Democratic Conditionality: Transnational Party Linkages and Regime Change in Slovakia, 1993–1998." *Europe–Asia Studies* 51 (7): 1221–1244.

―――. 2008. "The EU's Political Conditionality and Post-Accession Tendencies: Comparisons from Slovakia and Latvia." *JCMS: Journal of Common Market Studies* Vol. 46, Issue 2, March 2008: 365–387.

Purvaneckiene, Gierda. 2005. *Gender Equality Policy Stance in Lithuania. Public Policy on Gender Equality Perspectives*. Vilnius: University Publishing Center.

Ray, Raka. 1999. *Fields of Protest: Women's Movements in India*. Minneapolis, MN: Minnesota University Press.

Regulska, Joanna, and Magda Grabowska. 2008. "Will It Make a Difference? EU Enlargement and Women's Public Discourse in Poland." In Silke Roth, ed. *Gender Politics in the Expanding European Union: Mobilization, Inclusion, Exclusion*. New York and Oxford: Berghahn Books: 137–154.

Regulska, Joanna, and Magda Grabowska. 2011. "Post-1989 Women's Activism in Poland." Unpublished Manuscript.

Reingold, Beth.1996. "Conflict and Cooperation: Legislative Strategies and Concepts of Power among Female and Male State Legislators." *Journal of Politics* 58 (1996): 464–485.

Renc-Roe, Joanna.2003. "The Representation of Women in the Political Decision-Making Process in Poland: Existing Problems and Advocated Solutions." Paper presented at the European Consortium for Politics and Gender. Edinburgh, UK, March 28–April 2, 2003.

Renne, Tanya. 1996. *Ana's Land: Sisterhood in Eastern Europe*. Boulder, CO: Westview Press.

Reuters. 2000. "Bulgarian PM Admits long, Hard Way Ahead to EU." *Reuters Wire Service*. April 14, 2000.

Reynolds, Michael. 2005. *United Nations Development Programme: Review of UNDP's Partnership with Lithuania (1992–2005)*. Vilnius, Lithuania.

Risse, Thomas. 1999. "International Norms and Domestic Policy Change: Arguing and Communicative Behavior in the Human Rights Area." *Politics and Society* 27 (4): 529–559.

Risse, Thomas. 2000. "Let's Argue! Communicative Action in World Politics." *International Organization* 54 (1): 1–39.

Risse Kappen, Thomas, ed. 1995. *Bringing Transnational Relations Back in: Non-state Actors, Domestic Structures and International Institutions*. Cambridge: Cambridge University Press.

Rochon, Thomas R., and Daniel A. Mazmanian. 1993. "Social movements and the policy process." The Annals of the American Academy of Political and Social Sciences, 528 (July).

Röder, Ingrid. 2007. *Gender Equality, Pre-Accession Assistance and Europeanization: Two Post-Socialist Countries on their Way to the European Union*. Berlin: Logos.

————. 2009. "Gender+ Equality Policies A Europeanization of Old and New Member States? An Ongoing Process." QUING Working Paper. Vienna: Institute for Human Sciences.

Ross, Michael. 1996. "Conditionality and Logging Reform in the Tropics." In Robert Keohane and Marc Levy, eds. *Institutions for Environmental Aid: Pitfalls and Promise*. Cambridge: Cambridge University Press.

Ross, Karen. 2002. "Women's Place in 'Male' Space: Gender and Effect in Parliamentary Contexts." *Parliamentary Affairs* 55, no. 1 (2002): 189–201.

Roth, Silke. 2007. "Sisterhood and Solidarity? Women's Organizations in the Expanded European Union." *Social Politics: International Studies in Gender, State & Society*. 14 (4): 460–487.

Roth, Silke, ed. 2008a. *Gender Politics in the Expanding European Union: Mobilization, Inclusion, Exclusion*. New York and Oxford: Berghahn Books.

Roth, Silke. 2008b. "Introduction: Gender Politics in the Expanding European Union: Mobilization, Inclusion, Exclusion." In S. Roth, ed. *Gender Politics in the Expanding European Union: Mobilization, Inclusion, Exclusion*. New York and Oxford: Berghahn Books: 1–16.

Rothstein, Bo. 2005. *Social Traps and the Problem of Trust*. Cambridge: Cambridge University Press, 2005.

Sainsbury, Diane. 2001. "Gender and the Making of Welfare States: Norway and Sweden." *Social Politics* 8 (1): 113–143.

Sanbonmatsu, Kira. 2003. *Democrats, Republicans, and the Politics of Women's Place*. Ann Arbor: University of Michigan Press.

Sasse, Gwendolyn. 2008. "The Politics of EU Conditionality: The Norm of Minority Protection during and beyond EU Accession." *Journal of European Public Policy* 15 (6): 842–860.

Saxonberg, Steven. 2000. "Women in East European Parliaments." *Journal of Democracy* 11 (2): 145–158.

———. 2003. "Czech Political Parties Prefer Male Candidates to Female Votes." In Richard E. Matland and Kathleen E. Montgomery. *Women's Access to Political Power in Post-Communist Europe.* Oxford: Oxford University Press: 245–266.

Schimmelfennig, Frank. 2007. European Regional Organizations, Political Conditionality, and democratic Transformation in Eastern Europe. East European Politics and Societies Vol. 21 (1): 126–141.

Schimmelfennig, Frank, and Ulrich Sedelmeier. 2004. "Governance by Conditionality: EU Rule Transfer to the Candidate Countries of Central and Eastern Europe." *Journal of European Public Policy.* 11 (4): 661–679.

———, eds. 2005a. *The Europeanization of Eastern Europe: Evaluating the Conditionality Model.* Ithaca, NY: Cornell University Press.

———. 2005b. "Introduction: Conceptualizing the Europeanization of Central and Eastern Europe." In Frank Schimmelfennig and Ulrich Sedelmeier, eds. *The Europeanization of Eastern Europe: Evaluating the Conditionality Model.* Ithaca, NY: Cornell University Press.

———, eds. 2005a. *The Europeanization of Eastern Europe: Evaluating the Conditionality Model.* Ithaca, NY: Cornell University Press.

Schimmelfennig, Frank, Stefan Engert, and Heiko Knobel. 2003. "Costs, Commitment and Compliance: The Impact of EU Democratic Conditionality on Latvia, Slovakia and Turkey." *JCMS: Journal of Common Market Studies* 41 (3): 495–518.

Schimmelfennig, Frank. 2001. "The community trap: Liberal norms, rhetorical action, and the Eastern enlargement of the European Union." *International Organization* 55:47–80.

Schulze, Marianne. 2008. "Slovakia." In Gerda Faulkner, Oliver Traub, and Elizabeth Holzleithner, eds. *Compliance in the Enlarged European Union: Living Rights or Dead Letters?* Ashgate: Aldershot, Hampshire: 93–124.

Schwellnus, Guido. 2005. "The Adoption of Nondiscrimination and Minority Protection Rules in Romania, Hungary and Poland." In Frank Schimmelfennig and Ulrich Sedelmeier, eds. *The Europeanization of Eastern Europe: Evaluating the Conditionality Model.* Ithaca, NY: Cornell University Press: 51–70.

Schwindt-Bayer, Leslie A., and William Mishler. 2005. "An integrated model of women's representation." *Journal of Politics* 67, no. 2 (2005): 407–428.

Sedelmeier, Ulrich. 2008. "After Conditionality: Post-Accession Compliance with EU law in East Central Europe." *Journal of European Public Policy.* Vol. 15, Issue 6, 2008: 806–825.

———. 2009. "Post-Accession Compliance with EU Gender Equality Legislation in Post-Communist New Member States." European Integration Online Papers. Special Issue 2 (13), art. 23.

———. 2012. "Is Europeanization through Conditionality Sustainable? Lock-in of Institutional Change after EU Accession." *West European Politics* 35 (1): 20–38.

Seibert, Anita. 2005. KARAT Coalition. Interview with the author. February 15, 2005. Warsaw: Poland.

Shannon Vaughn, P. 2000. "Norms Are What States Make of Them: The Political Psychology of Norm Violation." *International Studies Quarterly* Vol. 44, Issue 2, June 2000: 293–316.

Siemienska, Renata. 1996. Kobiety: nowe wyzwania. Starcie przeszłości z teraźniejszością. (Women: New Challenges. Clash of the Past and the Present). Warszawa: Instytut Socjologii-Uniwersytet Warszawski.

———. 2004. "The Implementation of Quotas: European Experience." A paper presented at the International Institute for Democracy and Electoral Assistance/CEE Network for Gender Issues Conference. Budapest, 22–23 October 2004.

Šilović, Daša Š. 2004. "Lobbying for Quotas: The Experience of the CEE Network for Gender Issues." Paper presented at the International Institute for Democracy and Electoral Assistance/CEE Network for Gender Issues Conference. Budapest, Hungary, 22–23 October 2004.

Simmons, Beth. 2000. "International Law and State Behavior: Commitment and Compliance in International Monetary Affairs." *American Political Science Review* 94 (4): 819–835.

Singh, Rina. 1998. *Gender Autonomy in Western Europe: An Imprecise Revolution.* London: Macmillan Press.

Sloat, Amanda. 2004a. "Mapping Women's Campaign for Change: Comparative Report." Work Package 3. Executive Summary. Enlargement, Gender and Governance (EGG). EU Framework 5, Project No: HPSE-CT-2002-00115.

———. 2004b. "Legislating for Equality: The Implementation of the EU Equality Acquis in Central and Eastern Europe." Jean Monnet Working Paper 08/04. New York: New York School of Law.

———. 2005. "The Rebirth of Civil Society: The Growth of Women's NGOs in Central and Eastern Europe." *European Journal of Women's Studies* 12 (4): 437–452.

Šmiszek, Krzysztof. 2005. Specialist, Office of Government Plenipotentiary for Women and Men. Personal Interview. February 17, 2005. Warsaw.

Soule, Sarah A., and Brayden G. King 2006. "The Stages of the Policy Process and the Equal Rights Amendment, 1972–82." *American Journal of Sociology* 111 (6): 1871–1909.

Stadejek, Maciej. 2005. Specialist, Office of the Government Plenipotentiary for Equal Status pf Women and Men. Personal Interview. February 17, 2005. Warsaw.

Stanley, Ben. 2011. "Poland 20 Years Later: The Long Arm of Transition." In Ronald Tiersky and Erik Jones, eds. *Europe Today.* 4th ed. New York: Rowman and Littlefield Publishers, Inc.: 243–276.

Stetson, Dorothy McBride, and Amy G. Mazur. 2003. "Reconceptualizing the Women's Movement: Discourses, Actors, and States." Unpublished manuscript. Paper presented at the 2003 International Studies Association Annual Convention.

———, eds. 1995. *Comparative State Feminism.* Newbury Park, CA: Sage.

Studlar, Donley T., and Gary F. Moncrief. 1999. "Women's Work? The Distribution and Prestige of Portfolios in the Canadian Provinces." *Governance: An International Journal of Policy and Administration* 12 (4): 379–395.

Swers, Michele L. 2002. *The Difference Women make: The Policy Impact of Women in Congress.* Chicago: Chicago University Press.

Taljunaite, Meilute. 2003a. *Executive Summary for Lithuania.* Enlargement, Gender and Governance (EGG). EU Framework 5, Project No: HPSE-CT-2002-00115.

———. 2003b. *Implementing Equality Acquis.* Executive Summary for Lithuania. Enlargement, Gender, and Governance (EGG).EU Framework 5, Project No: HPSE-CT-2002-00115.

———. 2005. "The Women's Movement in Lithuania: Discourses and Lobbying Strategies." In Julie Ballington and Francesca Binda, eds. *The Implementation of Quotas: European Experiences.* International IDEA. Stockholm, Sweden.

Tarrow, Sidney. 1998. *Power in Movement.* 2nd ed. Cambridge: Cambridge University Press.

Toshkov, Dimiter. 2008. "Embracing European Law: Compliance with EU Directives in Central and Eastern Europe." *European Union Politics* 9 (3): 379–402.

Transformation Index Report. 2012. "Lithuania: Country Report 2012." Accessed January 2013 at http://www.bti-project.org/reports/country-reports/ecse/ltu/2012/index.nc.

Trinkūiene, Inija, and Jonas Trinkūnas. 1999. "Patriarchalizmo apraiškos lietuviškoje tradicijoje" (Manifestations of paternalism/patriarchalism in the Lithuanian tradition) In Gierda Purvanecikiené, ed. *Moterys: Tapatumo Paieškos* (Women: Search for Identity), Vilnius: Moterų informacijos centras (Vilnius: Women's Information Center).

True, Jacqui. 2003. *Gender, globalization, and postsocialism: The Czech Republic after communism.* New York: Columbia University Press.

True, Jacqui, and Michael Mintrom. 2001. "Transnational Networks and Policy Diffusion: The Case of Gender Mainstreaming." *International Studies Quarterly* Vol. 45: 27–57.

Tsebelis, George. 1995. "Decision Making in Political Systems: Veto Players in Presidentialism, Parliamentarism, Multicameralism and Multipartyism." *British Journal of Political Science* 25/03/: 289–325.

Underdal, Arild. 1998. "Explaining Compliance and Defection: Three Models." *European Journal of International Relations* 4 (March): 20–23.

Vachudova, Milada Anna. 2005. *Europe Undivided: Democracy, Leverage, and Integration after Communism*. Oxford: Oxford University Press.

Van der Lippe, Tanja and Eva Fodor. 1998. "Changes in Gender Inequality in Six Eastern European Countries." *Acta Sociologica*. Volume 41: 131–149.

Van Evera, Stephen. 1997. *Guide to Methods for Students in Political Science*. Ithaca and London: Cornell University Press.

Vermeersch, Peter. 2002. "EU Enlargement and Minority Rights Policies in Central Europe: Explaining Policy Shifts in the Czech Republic, Hungary and Poland." *Journal of Ethnopolitics and Minority Issues in Europe* Issue 1 (2003). Accessed at http://heinonline.org/HOL/LandingPage?collection=journals&handle=hein.journals/jemie2003&div=12&id=&page=.

Vidovic, H. 2002. "Labour Market Trends in Central and Eastern European Countries." In B. Funck and L. Pizzati, eds. *Labour, Employment, and Social Policies in the EU Enlargement Process: Changing Perspectives and Policy Options*. Washington, DC: The World Bank: 292–314.

Wahl, Angelika von. 2008. "The EU Enlargement: Conceptualizing Beyond 'East and West.'" In Silke Roth, ed. *Gender Politics in the Expanding European Union: Mobilization, Inclusion, Exclusion*. New York, Oxford: Berghahn Books.

Walby, Sylvia. 2004. "The European Union and Gender Equality: Emergent Varieties of Gender Regime." *Social Politics* 11 (1): 4–29.

Wängnerud, Lena. 2000. "Testing the Politics of Presence: Women's Representation in the Swedish Riksdag." *Scandinavian Political Studies* 23 (1): 67–91.

Warleigh-Lack, Alex, and Ralf Drachenberg. 2010. "Policymaking in the European Union." In Michelle Cini and Nieves Pérez-Solórzano Borragán, eds. *European Union Politics*. 3rd ed. New York: Oxford University Press: 209–223.

Watson, Peggy. 2000. "Politics, Policy and Identity: EU Eastern Enlargement and East-West Differences." *Journal of European Public Policy* 7:3, Special Issue: pp. 369–384.

Watson, Nicole, and Ursula Lindenberg, eds. 2002. *Monitoring the EU Accession Process: Equal Opportunities for Women and Men*. Budapest: Open Society Institute.

Watson, Nicole, and Miklós Vörös, eds. 2005. *Equal Opportunity for Women and Men: Monitoring Law and Practice*. Budapest: Open Society Institute and Network Women's Program.

Waylen, Georgina. 2007. *Engendering Transitions: Women's Mobilization, Institutions, and Gender Outcomes*. Oxford: Oxford University Press.

Weiner, Elaine. 2009. "Eastern Houses, Western Bricks? (re)Constructing Gender Sensibilities in the European Union's Eastward Enlargement." *Social Politics*: 303–326.

———. 2010. "Morality, Biology, and the Free Market: (De)Naturalizing the EU's Gender Equality Agenda in the Czech Republic." *Women's Studies International Forum* 33 (2010): 13–20.

Weldon, S. Laurel. 2002. *Protest, Policy, and the Problem of Violence against Women: A Cross-National Comparison*. Pittsburg: University of Pittsburg Press.

———. 2004. "The Dimensions and Policy Impact of Feminist Civil Society: Democratic Policymaking on Violence against Women in the Fifty U.S. States." *International Feminist Journal of Politics* 6 (1): 1–28.

———. 2011. *When Protest Makes Policy: How Social Movements Represent Disadvantaged Groups*. Ann Arbor: University of Michigan Press.

Wiedermann, Clemens. 2008. "Czec Republic." In Gerda Faulkner, Oliver Traub, and Elizabeth Holzleithner, eds. *Compliance in the Enlarged European Union: Living Rights or Dead Letters?* Ashgate: Aldershot, Hampshire: 27–60.

Wilkowska, Anna. 2003. "Gender Equality Standards in Poland: the Results of the Enlargement Process." NEWW-Polska. http://www.eonet.ro (April 14, 2005).

Wolbrecht, Christina. 2000. *The Politics of Women's Rights: Parties, Position, and Change*. Princeton, NJ: Princeton University Press.

Wolbrecht, Christina, and Rodney Hero, ed. 2005. *The Politics of Democratic Inclusion*. Philadelphia: Temple University Press.

Wolchik, Sharon L. 2011. "The Czech and Slovak Republics: Two Paths to the Same Destination." In Sharon L. Wolchik and Jane L. Curry, eds. *Central and East European Politics: From Communism to Democracy*. 2nd ed. New York: Rowman and Littlefield Publishers, Inc: 187–212.

Women's Information Center. 2009. "Moterys ir vyrai Lietuvos visuonemėje—2009." [Women and Men in Lithuanian Society—2009]. Research Report. Vilnius, 2009.

Young, Iris Marion. 2000. *Inclusion and Democracy*. Oxford: Oxford University Press.

Zhiriková, Klara. 2005. Unit on Gender Equality, The Ministry of Labor and Social Affairs of the Czech Republic. Personal interview. March 7, 2005, Prague.

Zieliński, T. 1995. Pozycja kobiety w rodzinie I w żiciu politycznym. [Women's role in the family and political life]. Warsaw: Centrum Europejskie Uniwersytetu Warszawskiego [European Center of Warsaw University], Bulletin 5, 1995.

Zielińska, Eleonora. 2002. *Monitoring the EU Accession Process: Equal Opportunities for Women and Men in Poland*. Budapest: The Network Women's Program and The Open Society Foundation Romania.

Zippel, Kathrin S. 2006. *The Politics of Sexual Harassment: A Comparative Study of the United States, the European Union, and Germany*. Cambridge: Cambridge University Press.

Index

abolition, 117, 126, 135, 156
acculturation. *See* social pressures
acquis communautaire, 86–87
Act on the Implementation of
  Certain Provisions of the
  European Union in the Field of
  Equal Treatment, 134–35
Amsterdam Treaty, 10–11
anti-discrimination laws, 55–56, 71,
  92, 96, 99, 165
  in Czech Republic, 151, 158–62,
  164, 167
  in Poland, 134–35, 139–40
anti-discrimination policies, 95

Balcerowicz, Leszek, 120
Balcerowicz Plan, 119–20
Beijing Platform for Action, 105,
  107, 131, 135, 162, 166. *See also*
  Fourth World Conference on
  Women
blueprint policy against
  discrimination, 53, 55–56, 56t,
  133
  adoption of a, 221t
  defined, 222
Borza, Iona, 89
Brazauskas, Algirdas, 174
Buchowska, Stana, 94
Bulgaria
  institutions on gender equality,
  217t

laws and legislative acts reviewed
  in, 209t
maternity leave provisions in, 215t
burden of proof in discrimination
  cases, 19
Buzek, Jerzy, 123

Catholic Church, 117–19, 126, 131,
  135, 138
CEDAW (Convention on the Elimi-
  nation of All Forms of Discrimi-
  nation against Women), 101–2,
  105, 111, 114, 157, 191, 200
CEDAW Optional Protocol (OP),
  105, 107, 107t, 111, 114
Central and Eastern Europe (CEE).
  See specific topics
Charter of Fundamental Rights of
  the European Union, 11, 159–60
Christian Democratic parties, 45, 120,
  147, 152, 160, 188
Commission of the European
  Communities. *See* European
  Commission
communism, Czech Republic's
  transition from, 145–46
Communist Party of Bohemia and
  Moravia (KSBM), 147, 151
communist states, 185
  gender equality in, 8–9, 103–4,
  143–44, 166, 200
  women's movement and, 152–54

263